The Great
German Wine Book

Kuno F. Pieroth

The Great German Wine Book

STERLING PUBLISHING CO., INC.   NEW YORK

SOURCES OF ILLUSTRATIONS

Agentur Foto-Center, Braunschweig
Archiv für Kunst und Geschichte, Berlin
Bayerische Staatsgemäldesammlung, Munich
Bayern Verlag, Bildagentur, Gauting
Lothar Beckel, Bad Ischl
Bildarchiv Preussischer Kulturbesitz, Berlin
Willy Bottler, Bernkastel-Andell
Paul Claus, Geisenheim
Deutsche Weininformation, Mainz
Heinen Verlag, Essen
Heisterkamp, Bad Kreuznach
Historisches Museum der Pfalz, Speyer

Hans Huber, Garmisch
Keystone Pressedienst GmbH Bildarchiv, Hamburg
Kiedrowski, Ratingen
C. H. Krüger-Moessner, Munich
Länderpress, Düsseldorf
Joachim Michels, Stromberg
Rheinisches Landesmuseum, Trier
Schott, Zwiesel
M. V. Wagner-Museum, Würzburg
Weinmuseum, Burg Layen
Heinz Gert Woschek, Mainz
ZEFA, Düsseldorf

Library of Congress Cataloging in Publication Data

Pieroth, Kuno F., 1937–
    The great German wine book.

    Translation of: Das grosse Buch der deutschen
Weinkultur.
    Includes index.
    1. Wine and wine making—Germany (West)   I. Title.
TP559.G3P5313   1983   641.2′22′0943   82-61708
ISBN 0-8069-0254-X

Copyright © 1983 by Sterling Publishing Co., Inc.
Two Park Avenue, New York, N.Y. 10016
Originally published in Germany under the title *Das grosse
Buch der deutschen Weinkultur*, copyright © 1980
mvg Moderne Verlags GmbH, Munich
Distributed in Australia by Oak Tree Press Co., Ltd.
P.O. Box K514 Haymarket, Sydney 2000, N.S.W.
Distributed in the United Kingdom by Blandford Press
Link House, West Street, Poole, Dorset BH15 1LL, England
Distributed in Canada by Oak Tree Press Ltd.
c/o Canadian Manda Group, 215 Lakeshore Boulevard East
Toronto, Ontario M5A 3W9
Manufactured in the United States of America
All rights reserved

Lithos: Krammer, Linz, Austria

Contents

I. WINE HISTORY AND CULTURE
A Gift of the Gods to Mankind 9
The Vineyard, Cradle of Culture 34

II. A JOURNEY THROUGH GERMAN WINE COUNTRY
Its Infinite Variety 53
The Character of Wine Comes From the Grape 57

The Middle Rhine: *Castles and Wine* 63
The Ahr: *River of German Burgundies* 71
Moselle-Saar-Ruwer: *A Splendid Chain of Vine-Covered Hills* 77
The Rheingau: *Home of World-Famous Wines* 87
The Nahe: *Germany's Testing Area* 95
Rheinhessen: *Historic Region Between Worms and Bingen* 103
The Rhine Palatinate: *"The Wine Palatinate"* 111
The Hessian Bergstrasse: *A Garden of Eden* 119
Württemberg: *"Oh blessed land! No hill without its vines!"* 125
Baden: *Nearly Two Thousand Hours of Sunshine* 133
Franconia: *The Monks Were Their Teachers* 141

III. THE LONG ROAD FROM VINE TO GLASS
From Grape to Wine 149
From Bottle to Glass 157
Varieties of Wine 166
The Sparkling Cousins: *Schaumwein, Sekt, Champagne* 169
Wine Law and Official Quality Levels 172
The Wine Label: *Birth Certificate and Calling Card* 179
The Great Vintages 181
Wine-Tasting 187
Wining and Dining: *A Double Pleasure* 191
"Zum Wohle!" ("To Your Health!"): *Wine and Health* 195

German-English Wine-Tasting Glossary 200
Twentieth Century Vintages 202
Index 204

Dear Reader,

Let me take you on a far-ranging journey through world history, in which we will explore the legends, folklore and romance of wine, especially the fine drinking wines of Germany. Wine has played an important, integral part in history and culture for at least eight thousand years. It has enlivened the work of great philosophers, poets and other artists and the lives of everyone.

We shall stop over in each of the wine-growing areas of Germany and learn how wine figures prominently in its heritage and become acquainted with the characteristics of wines from the major growing regions. How wine has helped shape developments in these regions is a fascinating sidelight to our knowledge of history and culture.

It will be my pleasure to acquaint you with the wide variety of German wines and thus enable you to satisfy that basic need of almost every wine lover—namely, to know more about this drink in order to fully appreciate it.

May a glass of this "gift of the gods" be your chosen companion while you read this book, and may your pleasure in each be mutually enhanced.

Kuno F. Pieroth

I.
Wine History and Culture

A Gift of the Gods to Mankind

It is an understatement indeed merely to call wine a beverage—or even a luxury. Without doubt, the fermented juice of the grape is one of the most remarkable products of civilization. It has been extolled by kings and commoners alike as one of the most exquisite sources of joy. We must not forget the "secondary function" of wine, which in the past was even more important—namely, its ritualistic role in the world's great religions.

No product is wreathed in more legend and story than wine. Mythic tradition tells us that it was "invented" not by man, but by the gods, a great number of whom are credited with this feat—Bacchus, the Roman wine god; Dionysus, the Greek wine god; Shiva, the Indian god of fertility (among other things); and the Egyptian god Osiris, responsible for the Nile floods which brought fertility to the fields.

In Judaism and Christianity, wine is con-

nected with the word of the Lord: Noah is said to have been bidden by Jehovah to take a vine onto the Ark, a vine which later served as the basis for a vineyard.

We shall return later to wine's "divine origins." Now let us have a look at the findings of archeologists and other scientists. Plants with foliage resembling vine leaves existed 30 million years ago. Seeds of vines have been found in 60-million-year-old geological layers in southern England, America and even Greenland. Evidence has been discovered that wild vines also abounded in the region from the reaches of the Lower Rhine to Lake Constance before anyone could have cultivated this plant. The habitat of the wild vine, a creeper which is still found in a few isolated places along the old course of the Rhine in the Palatinate, was limited by the onset of an ice age about 1 million years ago.

About 6000 B.C., when the post-glacial warm climate encouraged a luxuriant vegetation, the first signs of a primitive wine

A beautiful youth: the wine god Dionysus in marble. Roman copy of the Greek original from the fourth century B.C. Glyptothek, Munich.

culture appear, evidently originating in Asia Minor. In 1969 a fruit and wine press, almost eight thousand years old, was found in the vicinity of Damascus, and another, estimated at six thousand years old, on the southern slopes of the Caucasus. Sumerian roller seals on amphoras, also six thousand years old, may be considered the precursors of today's labels.

While there is no record of the first time wine was obtained from grape juice, there is a wealth of amusing legends about its debut.

When Noah, the forefather of winegrowers, enjoyed his first taste of "virgin wine" (the first wine from a new vine, usually pressed after three years' growth), the alcohol hit him pretty hard: As described in the First Book of Moses, "he drank of the wine, and was drunken; and he was uncovered within his tent."

Biblical legend also has it that Satan cursed Noah's love of the vine by fertilizing it in a truly devilish manner, slaughtering a lamb, a lion and a pig for this purpose. The parable says that as long as man drinks wine sparingly, he has the mind of a lamb; if he drinks generously, the savage passion of a lion awakens in him; and if he drinks too much, he behaves like a pig and loses his dignity as a human being.

The Bible has quite a few more things to say about wine. In the miracle of Cana Christ turns water into wine (hardly a method of production to emulate). The Book of Judges describes how the vine renounced the honor of being appointed king of the trees, saying, "Should I leave my wine which cheereth God and man and go to be promoted over the trees?" During the Exodus, the scouts sent ahead by Moses took the sighting of vines as the longed-for sign of having finally reached the Promised Land: "And they came unto the brook of Escol and cut down from thence a branch with one cluster of grapes and they bore it between two upon a staff."

Dire stories about the birth of wine can be found in Greek mythology: Zeus had fathered with his (illegitimate) daughter Persephone a son whom he called Dionysus. Hera, Zeus's ever-jealous wife, in a fit of rage set Titans upon the boy. They tore him to pieces and scattered his limbs to the four winds. But kind-hearted Pallas Athena found the infant's still-beating heart and made the vine spring from it. Thus Dionysus was virtually begotten a second time and was received into the circle of the gods, from which time he has been venerated as the god of wine.

There is a lovely tale about the birth of wine in Persian literature. It tells of a king named Jemshed who had a partiality for wild grapes and sometimes also quenched his thirst with their juice. In order to be prepared for times of scarcity, grape juice and grapes were preserved in sealed amphoras on which—because Jemshed had reservations about his nearest and dearest —a warning was inscribed that they contained poison.

One day, however, his favorite wife felt very ill and decided to end her life by using the "poison" in the amphoras. Of course, the grape juice had in the meantime fermented to wine, so that the young lady was transported to heavenly spheres but not to the hereafter. When she awoke— quite recovered from her illness—she told the king of her intoxicating experience, whereupon he took a cautious sip—and enjoyed it. Even though this is only a fairy tale, in Persia the date of the birth of wine is set at about 3000 B.C.

Bruno Götz, a wine expert from Baden, reports an Afghan legend about the discovery of wine which might well be a tale

Water into wine: the Biblical miracle, at the wedding in Cana, portrayed in a painting from about 1500.

from *A Thousand and One Nights*: In ancient times there lived a powerful ruler in Herat whose son, Bâdân, was the best archer in the land, respected far and wide. One day an eagle landed in front of the two men, and as they watched a snake approached and threatened the bird. The mighty shah feared for the life of the proud eagle, so his son killed the snake with one shot from his bow and the eagle, freed, took off.

One year later, the eagle reappeared and, after landing, struck the ground with his beak several times. On this very spot a few grains were found. The ruler thought the eagle had made him a present and ordered the grains to be sown. After a while a little green plant appeared, the like of which had not been seen before.

A few months later the plant bore very juicy blue berries, but, for fear of poison, nobody dared eat them or drink their juice.

A servant was ordered to observe the juice, which had been stored in vats, and soon afterwards he went to the shah reporting excitedly that the juice was boiling and bubbling without a fire. A short time later the liquid quieted down and turned a rich purple, but still nobody knew whether it was poisonous or perhaps had healing powers.

The shah, anxious to know more about the grape juice, decided to have a condemned murderer taste it so that he could learn the truth about its properties. The prisoner drank, grimaced, drank again and started to laugh, quite oblivious of his situation. Eagerly he obeyed the order to go on drinking, and drank until he fell into a deep sleep. When he awoke, he told how this liquid filled his heart with joy and all his problems had seemed to vanish into thin air. Upon hearing this tale, the ruler hesitated no longer, and, from that time on, wine drinking was popular in the region.

It is quite possible that through a similar kind of accident mankind discovered what was hidden in those plain-looking berries. Unfortunately, too little is known about the tribes of Asia Minor, who were obviously already wine-growers, to get an insight into their procedures and habits.

A mosaic of fragments of archeological findings in Egypt from around 3000 B.C., however, affords a much better view. Thus it can be said that viticulture was important in the time of the first Egyptian dynasties. In the land on the banks of the Nile, where climatic conditions approximated those prevailing on the Rhine today, wine-growing was a thriving industry.

The Egyptians were born gardeners, and their paintings and scripts show that they knew how to process the grape juice. The press being still unknown, people squashed the grapes with their bare feet (as is still sometimes done in remote southern regions). Fermentation was set in motion by yeast plants, although their properties were then not understood and were only grasped as late as the eighteenth century. The wine was then filtered and poured into large amphoras which were sealed with oil, clay or beeswax and stored in special chambers. Apparently it could be stored for a long time without losing its taste. Wine historians have even reported that Egyptian wine had a storage life of up to two hundred years! No wonder that the cellarers, who must have used very advanced methods of preservation, were held in high regard.

Incidentally, Egypt was not the cradle of the vine; it had to have been imported from other places, probably Asia Minor. In those times six different types of wine were known, and were mainly used for religious purposes.

But in the long run, the Egyptians felt that wine was too glorious to be used only as an offering to the gods. Songs inscribed on limestone shards disclose that they held feasts where wine was the focus of attention and inebriation considered to be a state blessed by the gods. One toast which has been handed down to us reads:

> To your health! Drink until you are
> drunk!
> May your life be beautiful.
> Celebrate a good day
> In life and health
> Until you reach the City of Eternity!

The Egyptian court officials received a daily wine allowance which encouraged consumption and necessitated the impor-

Egyptian wine planting and production. Tomb of the Night (1400 B.C.) in Thebes.

tation of wine from Asia Minor to satisfy increasing demand. To avoid any loss of the precious liquid, new production methods were introduced: After the grapes had been pressed, the marc (i.e., the residue of skins and stalks) was put into a cloth and pressed again.

With the progress in wine-growing, the marking of the amphoras was improved, too. Seals or inscriptions gave exact information about the year, the growing region, the wine-maker and storer. The custom of placing such amphoras in the tombs of pharaohs has in some cases enabled archeologists to fix the time of the reign of certain kings exactly.

The Egyptians, of course, held no monopoly on wine cultivation. Some two thousand years before the birth of Christ the art of turning grape juice into wine was known not only all through Asia Minor but on the eastern shores of the Mediterranean as well. There was a particularly brisk wine trade between Assyria and Babylon at this time.

The great code of Hammurabi, the famous king of Babylon (1728–1686 B.C.), even contains a law on the sale of wine, probably the first in recorded history. It fixed prices and prohibited under the pain of death undue noise-making and orgies in connection with the sale of wine. Priestesses who thoughtlessly entered an inn were also subject to the death penalty.

In time, viticulture extended further and further. Migrating Semitic tribes brought the vine from their original homesteads on the southern slopes of the Caucasus further south to the lower reaches of the Euphrates and to the deserts and lush pastures of the southwestern regions. From Syria wine culture spread over the whole of Asia Minor and reached the Greek peninsula from the north. At the same time Phoenician merchants brought vines and wine to Greece by sea.

The introduction of wine-growing into Greece must be considered fortunate, since it initiated a development from which we still profit—the lovely sight of a full glass of wine! Greece was certainly the cradle of European wine culture.

The history of Greek wine alone would fill a book; therefore we will content ourselves with essentials. We must distinguish between mythology and reality. Let us start with mythology.

In ancient Greece, the gods were responsible for everything. The supreme god, Zeus, was enthroned upon Mount Olympus. One of his sons was Dionysus, who, as has already been mentioned, allegedly gave the vine to man. Apart from the legend that the vine grew out of his heart, there is another myth, according to which the revivified Dionysus was dressed as a girl and raised by women. At the command of Zeus, father of the gods, Dionysus' half-brother Hermes turned him into a goat or a ram. Thus he lived with the nymphs in the Helicon Mountains, where he is said to have discovered wine.

The claim that Dionysus spread viticulture over at least half of our globe originates in the myth about Hera, Zeus's wife, and her discovery of the hideout of her husband's illegitimate son, whom she then vengefully afflicted with madness. Thereupon Dionysus sailed the seas like a man possessed, and wherever he landed he left traces of wine.

But the wine god could not have been all that mad, because apart from wine he had other responsibilities. He was also the god

The wine god has drunk too much: a drunken Dionysus supported by a youthful satyr. Floor mosaic A.D. 160. Röm.-Germ. Museum, Cologne.

14

of games, the theatre and masquerades, and lord over the dead and the souls of men.

The reason for connecting Dionysus with madness probably has its roots in the "influence of this narcotic beverage" (Nietzsche), which the Greeks consumed in more than ample quantities in a form said to have been very strong. The wine of ancient Greece was drinkable only when diluted, and whoever did not keep this rule apparently died raving mad, like the Spartan king Cleomenes (ca. 500 B.C.). However, wine-drinking occupied a special place in the dining customs of ancient Greece. During banquets the guests hardly drank at all. But afterwards! In high spirits from philosophical as well as lighthearted discussions, jokes, music, dancing and sensual games, they awaited the "playtime" after the meal as the most important part of the feast. Usually a speaker was chosen to give instructions regarding the pattern of drinking. The Greeks also knew the custom of drinking toasts.

Normally, women were not invited to these feasts, but every rule has exceptions. The courtesans, frivolous women who sold their services for money and were quite able to hold their liquor, were sometimes invited, and, more often than not, they challenged the men to drinking contests.

In contrast to such debauchery are the roles of wine in philosophy and in the art of healing. The great philosopher Plato (427–347 B.C.), a disciple of Socrates, expressed strong feelings about drunkards in his dialogue, *Symposium*. Plato's collection of laws, too, touched upon the subject of wine. The philosopher intended to make use of wine as an excellent medium to test the minds of citizens. He emphasized that wine-drinking encourages the feelings and aspirations of the heart and endows man with a powerful self-awareness and a belief in his own knowledge:

> When this takes place, the souls of the drinkers turn softer, like iron, through being heated, and younger too; whence they become ductile, just as when they were young, in the hands of the man who has the skill and ability to train and mould them. And now, as then, the man who is to mould them is the good legislator; he must lay down banqueting laws able to control the banqueter who becomes confident and bold and unduly shameless, and unwilling to submit to the proper limits of silence and speech, of drinking and music, making him consent to do in all ways the opposite. . . .

Wine-drinking was carefully controlled:

> No soldier on the march should ever taste of this potion, but confine himself for the whole of the time to water-drinking only. I would add this, that in the city also no bondsman or bondsmaid should ever taste of it; and that magistrates during their year of office, and pilots and judges while on duty, should taste no wine at all; nor should any councillor, while attending any important council; nor should anyone whatever taste of it at all, except for reasons of bodily training or health, in the day-time; nor should anyone do so by night—be he man or woman—when proposing to procreate children. Many other occasions also might be mentioned when wine should not be drunk by men who are swayed by right, reason and law. Hence, according to this argument,

Athena serves Heracles with wine: an Attic dish from about 470 B.C., in the
Staatliche Antikensammlung in Munich.

there would be no need for any State to have a large number of vineyards; and while all the other agricultural products, and all the foodstuffs, would be controlled, the production of wine especially would be kept within the smallest and most modest dimensions.

Certainly no great wine lover, our Plato!

His opinion that wine should have no place in important transactions was not shared by contemporaneous Persia. According to the Greek historian Herodotus (484–420 B.C.), the ancient Persians liked to discuss important problems while under the influence of alcohol. The decisions thus arrived at were examined the next day in a sober state and put into force only if they were still found practicable. On the other hand, the Persians also reversed the process, examining problems when sober and then checking their findings when intoxicated. It is said that in the latter case, many more decisions were revised.

His principles put Plato into disagreement with his teacher Socrates, who enjoyed his wine—with moderation:

> Drinking—that comforts me too. It seems to me that it is the same with men and their drinking bouts as with the crops in the fields; because they also, when God gives them too much to drink, cannot stand upright; when they are given what they can take, then they grow straight, blossom, and come to maturity.

The wise Greek physician Hippocrates (460–377 B.C.) also had a benevolent opinion of wine. The founder of Greek medicine and the originator of the Hippocratic Oath—which is still the code of medical ethics—considered wine an effective remedy in the treatment of headache, sciatica, constipation and edema:

> Wine is a thing which in a miraculous way is suitable for people, provided that it is used, in good and bad health, sensibly and in the right amounts appropriate to the individual's condition.

But the Greeks were not only philosophers about wine; they were also masters in processing it. They fermented it in special vats made of clay or wood and stored it in large earthen containers which were sealed with tar and resin. The Greeks treated their wine with all sorts of additives until well into the nineteenth century: sea water to make it more acidic, honey to make it sweeter, resin to prolong its storage life

(today's treatment of Retsina is based on a method developed thousands of years ago). Herbs and mysterious essences were added, too, and wreaths of parsley and flowers were wound around the heads of the drinkers because it was believed that they were a good cure for a hangover.

We are indebted to the Greeks for not keeping their knowledge of wine to themselves. Along with a considerable part of their culture, they gave the art of wine-growing and wine-making to the Romans when they came in contact with Southern Italy (which they called *Oinotria*, i.e., "wine land," from its abundance of wild vines).

The Romans, too, had among their numerous gods the wine god Bacchus. Today, the Greek Dionysus and Roman Bacchus are considered one and the same god with, so to speak, two domiciles. There are, however, some differences. While the Greek Dionysian cult kept mostly within acceptable limits, the Roman Bacchic feasts, the Bacchanalia, degenerated into licentiousness and were forbidden by the Senate in 186 B.C.

Obviously, the Romans were given to excess and intemperance. They drank the heaviest wines undiluted or even mixed with liqueurs. When Caesar gave a banquet, hardly any men of intellect and sensibility were present. The philosopher Epictetus (50–138) judged Roman revelry as follows: "The vine bears three grapes: The first brings sensual pleasure, the second, inebriety, and the third, crime." Crimes committed in a state of drunkenness never found clemency; the culprit had to pay for his misdeeds in full measure.

The Romans invented a custom which is still popular today—the "morning drink" —and they had so-called "drink masters" who watched for offences such as the spilling of wine and meted out judgment on the spot.

But to return to Bacchus: It simply will not do to measure Greek and Roman gods by the same yardstick. While the Greek Dionysus is always depicted with well-groomed hair and beard as an apparently mature god, Bacchus is always shown running around naked and seems to have been an immature youth.

No wonder he was never a favorite with scholars and theologians. The humanist Erasmus of Rotterdam wrote in the sixteenth century:

> Why does Bacchus always look like a long-haired rogue, fitting the imagination of the old? Because he is always wild and spends his whole life gorging himself, dancing and full of exuberance, so that he is totally unacquainted with Pallas Athena, the goddess of wisdom.

Luckily for her, Athena was of Greek blood. As a Roman lady, she would have encountered certain difficulties regarding wine. One can only pity the fair ladies of ancient Rome, for exceedingly rough customs prevailed in those times.

Romulus, the founder of Rome, simply condemned to death all females who were caught drinking wine. The moralist and statesman Cato (234–149 B.C.) decreed that any man had the right to kiss his servant-women if he wanted to check that they hadn't been drinking. Whether he would have had only this purpose in mind is not certain.

Many centuries later, the city of Heilbronn demonstrated that intemperate women still met with disapproval. The city council decreed, "Women who are addicted to drink shall have a notice pinned on their heads ... with the words 'drunken hag.' "

Human nature being what it is, prohibitive measures provoke violations. Thus in Italy, wine-growing advanced steadily, although women were forbidden to drink at all, and, in some parts of the country, men were allowed to drink only on completion of their thirty-fifth year. Around the beginning of the Christian era, the technique of wine-making had reached a relatively high standard. At that time, Rome could offer eighty types of wine, and Italy had taken first place among wine-producing countries.

The Romans also knew a lot about the importance of climate, the location of the vineyard and the times for grape harvesting. When we say today that Spätlese ("late-picked") wine was "invented" in 1775, this is only partially correct: Some two thousand years previously it was known that the quality of the wine could benefit from a late harvest. But, of course, then one did not pick withered grapes affected by "noble rot," as was done in 1775.

In ancient Rome there were also explicit directives on how to fertilize the vineyards. Columella, a Roman agricultural expert who lived in the first century A.D., wrote,

> One should not use any of the normal animal manures for vines because it will spoil the taste of the wine. The quality as well as the quantity of the harvest will benefit if soil from hedges and the like is mixed into the soil of the vineyard.

Shortly before the beginning of the Christian era, the Romans had a lucky windfall in conquering a wine-growing region that owed its existence to the Greeks. In the sixth century B.C., Greek refugees had reached the southern coast of Gaul and settled there. At that time, Gaul extended over present-day France, Belgium and upper Italy. The Greeks founded Massilia (which later became Marseilles), and as a "christening gift" brought the vine with them.

The wild Celtic tribes then roaming Gaul received news of an "indescribable drink" which was being produced on the southern coast. Thus the way was paved for the expansion of wine-growing, for even then the ancestors of the French enjoyed tasty foods. However, the actual spread of the vine in Gaul occurred after Caesar conquered the country (58–51 B.C.). One century after this, even Italy with its wealth of quality wines appreciated the wines from Bordeaux, Vienne and Narbonne.

The Roman historian Pliny (23–79), discovered to his surprise that the people in Gaul preferred wines from Italy and those in Italy, wines from Gaul. Being a patriot, Pliny condemned his fellow countrymen harshly:

> They castrate the wine in order to be able to drink more. They even prepare poisons which cause thirst. Some drink hemlock so that the fear of death forces them to drink. The drinking vessels are covered with adulterous pornographic scenes, as if drinking alone does not invoke enough lust.

In the twentieth century, many people feel the urge to put their thoughts about certain wines into writing, and often their opinions differ widely. It was just the same two thousand years ago. The two great Roman poets, Virgil (70–19 B.C.) and Horace (65 B.C.–A.D. 8), praised wine wholeheartedly. It is quite possible that wine contributed to the success of Caesar's campaigns, for upon his orders, the legionaries received daily rations of it. Perhaps that is why the armies were spared the scourges of typhoid fever, dysentery and cholera.

As mentioned earlier, Caesar found the Greek legacy of cultivated vineyards in Gaul, and when the Roman legions invaded Germany, they probably brought the vine there.

For a short time the spread of the vine was halted when the despotic ruler Domitian (51–96) ordered a frontier wall, the *Limes Germanicus*, to be built to mark the northern borders of southern Germany and Gaul, in order to turn the whole of those regions into a great flower garden. He also prohibited any wine-growing north of the Alps. But those who had learned to appreciate the taste of wine paid no heed to this restriction. Rome was far away, and the legionaries were grateful to get locally the drink they were used to.

Under the Emperor Probus (276–282) the law was rescinded, but this wine lover and vintner was ill-rewarded for his action. Probus, born in Croatia, grew wine in the region betwen Bosnia and Slavonia, and had detailed a troop of legionaries to work in the vineyards. This enraged the soldiers so much that they slew the emperor when he visited one of his vineyards.

At that time, viticulture was progressing well in Germany. Earlier, when the Romans had reached Lake Constance for the first time and had planted vines in this region, the local people were still drinking mead or a beverage similar to beer. But this state of affairs changed very quickly. Tacitus (50–116) writes in his *Germania* that the Teutons were so keen on the new beverage that they would willingly sacrifice all their goods and even hire themselves out as slaves in order to get it. They suffered from a well-nigh unquenchable thirst which compelled them to drink day and night.

Little by little, vine cultivation spread further north, and in some regions wine-

The famous Wine Ship—tombstone of a wine-trader, ca. A.D. 200. Found in
Neumagen and on display in the Rheinisches Landesmuseum in Trier.

making and the wine trade became main sources of income. Marble sculptures from the tombs of wealthy wine dealers have been found near Neumagen (on the Moselle River), showing young dancing girls with swirling veils holding large clusters of grapes in their uplifted hands in praise of the continuance of life after death.

The Roman poet Decimus Magnus Ausonius, a native of Bordeaux, described the charm of the Moselle region in glowing terms in his poem *Mosella*. In view of this, some vintners still claim that Moselle wine has always been superior to Bordeaux because Ausonius's search for a really good wine led him to the Moselle, where he stayed. Regional rivalry can sometimes prompt such precipitate statements.

But the Teutons must be credited with one revolutionary invention. The Greeks and the Romans did not use wooden vats for storage, but rather earthen amphoras with a capacity of up to 600 litres. The beer-drinking Teutons now remodelled their wooden beer casks into storage vats for wine, which distinctly improved its quality. In the wooden containers, which were permeable by air, flavor and taste could develop much better. The craftsmen who made these casks were called *cuparius* (from which our term "cooper" stems).

Apart from earthenware and wooden containers, glass bottles were coming into use, and we can today still marvel at an original relic from those times. Probably the oldest liquid wine so far discovered has been found in a glass amphora in a Roman stone coffin. The small residue of wine under a strongly resinated oil layer is approximately seventeen hundred years old. It is the main attraction in the Wine Museum in Speyer. A few decades ago, an examination showed that some of the main components of wine were still present; as one would expect, it is no longer fit for consumption.

In the course of time, the Romans withdrew from the conquered territories, and although during the Germanic migrations around 500 viticulture in Europe suffered a considerable setback, it was not completely given up. The advance of Christianity contributed largely, even decisively, to the recovery of wine production. And in the meantime, the wine gods of the Greeks and Romans had been augmented by Christian patron saints of wine.

Today, we still have our wine patron saints, e.g., Saint Gall in Switzerland, particularly in St. Gallen, Saint Urban in Swabia, Saint Cilian in Main-Franconia and Saint Roch in the Rhineland. Among these Urban, who became Pope in 223, had an especially close relationship with the grape. During a persecution of Christians he allegedly hid in a vineyard and escaped. As an expression of gratitude, he took the grape as well as the vine under his special protection. Saint Urban's Day (May 25) is an important date for growers because it gives some predictions about the quality of the harvest. An old saying goes:

Scheint die Sonne klar am Sankt Urbanitag,
Wächst guter Wein nach alter Sag;
Ist aber Regen, dann bringt's den Reben Schaden,
Daher Urbani Bild muss in dem Wasser baden.

If the sun shines clear on Saint Urban's day,
There grows good wine the people say,
But if there be rain it brings the vine scathe,
And therefore Saint Urban must go for a bathe.

In the vintners' villages, the statues of saints were indeed quickly removed from their pedestals when rain fell on the twenty-fifth and were ducked in a brook or in the village pond—no escaping the rule, even for saints!

The German monks did a tremendous job. The Benedictines and Cistercians were missionaries of agriculture and viticulture, and that was really no wonder, because they needed sacramental wine for the celebration of mass. Since it was too cumbersome to take wine along, and since it often took months for goods to reach their destination if they got there at all, the monks simply grew their own wine near their homesteads (which became the origins of monasteries).

Special credit must go to the "Apostle of Germany," Winfrid, later Saint Boniface (717–754), who, according to Rhenish folklore, initiated the creation of many vineyards when he was Archbishop of Mainz. In 742 vineyards were also set up in Franconia. His activities laid the basis for the foundation of the diocese of Würzburg which promoted wine production in this region. In 1979 Würzburg celebrated the anniversary of "Twelve Hundred Years of Wine-growing."

The monasteries also received many vineyards as donations. The documents of such transactions constitute important evidence in tracing the development of wine-growing on the east bank of the Rhine.

Christianity disseminated a new morality

and the monks participated actively in the rebuilding of destroyed cities. Bishop Nicetius initiated the reconstruction of the totally ruined cathedral in Trier and built a large castle on a formerly densely wooded hill near Coblenz (Roman name: *Confluentes*, i.e., "confluence"), where very soon vines were growing, replacing the former wilderness.

Wo sonst wildes Gesträuch,
Grünt wohgepflegt jetzt der Weinberg.
Apfelbäume steigen empor in zierlicher
*   Pflanzung. . . .*

Where otherwise wild thickets,
Now sprouts well-cultivated the vineyard.
Apple trees rise up in graceful
    cultivation. . . .

As can be seen, wine-growing in Germany and France kept pace with the improvement of cultural conditions; at the same time it deteriorated in those southern countries where it had had so splendid a start. Charlemagne (742–814) had a decisive influence on the development of the new high culture of wine-growing. This king of the Franks (from 768) and later emperor (from 800) was a great patron of the arts and sciences.

While in the past the Franks had vandalized the conquered territories and spread terror wherever they went, under Charlemagne conditions improved. As regards wine-growing, he promoted the planting of new grape varieties and passed many laws. He prohibited the pressing of grapes with bare feet and ordered that henceforth the grapes should be pressed in *Truttas* ("wine presses").

The still-popular *Strausswirtschaften* ("wreath inns"), too, owe their existence to a decree by Charlemagne which pre-scribed that every innkeeper who also managed vineyards had to hang a conspicuous sign, in the form of a bunch of flowers or a wreath, outside his inn if he dispensed his own wines.

The vineyards on the Johannisberg overlooking the Rhine are another achievement that must be credited to Charlemagne. From his palace in Ingelheim the emperor had observed that the snow melting always started on this hill, and he took this as a favorable sign—with good reason, as we know today.

That viticulture continued to prosper after the era of Charlemagne was again due to the monasteries. Wherever new monastic orders were founded, vines were planted, even in Thuringia and Pomerania. The wine from these northern regions, however, was often the subject of satirical verses:

Wein aus Mark Brandenburgs Gehege
Fährt durch die Kehle wie eine Säge.

Wine from Brandenburg plantations
Goes down the throat like a saw.

The monks set the trend in wine-growing, especially the Cistercians, who in 1135 founded the Eberbach monastery in the Rheingau. This is one of the most impressive monuments built by the order and in the Middle Ages was an important wine-growing and wine-trading center, with 200 marketing yards, wine cellars and its own fleet of barges.

Not only was the wine-growing area extended, but vintners also enlarged their knowledge. Steep slopes were terraced and diverse methods of training the vines introduced (stake training, wire training, high training on a pergola system).

More attention was paid to the quality of the wine. Until the time of Charlemagne, mixed blends prevailed. There were two classes of wine, the *vinum hunicum* and the *vinum francium*, of which the latter cost twice as much as the former.

"Theological wine" from the monasteries was especially valued because for the monks it was quality, not quantity, that counted. They changed their attitude, however, when they discovered that their wine was a lucrative commodity. Although the economic boom continued and wine-growing spread further—in the twelfth century, wine-growing was carried on even in Schleswig-Holstein and Denmark—the wine's quality deteriorated markedly.

By 1400 the total wine-growing area covered approximately .75 million acres. Wine had become cheap due to a surplus of production, and had replaced beer as the favorite thirst-quencher. The average annual per capita consumption came to 150 litres of wine or more. Many a worthy Würzburger even polished off 1,000 litres per year! Apparently, the wine's diminishing quality had no effect whatsoever on demand. Anyone now praising the wine culture of those good old times, still laboring under the delusion that only unadulterated dry wines were on the market, knows nothing about the methods then practiced to improve the wine. The following additives were officially recommended: egg white, egg yolk, milk, cheese, yeast, boiled wine, brandy, honey, bacon, pork, staghorn, wheat flour, barley flour, starch, olive oil, beechwood chippings, oak gall, clay, sand and table salt. As preserving agents, hops, juniper wood, juniper berries, valerian, garlic seeds, sour cherries, almonds, mustard, aniseed, nutmeg, pepper, vermouth, elder blossoms, cinnamon, caraway and lemons were used. Mead was often added to sweeten wine.

When around 1350 a nephew of the Holy Roman Emperor, Louis of Bavaria, visited the grandmaster of the Teutonic Order in Marienburg, he was served wine from the vineyards on the hills near Thorn (western Prussia). The guest found the wine so excellent that his "snout was sticky" and he demanded more. The chronicler tactfully kept silent about the after-effects.

Apart from the officially recommended additives, there were some which the law prohibited. But in the Middle Ages the adulteration of wine was such a common practice that the Prince Bishop of Würzburg, Otto von Wolfskeel (who officiated 1333–1345), insisted that it should be forbidden to use anything but grapes for wine-making.

But however exotic the mixture, it was poured down the throat. Drunkenness was a sign of belonging to the fashionable world. Only some clear-headed men harshly condemned the drinking habits of the day. In the sixteenth century Hans Turmaier of Abensberg said of the Bavarians, "The Bavarian people are spiritual, wicked and righteous. . . . They drink a lot and sit day and night over their wine."

Even more outspoken was Martin Luther (1483–1546). The reformer and founder of German Protestantism complained:

> Unfortunately the whole of Germany is plagued by drunkards. We preach and shout about this, but all in vain. It is a bad old tradition. In Teutonic countries . . . it has increased and still is increasing.

Wine, once praised as the drink and the gift of the gods—according to Luther, "Beer is the work of man, wine comes from God"—had lost much of its prestige. It is an idle thought whether the gods may have

An old engraving of the monastery at Eberbach in the Rheingau, an important medieval wine-trading center.

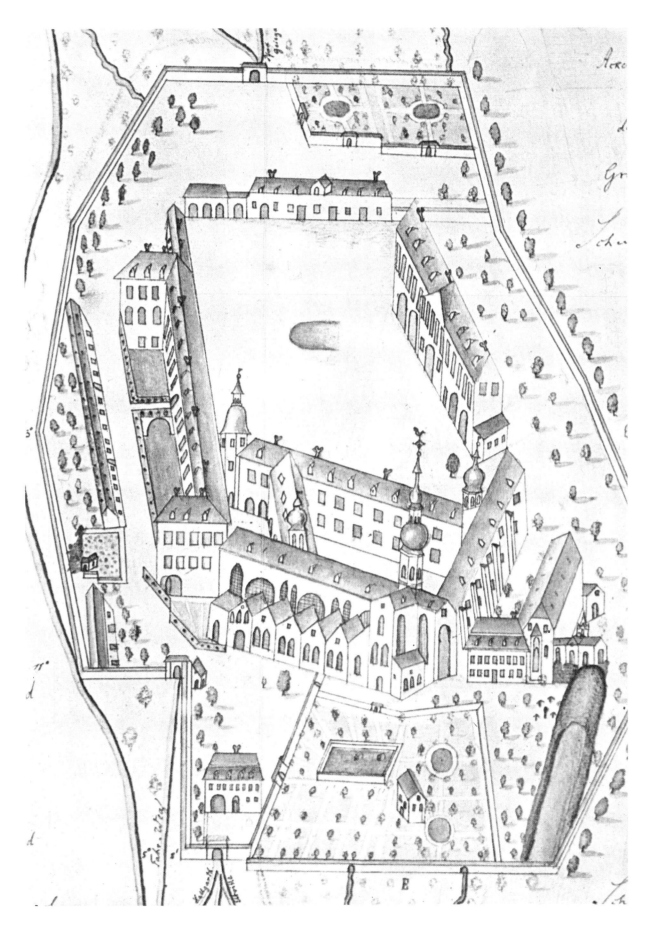

wanted to get rid of the ghosts they had summoned. Anyway, after the "century of carousing," the seventeenth century represented a turning point.

The price of beer went down. Through the trading activities of the Hanseatic League, cheaper and sweeter wines from the Mediterranean regions gained access to the German market. The Central European climate worsened, and more and more pests spread.

Moreover, the expansion of wine-growing had led to overproduction. Empty casks were sparse. After good wine years (a rarity in the Middle Ages), many casks were emptied in order to make room for the new, better vintages. Thus, in 1484 the vintners around Lake Constance poured approximately 1 million litres of wine into the lake.

The trade in homegrown wine had become unprofitable, not least through the proliferation of customs barriers between the ever more separate German states. Countless rulers cashed in on each transit of goods across the border. Many of the castles today standing as picturesque ruins were nothing but troublesome customhouses, such as the beautiful Pfalz Castle near Kaub.

In the sixteenth century, southern and western Germany were shaken by the Peasants' War. In the conquered palaces and castles, such as the Hambach Castle, the peasants smashed all the big wine casks. The peasants, who were then nothing but miserable slaves, being fully occupied with making war on their oppressors, had neither the time nor the inclination to work in the vineyards, which in consequence deteriorated.

Sometimes, though, wine protected the nobility and their castles from destruction. When the peasants appeared in Leiningen, in the Palatinate, to ravage the castle, they were amazed to see the gates wide open and the lady of the castle in person invite them to a merry feast with plenty of wine. The peasants fell to with a will and forgot all about the purpose of their visit.

The peasants in the Rheingau did not suffer as much as those in southern Germany. In this region, neither slavery nor compulsory duty existed. For centuries, the peasants had been yeomen whose rights had been confirmed in the "Weistum" of 1324, the first constitution of the Rheingau. Despite this, they too rebelled, and threatened the Eberbach monastery.

On May 2, 1525, peasants gathered on the juniper heath bordering the monastery. Their blood was up because the clerical lords had recently imposed local taxes on them. Moreover, the monks sold their own wine free of tax, which was a thorn in the side of the vintners. They demanded the same right for themselves, and in addition they had another pressing request: They did not want to go on paying duty on their wine at the Ehrenfels customs station.

The Rheingau peasants had sent their demands to Mainz and asked for a speedy decision. The gathering on the juniper heath was meant to emphasize their wishes. But the authorities in Mainz took their time, and thus the monks of Eberbach got a taste of the peasants' angry mood and violent behavior. They were compelled to feed their uninvited guests, which meant that six thousand bushels of flour and grain and nearly all the cattle, poultry and stored meats were devoured. The ample meals must have made the peasants enormously thirsty, because the great vat of Eberbach

The wondrous history of the driving force of a wine in Franconia, preserved in a print from the year 1577.

26

Ein Neuye Wunderbare vnnd Warhafftige geschicht / von einem

Weintrauben / Welcher sich durch Gottes Segen wunderbarlich erzeyget hat. Geschehen Anno LXXVII.

Als tausent vnd fünffhundert Jar
Sibensibßig die jarzal war/
Begab sich warhafftig die geschicht
Wie ich den albie thu bericht/
Geschehen in Ochsenfort der Stadt
Im Franckenlandt welchs auch krat/
Ligt am Wasser mit nam der Mayn
Gantz weit erkandt / von groß vñ klein/
Drin wont ein Herr gantz wol bekandt
Michael hinderdössfer gnandt/
Derselbig ein Weingarten hat
Derselbig ligt nit weit vor der Stadt/
Auff der Frickheuser marck eben
Drin steht ein Weinstock hat zwu reben/
Sambt andren klein reben endtsprossen
Auß obgmelter Stock herauß gschosse/
Der einig obgmelt Reb versteht
Der zur rechten hand hinauß geht/

Angebunden an einen pfal
Der hat getragen dazu mal/
Den schön Weintrauben der gestalt
Wie er albie steht abgemalt/
Vnd diser Reb da das Aug rauß
Entsprossen ist/hat sich vor auß
Voneinander zutheilet fein
Also das achtzehn Weintreiblein/
Sein worden welchs nit verwundrung
Haben gesehen alt vnd jung/
Vil Würtzburger / vnd andre warn
Kamen geritten vnd gefarn/
Sahen den Treubel mit verlangn
Das ein Aug / wie man pfleget zusagn/
Solt allein achtzen treublein tragn/
Denn zwischen jeden Trauben fein
Sein gewachssen schöne weinbletlein/

Letzlich hat der Herr des Weingarten
Jn lassen verzeun/das dem zarten/
Gwechs /kein schad nit zu handen kem
Nun hat sich begeben nach dem/
Das ein böß Mensch sich hat beflissn
Das schön gwechs heimlich abgerissn/
Welchs vnzeitig /jhm nichts nutz war
Zwu ander Perschon kamen dar/
Zu sehen auch das göttlichwunder
Funden den Treubel liegen wunder/
Dem Weinstock /vnden auf der Erdt
Den hubens auff/mit beschwerdt/
Trugens jn gen Ochsenfurt
Vnd gaben dem Herrn zeisein/
Den empfieng er mit grossen schmertzen
Also wenn Gott ein frommen hertzen/
Noch etwas guts gibt zugeniessen
Das thut dem Teuffel hartverdriessen/

Schaut wie er richt ein schaden an
Wo ers selbst nicht außrichten kan/
So schickt er seinen botten dar
Drumb sol wir billich gantz vnd gar/
Zu Gott rüffen das er bewar
Die Frücht auff dem Feldt jmmerdar/
Vnd auch dieselben laß erspriessn
Das wirs mögen mit danck geniessn/
Vnd außtheilen gantz Brüderlich
Vnd dem geitz Teuffel wehr gwaltig
Sambt allem vnglück vnd elendt
Helff vns jmmer ewig/ Amende.

Gedruckt zu Nürnberg / durch
Alexander Pfeiffer.

containing 74,000 litres of wine was emptied save for a negligible residue.

Lucky Rheingau, where a lot of wine but very little blood flowed during the Peasants' War! While the Rheingau peasants feasted merrily on the juniper heath, elsewhere the rebels fought against the troops of the Swabian League and were disastrously beaten. They were executed by the thousands.

Perhaps the generous wine supply had cooled the anger of the Rheingau peasants; anyway, they surrendered unconditionally to the troops of the ruling princes, paid the fees and taxes demanded and relinquished their privileges. Some of their leaders were executed, but the majority got away unharmed. For a long time the spring of 1525 was a painful memory, as is witnessed by a song about these events:

> *Als ich auf dem Wacholder sass,*
> *Tranken wir aus dem grossen Fass.*
> *Wie bekam uns das?*
> *Wie dem Hund das Gras!*
> *Der Teufel gesegnet uns das!*

> When on the juniper I sat,
> We drank from the great vat.
> How did we like that?
> Like a dog the grass.
> The Devil blessed us, at that!

But to return to the vat at Eberbach, the custom of making bigger and bigger wine casks developed during the heyday of feudalism, when the absolute princes tried to outdo each other. The last of these mammoth casks can still be seen in the castle at Heidelberg. It was made in 1750 by order of the Elector Charles Theodore of the Palatinate and has a length of 10 metres, a height of 7 metres and a capacity of 221,726 litres. (It was in use for only twenty years.)

There was a very simple reason for the extreme size of the vats. They served as storage tanks for the vintner's "tithe" (up to 80 percent of the total yield). From these casks civil servants and workmen were paid in kind. The wines were not separated according to their origin, so as to preclude some people receiving better quality than others. One can safely assume that the casks contained quite an exotic mixture.

Wine-growing was affected badly by the rising taxes. Even the Reformation, initiated by Martin Luther in the sixteenth century, was not exactly a blessing for the vintners. While it was true that the re-establishment of the Communion—i.e., bread and wine—promoted the sale of wine, the secularization caused many monasteries and their vineyards to be confiscated by princes who had embraced Protestantism. Thus many superbly situated vineyards passed into incompetent hands. The result was that in many regions wine-growing stopped altogether or was administered inefficiently and indifferently.

The religious controversies in Central Europe escalated steadily until they erupted in the Thirty Years' War (1618–1648). By that time, the theological differences between Protestantism and Catholicism were no longer the issue. The conflict had turned into a political struggle, in which everybody brought forth his own claims to power. Foreign armies crushed fields and vineyards. Cellars were pilfered, peasants slain. Only in some relatively safe places was wine still being produced, but then only in small quantities and of inferior quality. When at long last the Peace of Westphalia ended the horror of the war, the wine-growing areas, formerly so carefully tended, had turned fallow.

What had been left was destroyed by year-round hunts held by the ruling princes, who immediately resumed their former way of life. They thought only about whiling away the time agreeably and filling their bellies; one Duke of Württemberg was so fat that he had a section sawed from his dining table to fit his potbelly. Peasants and vintners had to serve as beaters—after all, they were nothing but slaves. Many of them froze to death in winter, because they had no warm clothes. Regardless of the damage to fields, the hunt went merrily over hedge and ditch. And whatever was not ruined by the caprice of the princes was destroyed by famine and the plague.

But the production of wine had not come to a standstill in all parts of Germany. While northern Germany and Bavaria (with the exception of Franconia) abandoned wine-growing altogether, the damage along the Main and Rhine and their tributaries was not quite so severe. Thus a promising new start was made—which was, however, halted by another war in some regions.

When Louis XIV of France, the "Sun King" (1643–1715), felt the urge to enlarge his power and started predatory wars, his armies invaded the Rhineland. The Rhine Palatinate was hit especially hard when it was vandalized between 1688 and 1697.

But this did not stop the replanting of the vineyards. At first, vines were chosen with a view to maximizing the quantity harvested; however, the quality of the wine was so inferior that progress was slow.

The fact that wine-growing did recover in the eighteenth century was due not only to the popularity of the drink, but also to the support it received from progressive-minded princes and the clergy. One of the foremost promoters was the Elector Charles Theodore.

Around this time, new scientific discoveries also began to bear fruit. Systematic pest control was initiated. High-quality vines were chosen and propagated, and cellaring methods improved. The monasteries made use of the findings of ancient Roman agricultural authors, who reported large yields of up to 120 hectolitres per hectare (49 hectolitres per acre), in contrast to a maximum in the Middle Ages of only 40 hectolitres per hectare (16 hectolitres per acre) in the wine-growing regions of Germany.

A large harvest does not necessarily mean one of good quality, while a small harvest does not necessarily improve the quality of the wine. At that time, the vines yielded only small harvests because the methods of cultivation were extremely poor.

It was eventually realized that the site of a vineyard plays an important role and that geographically determined cultivation can bring a marked improvement in quality.

The year 1775 is a milestone in the history of wine-making. It was virtually the start of the era of the Qualitätswein mit Prädikat ("specially graded quality wine"). In that year, the value of "noble rot" was discovered accidentally. It happened in the monastery of Johannisberg, which was then owned by the Diocese of Fulda. The prince bishop had reserved the right for himself to determine the moment for grape picking. A mounted courier brought the ripe grapes to him for tasting. But as it happened, the courier was a few weeks late. (We do not know whether he was held up by robbers or others or whether he succumbed to the charms of a fair maiden.) Anyway, the monks waited impatiently but obediently for permission to start picking. Meanwhile, the ripe grapes were left hanging on the vines. They withered and became even more unsightly when a fungus (*Botrytis cinerea*) started to cover them. Nevertheless, after the return of the courier, the thrifty monks harvested the grapes and pressed them. On February 26, 1776, the new wine was sampled. What a surprise when it was found that these overripe and partly rotten grapes yielded the finest wine! Thus the term "noble rot" (*Edelfäule*) was coined and Spätlese, Auslese, Beerenauslese and Trockenbeerenauslese entered the wine scene, even though these terms were introduced much later. As mentioned earlier, late harvesting had been practised by the Romans, but German vintners cultivated and perfected this method after 1775.

In the Rheingau, the first important classification was introduced: "Cabinet" wine. This term had already been used by the monks of Eberbach who stored the best wines in a *Cabinetkeller* ("cabinet-cellar"). Now, for the first time, it was applied in "sales promotion": In 1779 the Johannisberg monastery sold an especially noble wine under the term "Cabinetwein."

The name persisted even after the Napoleonic secularization of 1802 and 1803, and it gained in value when a few clever princes like the Duke of Nassau (who had taken over the monastery of Eberbach) and Prince Metternich (the new owner of the former Johannisberg monastery, now Schloss Johannisberg) realized and exploited the advantages of such a classification.

In the nineteenth century, the physicist Christian Ferdinand Oechsle (1774–1852) initiated a new development when he invented the must scales to ascertain the exact measurement of the sugar content of the grape must. Today, the Oechsle system is a determining factor of how a wine will be handled in the cellar, and it also supplies the basis for the definition of its quality.

One degree Oechsle equals one gram above the specific gravity weight of water (1 litre)—i.e., 1 litre must with 80 degrees Oechsle is 80 grams heavier than 1 litre water.

However, thirty years after the introduction of Oechsle's scale, wine-growing in Europe—which had reached a peak in the first decades of the nineteenth century—seemed to have been dealt its death blow. This time the cause was neither a war nor the thoughtless ignorance of ruling princes but a plain-looking insect which in 1865 demonstrated its activity for the first time in the French province of Languedoc. For a long time the search for the cause of the terrible grape disease, which had devastated the vineyards and spread like a conflagration, brought no result.

Three years after its first appearance, the "vine louse" was discovered by Professor Planchon, of Montpellier. He named it "*Phylloxera vastatrix*," i.e., "devastating leaf-parcher." The question of its origin was also answered: Between 1858 and 1862, large shipments of vines from the eastern part of America had arrived in southern France, and with them came a most undesirable stowaway—the vine louse.

The vine louse which sucked the root of the vine dry—not the grapes, as was erroneously believed—spread all over Europe. For a short time it was stopped at the borders of Germany, because in 1873 Chancellor Bismarck prohibited the importation of vines. But because this scourge of the vineyards multiplied at a tremendous speed and was not necessarily dependent on the vine as its only means of transportation, it also invaded Germany. In 1881, it made its first appearance in the Ahr valley, with devastating results.

At the close of the century, the damage had become incalculable. Wherever the vine louse appeared, all vines had to be destroyed. And it was not only the vine louse which threatened to extinguish wine-growing in Europe; some other plagues had also been carried in from America, such as *Peronospora* (downy mildew) and *Oidium* (powdery mildew).

As a consequence, the German wine-growing region shrank from approximately 150,000 hectares (370,000 acres) in 1870 to 100,000 hectares (247,100 acres) in 1914. None of the remedies applied (such as flooding infested vineyards) was successful. Only when European vines were grafted onto immune American rootstocks could the vintners hope again. But it took many decades before adaptation was completed. As late as 1949 the well-known vine cultivator Georg Scheu wrote in his *Winzerbuch* (*"Winegrower's Book"*) about the "disastrous extent of vine-louse infestation."

One of the tasks of the viticulture institute in Geisenheim in the Rheingau—an academy of international standing—has been the elimination of this problem, for the vine louse is still living in our vineyards. The research division of the academy conducts large-scale testing in which rootstocks are matched to the various types of grapes. It is also concerned with the cultivation of vines.

The end of the nineteenth century brought decisive progress in the field of wine-making. The French chemist and biologist Louis Pasteur (1822–1895) had not only discovered the action of certain bacteria on fermentation, but also the fact that wine, just like must and other liquids, can be cleared of microorganisms by heating. These findings facilitated control of the fermentation process.

But not all new developments were so welcome. In those years, the adulteration of wine and the production of artificial wine became common practices. Even the first German Wine Law of 1892 was no help, for while it branded artificial wine as a falsification, it permitted its sale if labelled accordingly.

It was left to the Wine Law of 1901 to prohibit the sale of artificial or excessively sugared wines. That this law was frequently violated was demonstrated by the doctoral thesis of Theodor Heuss, written in 1905. The later president of the Federal Republic of Germany, who was then twenty years old, did not mince words:

> The combined growing of good and inferior qualities and the throwing together of black and white grapes was then—and to a considerable extent still is—an evil habit . . . because it destroys the individuality of a kind right from the start.

But in the course of time, the German vintners tried to preserve the character of their wines. The common practice of blending with imported wines (which was finally prohibited by the Wine Law of 1930) was also abandoned slowly but surely.

After the end of World War II, as after World War I, wine-growing in Germany suffered a considerable setback, partly due to the lack of qualified workers and partly because of the lack of insecticides. But in 1949, there was a revolutionary development which remedied most of the neglect and damage within an amazingly short period of time. It was a wine miracle within the economic miracle, so to speak.

Today, far more than half of the German wine-growing regions have been consolidated into larger and more economical areas, a prerequisite for an increase in profitability and an improvement in quality. Now approximately two thousand hectares (five thousand acres) are equipped with sprinkler systems as protection against drought, an achievement which was once virtually unheard of in wine-growing. Harvesting methods have also been refined so that they are now ruled by the laws of quality. The aim is no longer to delay the harvest as long as possible; instead, the grapes are gathered in accordance with their degree of maturity. The modern vintner knows that some varieties are ripe for harvesting in early September, while others, such as the Riesling, take a few weeks longer.

New grape varieties are being developed and tried out, and some, which give better yields of a good quality, have come to stay. The Müller-Thurgau, a grape developed in Geisenheim towards the end of the nineteenth century from a crossing by the Swiss Hermann Müller of canton Thurgau, is today the dominant variety in West Germany.

Some recently evolved crossings that have proved their worth and which we would be loath to miss are Scheurebe, Kerner, Huxel, Kanzler, Faber, Morio-Muskat, Bacchus, Optima, Ehrenfelser, Rieslaner and Ortega. Other newly developed varieties will disappear if the results of the tryout period, which covers a few decades, show that they do not meet the requirements.

Fertilizing has also been improved. These measures have had the affect of increasing yields two- or even threefold in only three decades. Today's average exceeds 100 litres per hectare (40.5 litres per acre), which is considerably more than in other leading wine-growing countries.

There have, of course, also been advances in wine-making techniques. Among the numerous new developments, the mobile horizontal centrifuge must be mentioned. This increases the yield from the juice and offers a gentler treatment of the skins and pips. In addition, there are now special vats for low-temperature and high-temperature fermentation. For improvement of the taste, especially with regard to alcohol and bouquet, pressure tanks have been designed in which the fermentation process can be controlled.

The cellarers have learned how to soften the high acidity of some wines by adding unfermented grape juice (*Süssreserve*). This method provokes criticism when used excessively, because the wine then loses its overall balance and simply tastes sweet. That is certainly not to the liking of even those who prefer a slightly sweet wine, and this holds true for the majority of wine-drinkers in Germany.

Anyway, the cellarer has not had too much latitude in blending wines, because the maximum quantity *Süssreserve* allowed has been strictly set down in the Wine Law.

There have also been changes with respect to the vats. The wooden cask has largely been replaced by receptacles made of other materials. The maturing process of the wine can now be controlled much better. Still, some romantically inclined wine-lovers may dream with sentimental longing of a cellar filled with wooden casks. For this reason many estates reserve at least a "representative corner" in their cellars where handsome old wooden casks are on show.

The Wine Law of 1971 abolished the terms "Naturrein" ("unadulterated") and "Originalabfüllung" ("estate-bottled"), and introduced a three-category scale of quality—namely, Deutscher Tafelwein ("German table wine"), Qualitätswein ("quality wine") and Qualitätswein mit Prädikat ("specially graded quality wine"). The old traditional term "Cabinet," which once served to signalize the special quality of a Spätlese or Auslese, has also found a place in the new legislation. The word "Kabinett" now signifies the lowest group of Qualitätswein mit Prädikat.

Fortunately for the German wine consumer the price of wine has been kept stable, particularly when compared with the prices of other luxury articles. It has even dropped in relation to national income over the past decades. The average pay for one working hour buys a considerably larger quantity of wine than it did in the early part of this century or even ten or twenty years ago. And thanks to the manifold advances discussed above, the quality of wine has much improved, so that it is now more beneficial to health. To support this latter claim it is no longer necessary to cite physicians of classical antiquity: Modern physicians share this opinion and have classified wine as a remedy in the broader sense of the word.

The Vineyard,
Cradle of Culture

Wine enhances human emotion and gives a sparkling lustre to festivities of any kind. This source of exuberance and strength has encouraged man to create works of art of imperishable value. At all times and throughout all periods of art, wine has been a subject of artistic inspiration. It has stimulated man's artistic genius to the full and roused him to great works.

A few lines in the great Sumerian epic *Gilgamesh*, which was created in the second millenium B.C., can be considered the first praise of wine in literature. In this poem, Utnapishtim, "eldest of the ancients," tells how he encouraged the men who helped him build the ark which was to save him from the great flood:

> Cattle I slaughtered for the people,
> Sheep I killed daily.
> With must, sesame wine, oil and wine
> I refreshed the workmen as with water
>   from the river,
> So that they feasted, like a New Year's
>   Day. . . .

The earliest permanent sculptural monuments on the subject of wine are the reliefs in the rock-cut tombs of El Kab, a site of ruins on the Upper Nile and once the metropolis of an independent kingdom. Many potsherds, dating 1300–100 B.C.,

show rich decorations picturing vine leaves and wine. So the burial chamber at Luxor (on the site of ancient Thebes) in Upper Egypt contains many sculptured reliefs decorated with drinking scenes. The wine sacrifice to the gods is also a common subject.

Also shown is how Egyptian society women used wine as an elixir to enrich their morning toilet. Instructive, and at the same time impressive, is a representation of highly enjoyable aspects of the life of the Egyptians, who had wine in plenty, found in a small grave dating back to the heyday of Thebes. (In the eighteenth dynasty, ca. 1500 B.C., Egypt was a great power.) At merry banquets the wine flowed like water. The harvesting of the grapes and a wine press are also represented. In a later portrayal, profane allegorical scenes showing cults as well as wine customs form the themes. The intoxicating strength and effect of the wine is not concealed.

Just as in the valley of the Nile, artistic work elsewhere in the Near East was abundant. Here too, time and again, wine, vines and grapes form the motif. It is above all the larger-than-life sculpted relief figures of the Hittites, dating from 1500 to 1200 B.C. and found to the east of Ankara, that show the way these people brought God, man, animals and wine together.

Symbolism of fertility is the central theme of a picture from about 730 B.C. in which the king is served wine by the Hittite god of fertility.

In the rocky "Garden of Babylon" very early and quite naturalistic portrayals of grapes have been found. And at Nineveh sculptures have been found showing themes connected with wine.

However, none of the civilizations following the Sumerians and ancient Egyptians were as involved with the mysteries of wine as the Greeks. Wine played a role not only in poetry and philosophy, but also to a considerable extent in the visual arts. In Greek classics from the fifth century B.C. on, the wine god Dionysus appears as the ideal figure of athletic youth.

The Greeks in fact managed, particularly in sculpture, to intensify the portrayal of Dionysus, while the Romans often portrayed their Bacchus as superficial, without depth and spirit. On this subject Hermann Jung, in his *Wine in Art*, says:

> In an ecstasy of both bliss and pain the devotees of Dionysus sought unification with the gods. And so they too were inspired by this cult, the art emanating from the mysticism of wine, deeply impressed with a high ethic and at the same time a touch of tragedy which at that time blessed the wine god.

From the mid–fourth century B.C. comes what is probably the most famous and artistically most perfect sculpture of the wine god, a marble bust of the child Dionysus. Its creator was the great sculptor Praxiteles.

Among the numerous statues relating to Dionysus must be mentioned a bronze satyr of the Hellenic-Roman epoch which can be admired in the National Museum in Naples. It typifies the type, Dionysus as drunken companion.

Hermann Jung points out that

> apart from Dionysus and the lascivious adjutants who accompanied him—the satyrs, originally woodland demons, and Silenus, rollicking, drunken, bloated companion of the wine god—other Dionistic exponents of Greek mythology were portrayed: Ganymede, the cupbearer and beloved favorite of Zeus, who according to Homer was carried off to Olympus because of his beauty and so that he could fill Zeus's cup and at the same time provide his amorous services. One of the most important statues of Ganymede from an artistic point of view is a bronze figure created by the Attic sculptor Leochares (fourth century B.C.). It shows how Ganymede is carried off by one of Zeus's eagles from among a group of people.

The Greek vase painters in the eighth century B.C. played a unique artistic role. In addition to vases, drinking vessels and plates were painted with similar motifs.

One of the most beautiful works of this kind of art is a bowl by Exekias (550 B.C.) which shows a sea voyage of Dionysus. Another—one of the most precious works of all time—is the plate painted by Psiax showing Anacreon with a drinking bowl and lyre. From this particularly productive Greek artistic era also came vase paintings using as a motif the symposium—the assembly of male intellectuals following a good meal with plentiful wine for the purpose of discussion and debate. Precious bowls and cups with magnificent symposium scenes can be seen in Europe's museums. In Vienna a relief sculpture of an ancient Dionysian theatre can be admired.

If one follows the path of wine from Mesopotamia and Assyria over Egypt to Greece and on to southern Italy, one comes to the Etruscans. It is very interesting to see, to experience, how the Greek influence was carried on here. The Greeks and Etruscans took part in a regular cultural exchange. We can to this day wonder at the majestic colors and clearness of their works of art. The most important and most perfect works of Etruscan artists come from the period straddling the fifth and fourth centuries B.C. We can find them above all in the decoration of their ostentatious tombs to the north of Rome.

Hermann Jung believes the tomb frescoes —designed to help the dead remember their happy earthly existence with sumptuous banquets together with scantily dressed women—to be the oldest, most unusual and largest collection of paintings representing bacchanalian scenes (Tomb of the Leopards, 470 B.C.).

These portrayals mirror the cheerful way of life brought about by wine for these ancient people. Later the Etruscans' optimism was overshadowed by the Greek-inspired belief in demons.

Etruscan amphoras and bowls show abundantly the joy these people had in wine. In Florence there is a drinking bowl from the second half of the fourth century B.C. with particularly charming Dionysian motifs.

The Romans inspired themselves with the spirit of Dionysus in their licentious Bacchus festivals; however, their Bacchanalia suffered increasingly from superficiality, even decadence. Neither the mystic liquid nor the spiritual exaltation was decisive, but rather the ever-increasing profane sensual enjoyment. From this time— A.D. 130–160 —comes the famous Bacchus temple at Heliopolis, the present Baalbek in Lebanon. Hermann Jung considers it the greatest monument still existing that was ever dedicated to the wine god. It is a showpiece on the old Acropolis of Baalbek, erected by Antonius Pius and his successor.

Around the birth of Jesus Christ, while many Roman monuments became increasingly superficial and even repeated themselves in copies, the art of sculpture received a new boost. Its motifs were mainly mythical and allegorical conceptions: Time and again new themes were created from the Bacchus myths. The sacrifice to the wine god found great importance as a motif. At this time Bacchus was eagerly connected with related gods— Venus, Amor, Ceres, Diana. Hermann Jung on this point has written:

> To the personification of wine through Bacchus was connected the personification of eroticism or love (Venus, Amor) at the same time as an allegory on the effect of wine or the symbolization of fertility through the connection with Ceres. Often as an accompanying phenomenon appeared the muse of music, upon which the festive motif of the Bacchanalia rested.

Wine lovers interested in history and art who visit Italy are strongly urged to visit the ruins of Pompeii. Nowhere else in the whole world are there such beautiful, perfect artistic portrayals dedicated to wine. Although the objects originating there now fill museums all over the world, a sheer, inexhaustible wealth remains in Pompeii. They all unite in a single glorification of wine, and bear witness to the happy way of life of the people of Pompeii. In the House of the Satyr, the House of the

Greek dish from around 530 B.C.: the wine god Dionysus on his sea voyage. Staatliche Antikensammlung, Munich.

Centenarian, the House of Golden Love, the House of the Silver Anniversary, the House of M. Lucretius Frontos—everywhere the god Bacchus triumphs. Hermann Jung describes one of many:

The most precious and expressive frescoes were discovered by archeologists during the excavation of the House of Mysteries near the city of Pompeii. It is the reproduction of an intoxicating series from the cult of Dionysian mysteries with sybaritical dances by satyrs, Silenus and agonizingly ecstatic, delirious women. As a document this imposing religious fresco is especially important as the last reflected splendor of the still etherealized Dionysus cult of Greek conception. This work of art is comparable to the swan song, a mystery anchored in culture which has been gradually degraded by the Romans to spiritlessness.

In Germany we have from this era a colored portrayal of Bacchus in a mosaic floor, created by Roman artists, which enchants with its beauty. It was found near the south door of the Cologne cathedral in 1941, during the building of an air-raid shelter. At forty-seven square meters it is one of the biggest and most beautiful to be seen north of the Alps. The motif shows a drunken Bacchus falling upon a satyr carrying Thyrsos, surrounded by satyrs who in bacchanalian dance are leading an amorous chase of Maenads.

With the Romans, as with the Etruscans, wine influenced the artistic decoration of burial monuments. Wine and the vine were always glorified. Particularly famous are the sculptures from Roman tombs. Two of these, the Neumagen Wine Ship and the Cheerful Helmsman, are to be found in their original form in the Landesmuseum in Trier. They were discovered in the 1890's on the Moselle.

By the time of the transition from the Roman period to the Christian era the religious significance of wine had become temporarily lost.

Christ raised wine to the symbol of eternal life, changing it into God's blood. ("Drink ye all of it; for this is my blood. . . .").

Thereby the religious importance of wine continued. Christian religious art has expressed this many times, as for example in the symbolic portrayal *Christus im Kelche* in the monastery of Neuberg near Vienna (ca. 1600). Leonardo Da Vinci's *The Last Supper* is indeed the greatest work on this theme.

In Germany to the present day, many artists, such as Albrecht Dürer, Fritz von Uhde and Emil Nolde, have created expressive portrayals of this theme.

In the Middle Ages Biblical wine motifs found more and more acceptance. This may be seen in the column shafts in the cathedrals at Cologne, Trier, Speyer, Mainz and Strasbourg. In their ornamentation the vine or the grape often appears. We admire the prelates' pew in the monastery church in Maulbronn (1146), a masterpiece of highly developed Gothic wood-carving, or the beautiful choir pews of the wood-carver Falkener von Abensperg (1510) in St. Valentine's Church in Kiedrich in the Rheingau. The side walls of the latter are a lively but harmonious interlaced ornament of vines and grapes. Here we can find a further architectural delicacy, a band of vines under the triangular gable-end of the west gate (1310).

In the wine museum in Speyer a sculpture one meter high made out of lime wood and dating from the eighteenth century is kept, depicting the first wine-grower, Noah, wearing a wine-grower's apron.

In the Biblical subject "The Scout," two men are carrying an oversized grape which they have brought back from their reconnaissance in order to prove the existence of the land of milk and honey. This subject is to be found in many artistic portrayals, as in the Verduner altar in Klosterneuburg near Vienna (1181).

In the Rheingau this subject is also very

The Last Supper **(Giotto di Bondone, ca. 1300). Christ says of the wine, "This is my blood. . . ."**

common. Its symbolism expresses, "From the Holy Virgin we have received the grape of life." One of the most beautiful madonnas is to be found in the Gothic church at Kiedrich. Mary smiles blissfully and carries a sceptre with vine leaves and a crown. This portrayal comes from the thirteenth century.

The "Schröter madonna" with child and grape from 1430 is also famous, as is the "grape madonna" in the Suermondt Museum in Aachen, the "rustic madonna" in the town hall in Lorch, the regal "radiant madonna" in the cathedral at Xanten and the especially precious and expressive madonna with child and grape from the famous altar of Mary in the same church (1536). One of the most beautiful madonnas must be the "heavenly queen with child and grape" in Rauenthal, made in the

Baroque style of the seventeenth century. Worth seeing also is the three-figure Anna-Selbdritt group which can be found in Cologne, Aachen, Trier and in Iphofen in Franconia. This shows Saint Anne with the Virgin Mary and child Jesus. One of the figures is always holding a grape. Lucas Cranach the Elder (1472–1553) has glorified this, too, with his painting *Madonna mit der Traube* (*"Madonna with Grape"*) to be found in Munich's Pinakothek.

Saint Urban with the grape, a variant of this madonna theme, is to be found in wood or stone in numerous churches in Germany's wine-growing areas. Special mention must be made of the column in the palace church at Vollrads in the Rheingau, which dates from the sixteenth century.

The bacchanalian themes of the previous centuries were resurrected once more in the fifteenth and sixteenth centuries. Here we must mention Titian (1477–1576), the master of the High Renaissance, whose *Bacchanale* is in the Prado in Madrid and whose lifelike *Bacchus and Ariadne* is in the National Gallery in London.

In Germany it was Albrecht Dürer, Hans Holbein the Younger and Hans Baldung who time and again in picture, carving or copper-plate engraving took up the Bacchus theme. Cranach also took the drunkenness of Bacchus as his theme. Holbein transformed mythological conceptions into rustic bacchanalia. In the sixteenth century Rubens fashioned bacchanalian motifs. The erotic is expounded as being the main content of bacchanalian themes. For one of the most beautiful, elegant and serene compositions concerning the secrets surrounding wine, we must thank Rembrandt for his self-portrait, in which, with his wife Saskia, he raises a small high-stemmed wineglass and drinks to the onlookers.

Spanish artists also took up the Bacchus theme. Velasquez created masterly portrayals, which can be found in the Prado in Madrid.

In the seventeenth and eighteenth centuries in Germany, numerous works on the bacchanal theme were created in, for example, Würzburg, Veitshöchheim, Bamberg, Ludwigsburg, Schwetzingen, Weickersheim and Trier. In the eighteenth century, Bacchus themes became increasingly important in the skilled crafts: in ivory carving, working wifh gold, porcelain- and sculpture-painting, ceramics, heraldry and decorative tiles as well as on drinking glasses and wine tankards. At this time, themes connected with wine take form in carpets, tapestries, and wood-carving on altars, choir pews, staircases, chests, cupboards, portals and elsewhere.

Without Bacchus and wine motifs many craftsmen would have found life difficult. We find Bacchus as a lusty goblin astride a barrel, as in the Ludwigsburg Schlosskeller and in the town hall in Bremen.

Since the sixteenth century we see for the first time in works of art, particularly paintings, Bacchus as a symbol of fall and the month of October.

From the eighteenth century into the nineteenth century, wine lost more and more of its popularity in Europe. Modern, fashionable drinks prevailed. With this the bacchanal in artistic presentations became rarer and rarer. When it does occur it is to be called more realistic than bacchantic, as, for example, in the almost severe portrayal by Francisco Goya in *The Wine Harvest*.

In the nineteenth century, Arnold Böcklin

The grape is to be found in many church motifs. Shown here is the madonna of Geisenheim.

40

first took up mythological bacchanalian themes, to be followed by Anselm Feuerbach, Johann Peter Hasenclever and Eduard Grützner, all painting in a contemplative and sober manner. Wilhelm Busch's illustrations and portrayals connected with wine are, on the other hand, full of humor.

Probably the most important painter of this period who devoted himself to wine—and did so in the best sense of the word—was Max Slevogt. His incandescent fall pictures of the Palatinate, his lusty and ironic pen-and-ink drawings and his frescoes in the town hall in Bremen of themes from Hauff's joyous fantasies radiate happiness, humor and bliss.

Pablo Picasso dedicated several of his paintings and drawings to wine. They are truly bacchanalian, joyful, voluptuous and expressive of wine-besotted sensuality. His *Bacchanal* can be seen as the triumph of intoxication, sensual pleasure and eroticism. Regarding this, Hermann Jung says:

> No other work of modern art would be more suitable to round off this theme than this work of Picasso: According to examples over the centuries a masterpiece of modern style has been created, which chooses the mysteriousness of wine in eternal, invariable symbolism as artistic subject.

Let us turn to music. Little has been written about the influence of wine on musical composition. Nevertheless, many pieces of music use the theme of wine.

What have wine and music in common? Both can intoxicate us. Comparisons have often been made by artists fond of wine. It has often been perceived that Mozart's music corresponds to a Moselle wine, Bruckner's to a full-bodied Palatinate and Haydn's to a rustic Burgenland (Austria).

Such comparisons don't sound too far-fetched.

Ludwig Kusche, pianist and writer, gave a now unfortunately almost forgotten address at the opening of German Wine Week in 1959 in Munich on the theme "Wine, Music and Musical Wine," an address full of humor and perception. "Among the musicians who encouraged composing, wine-drinking must have been considered for a very long time a beautiful custom."

Kusche has determined that Johann Sebastian Bach was a great wine-drinker, and that even during the sermon he went down into the cellar to get himself in the right frame of mind for further playing on the organ. Knowing this, one should perhaps not play Bach's fugues as dryly as is often the case.

Haydn was an enthusiastic wine-drinker. "The greatest mistake with the interpretation of Haydn's music is that one plays him to affectedly, too girlishly, too much à la Rococo," criticizes Kusche. The wines of Burgenland—Haydn lived in Eisenstadt—have a lot of body; this quality is often missed in interpretations of Haydn quartets and symphonies. In his worldly oratorio *Die Jahreszeiten* ("*The Seasons*") he composed, in "Der Herbst" ("Autumn"), one of the most beautiful drinking choruses in all of music.

Kusche has written particularly humorously about Mozart. An old literary source had reported that, during his work on *Die Zauberflöte* ("*The Magic Flute*"), Mozart, at his lunch breaks, which he mostly took with his lyricist Schikaneder, "worked lustily, laughed and drank champagne." Champagne combined with *Zauberflöte* is a little suspect to Kusche, for at that time champagne was an expensive drink that Mozart half a year before his death, as

Bacchanal in earlier times: debauchery without bounds. Painting by Titian (1477–1576).

poor as a church mouse, could never have afforded. Schikaneder must have treated him, because he was so sure of the success of *Zauberflöte*. (And he was right: In 1791 alone the opera was performed twenty-four times, bringing Schikaneder nearly 8500 gulden, which for those times was an incredible amount. Mozart, however, received practically nothing from this.)

And now to Beethoven, the Rhinelander from Bonn, and a surprising statement from Kusche:

The master must have understood very little about wine, because it is reported to us by his faithful secretary Schindler that he had a great liking for adulterated and artificial wine. An intimate friend of Beethoven in later years tells us that he drank a lot of wine at table, and could also take a lot, and liked to drink in lively company. He did not compose after drinking.

Kusche refers to a saying of Max Reger: "In a stupor nobody composes, not even a genius."

Weber and Lortzing paid homage to wine. Lortzing's aria "Im Wein liegt Wahrheit nur allein" ("The Truth Lies in Wine Alone") became one of the best-known drinking songs. Another is the champagne-aria from Mozart's *Don Giovanni*. (Champagne? Not at all! In the original Italian text of Da Ponte no mention of champagne is made; this can only be an error in the German translation.)

Much more could be said about music and wine. Hoffmann's narrations from Offenbach's *Tales of Hoffmann*, for example, and the drinking bout at the beginning of the opera. (However, the libretto is incorrect in implying that the students drank beer and wine in large quantities; at Lutter und Wegner, their gathering-place in Berlin, beer was taboo. E. T. A. Hoffmann himself had never drunk "flaming punch.") Let us content ourselves with these examples of musical composition. Schubert, Schumann, Wolf and Richard Strauss could also be mentioned as examples of the creative power of wine.

In literature it is naturally Goethe from whom an extraordinary number of quotations come. The greatest German poet is confirmation of the theory that wine has stimulated mankind with ideas and also kept him in good health. With all due respect to Goethe, he drank wine in scandalous quantities. Two or three litres daily was his norm, and often he drank even more. All this without Goethe ever being seen to be intoxicated!

Goethe's life began and ended with wine. After his birth on August 28, 1749, apparently due to clumsiness on the part of his nanny, he was pronounced dead, without any sign of life. An attempt was made, however, to bring him back to life by putting him in a bath of hot wine, whereupon his grandmother cried out, "He lives!"

Wine was also not absent when his last hour struck on March 22, 1832. Goethe sipped his wine and then asked, "You haven't put any sugar in the wine?"

The countless verses of Goethe and his intimate relationship to wine have been the material for many stories and essays. We will content ourselves with one or two quotations. Here is the wonderful acknowledgment of Brother Martin in *Goetz von Berlichingen*:

Der Wein erfreut des Menschen Herz,
Und die Freudigkeit ist die Mutter aller
*   Tugenden.*
Wenn ihr Wein getrunken habt,
Seid ihr alles doppelt, was ihr sein sollt:
Noch einmal so leicht denkend,
Noch einmal so unternehmend,
Noch einmal so schnell ausführend.

When thou hast eaten and drunken,
Thou art as it were new-born,
Stronger, bolder, more ready for action.
After wine thou art double what thou
    shouldst be!
Twice as ingenious,
Twice as enterprising,
And twice as active.

Goethe should have been very thankful that it was possible for him to consume great quantities of this noble drink without any effects. He was well aware that others were not blessed with such steadfastness:

There are in wine productive powers
of a very important kind: But it all
depends upon the condition, time and
hour. What is beneficial for one is
damaging for the other.

Quality was everything for him. Often he enthused about the wine of the millenium,

Rubens: *Drunken Silenus.* **Alte Pinakothek, Munich.**

the celebrated 1811 vintage. Disrespect was certain for those who weakened their wine with water. "Who has taught you this horrible custom?" he once asked in good company when he caught his host at this. His motto was:

Soll denn doch getrunken sein,
Trinke nur vom besten Wein!

If you are going to drink,
Then drink only of the best wine!

It is well known that Goethe liked to travel, and always looked for a circle of acquaintances with whom he could chat when animated by wine. The Rochusfest in Bingen in August 1814 was one such occasion. There his small talk about the preaching of a bishop on fasting and wine are evidence of this. They are recorded in Karl Christoffel's book *Der Wein in Goethes Leben und Dichtung* (*"Wine in Goethe's Life and Poetry"*):

Friendly people came together and we gladdened ourselves with pleasant neighborliness, yes, amiable company who had come from the banks of the Nahe to this festival. Lively children drank wine, like their elders. Brown mugs with white monograms were passed around the family groups. Nobody was ashamed about the desire to drink, to some extent they glorified the drinking. Pretty women admit that their children enjoy wine just as much as their mother's breast. We asked if it was true that ecclesiastical gentlemen, even electors, were able to drink eight Rhine measures of wine, which means sixteen of our bottles, in twenty-four hours. A seemingly serious guest passed the remark that to answer this question one must remember the fasting sermon of their bishop, who after having described the depravity and drunkenness of his congregation in the most colorful terms closed by saying, "Convince yourselves from this, piously, that those who commit the greatest sins misuse in such a way the magnificent gift of God. The misuse does not, however, rule out the use. It stands written 'Wine brings joy to people's hearts.' From this it becomes clear that for ourselves and to please others we can and indeed should enjoy wine. Now, perhaps among my male listeners are none who do not drink two measures of wine without sensing a certain confusion of their senses, who, however, by the third and fourth measure so wickedly sink into oblivion that they fail to recognize wife and children, hurt them with scolding, blows and kicks, treating them as they would their worst enemies, which makes them disparaged and despised by God and their contemporaries. Those, however, who after the fourth, fifth or even sixth measure remain so much themselves that they would lovingly help their fellow man, can understand domestic concerns and find themselves able to carry out the orders of ecclesiastical or temporal leaders enjoy their modest part and receive it with thanks. They cherish this without examining it very carefully, because here normally a limit is set for the weak. It is very rare that God in all his virtue grants anyone the special grace to be able to drink eight measures, as he has honored me his servant. As it cannot be said about me that I have ever unfairly shown anger to anyone, that I have misjudged members of my family or relatives or indeed neglected the ecclesiastical duties and business incumbent on me, rather as you can all certify that I am always prepared to praise and honor God to make myself useful to the advantage of my nearest, so I can with thanks and a good conscience continue to be glad about this gift entrusted to me by God. And you, my pious listeners, take your modest part that your body may be refreshed and your spirit gladdened. And remember to prevent excess by not forgetting the words of the dis-

Clear to see in many churches is the great sacred importance of wine. This stained-glass window is in the Evangelical church in Rüdesheim in the Rheingau.

46

ciples, 'Examine everything and keep the best.' "

So it couldn't be avoided that wine remained the main topic of conversation. A dispute then arose about the advantages of the various vines, and here it was pleasing to see that there was no difference of opinon about the best ones. Hochheimer, Johannisberger, Rüdesheimer remain above dispute, which is confined to those of the middle ranges where jealousy and envy prevail.

Eckermann, Goethe's partner in many discussions, has left us a lot of information about his attitude to wine.

> When I arrived in the evenings he at once had a bottle brought. Never, not even in his youth, did he make a cult out of drinking. He always regarded wine as a remover of worries and a mood improver which made him cheerful and youthful. To this he remained true until his last years, always drinking at midday a bottle of light Würzburger.

Friedrich von Schiller (1759–1805) had a friendly relationship with Goethe. Through his mediation Schiller received in 1789 a professorship in history and philosophy at Jena. He too was a wine lover, which has remained practically unknown; perhaps he was introduced to the grape by Goethe. There are several poetic examples of his glorification of wine.

> *Auf der Berge freien Höhen,*
> *In der Mittagssonne Schein,*
> *An des warmen Strahles Kräften,*
> *Zeugt Natur den goldnen Wein.*
> *Funkelnd wie ein Sohn der Sonne,*
> *Wie des Lichtes Feuerquell,*
> *Springt er perlend aus der Tonne,*

> *Purpurn und krystallenhell.*
> *Und erfreuet alle Sinnen*
> *Und in jede bange Brust*
> *Giesst er ein balsamisch Hoffen*
> *Und des Lebens neue Lust. . . .*

> On the free southern hills
> Where the full summers shine,
> Nature quickened by sunlight,
> Gives birth to the vine!

> As the child of the sunbeam,
> The wine leaps today,
> From the tune springs the crystal,
> A fountain at play.

> All the senses it gladdens,
> Gives hope to the breast;
> To grief a soft balsam,
> To life a new zest.

His judgment is still valid today: "Wonderful is Bacchus' gift, balsam for a broken heart."

Naturally, long before Schiller and Goethe great minds in poetry and prose had expressed themselves about wine. We can turn the wheel of time a long way back until we come to Homer, who lived in the eighth century B.C., and who described the wine harvest thus:

> Therein he set also a vineyard heavily laden with clusters, a vineyard fair and wrought of gold; black were the grapes, and the vines were set up throughout on silver poles. And around it he drove a trench of cyanus, and about that a fence of tin; and one single path led thereto, whereby the vintagers went and came, whensoever they gathered the vintage. And maidens and youths in childish glee

Wine influenced the work of the "waltz king," Johann Strauss, as this music title page proves.

48

Wein, Weib u. Gesang

Text von J. Weyl.

WALZER

für

Männerchor

mit Begleitung des Orchesters

(oder Pianoforte)

componirt und

Herrn Johann Herbeck,

K.K. HOFKAPELLMEISTER

freundschaftlichst gewidmet

von

JOHANN STRAUSS,

Hofball-Musik-Director.

OP. 333.

21.731.

Pr.	Für Piano allein	Mk 2
---	Für Männerchor mit Piano	Mk 5.40
	Für gemischten Chor mit Piano	Mk 5.30
	Für Piano zu 4 Händen	Mk 2
	Für eine Singstimme mit Piano	Mk 2

Leipzig, Aug. Cranz.
Brüssel, A. Cranz.   London, Cranz & Cº

49

were bearing the honey-sweet fruit in wicker baskets. And in their midst a boy made pleasant music with a clear-toned lyre, and thereto sang sweetly the Linos-song with his delicate voice —and his fellows beating the carts in unison therewith followed on with bounding feet, dance and shoutings.

Wine quotations are known to us from Shakespeare, Voltaire, Oscar Wilde, Christoph von Grimmelshausen and many others. The Swabian doctor and poet Justinus Kerner (1786–1862) who among other things wrote, "In good health still drunk the sparkling wine . . ." even had a very popular sort of grape named after him.

The more modern writers have praised wine for its creative effect: to mention only a few—Thomas Mann, Hermann Hesse, Kurt Tucholsky and the nowadays almost forgotten Roland Betsch. We should also not forget Rudolf Bindung and his delight-ful *Moselfahrt aus Liebeskummer* ("*Moselle Journey Because of Lovers' Grief*"). Without wine Carl Zuckmayer's *Fröhlicher Weinberg* ("*Happy Vineyard*") would never have been written. Zuckmayer, who lived literally on wine, mentions his home, the Rheinhessen wine area, in many of his texts and poems.

In closing, let us once again quote Schiller, in his *An die Freude* ("*To Joy*"):

Küsse gab sie uns und Reben. . . .
Freude sprudelt in Pokalen.
In der Traube goldnem Blut,
Trinken Sanftmut Kannibalen,
Die Verzweiflung Heldenmut.—
Brüder, fliegt von euren Sitzen,
Wenn der volle Römer kreist,
Lasst den Schaum zum Himmel spritzen:
Dieses Glas dem guten Geist!

Joy sparkles to us from the bowl.
Behold the juice whose golden color
To meekness meets the savage soul,
And gives despair a hero's valor.
Up, brothers! Lo, we crown the cup!
Lo, the wine flashes to the brim!
Let the bright fount spring heavenward!
   Up!
To the good spirit this glass! To him!

In the Wine Cellar of Herr Chlumecky. **Painting by Joseph Navratil (1798–1865), with a self-portrait of the artist.**

51

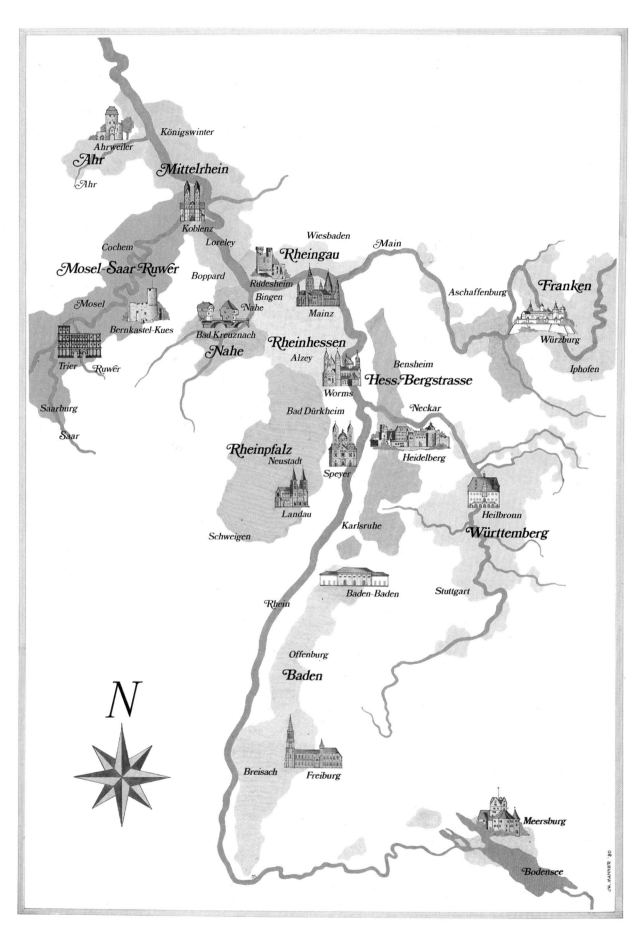

Ahr

Ahrweiler

Königswinter

Mittelrhein

Ahr

Koblenz

Cochem

Loreley

Wiesbaden

Main

Mosel-Saar-Ruwer

Boppard

Rheingau

Franken

Mosel

Rüdesheim

Aschaffenburg

Bingen

Bernkastel-Kues

Nahe

Mainz

Würzburg

Trier

Bad Kreuznach

Rheinhessen

Iphofen

Ruwer

Nahe

Alzey

Bensheim

Saarburg

Worms

Hess. Bergstrasse

Saar

Bad Dürkheim

Neckar

Rheinpfalz

Heidelberg

Neustadt

Speyer

Landau

Heilbronn

Schweigen

Karlsruhe

Württemberg

Baden-Baden

Stuttgart

N

Rhein

Offenburg

Baden

Breisach

Freiburg

Meersburg

Bodensee

II.
A Journey Through German Wine Country

Its Infinite Variety

The editor of *Wandsbeker Boten*, Matthias Claudius (1740–1815), a priest's son, raised his glass, drank it cheerfully and pronounced, "In the whole of Europe, you wine bibbers, is there no longer such a wine." He meant, of course, German wine. Naturally he was right, but not exactly—because really he should have said, "such wines," as there is not just one German wine. This great variety of wines is a fortunate thing for wine lovers.

It is impossible to say how many types of wine there have been, as every growing region, every vineyard, every vintage and every variety of grape produces a different wine, time and again. However similar they may be in origin, they will always differ in subtlety.

Even so, the majority of German wines

The eleven wine cultivation areas guarantee variety in German wine. English equivalents for German names: Coblenz ("Koblenz"), Lake Constance ("Bodensee"), Franconia ("Franken"), Lorelei ("Lorelei"), Middle Rhine ("Mittelrhein"), Moselle River ("Mosel"), Rhine Palatinate ("Rheinpfalz"), Rhine River ("Rhein").

have something in common: a limited alcoholic content and pure elegance. It is this that gives them their reputation of being wholesome and versatile, making them so desired the world over.

Approximately fourteen hundred wine villages in the German Federal Republic share a cultivated wine area of about ninety thousand hectares (ca. .225 million acres). In these villages about one hundred thousand firms grow wine. Small firms still predominate, 76 percent having a cultivated area of under one hectare (about two and one-half acres) and only 24 percent of one hectare (twelve and one-half acres) or more. Large firms are still a rarity, only nineteen hundred have five hectares or more. There has indeed been a clear change over to larger groups in the last decades, but the so-called "spare-time wine-growers"—many of whom have full-time jobs mainly in the industrial areas of Ludwigshafen, Rhein-Main, Coblenz, Karlsruhe, Freiburg and Stuttgart—still prevail.

Germany's vineyards cover a small area in comparison with the "wine giants" France and Italy, with 1.3 million hectares (ca. 3.25 million acres) each, and Spain, with 1.7 million (ca. 4.25 million acres). Germany has only one percent of the total world wine-growing area of 9 million hectares (ca. 22.5 million acres). From this global area, 280 to 350 million hecto-litres of wine are produced. Germany, with an average yield of 8–10 million hectolitres, produces a share of approximately 3 percent.

However, if we consider the average yield per year and per hectare then Germany and Luxembourg are at the top, which is a clear indication of how intensive wine cultivation is in these countries. In per capita consumption, on the other hand, France comes out on top, followed by Italy (100 litres per year), Portugal (90 litres), Argentina (77 litres) and Spain (70 litres). German consumption is in the medium range, with about 20–21 litres per head (excepting sparkling wine). That's not very much in comparison to consumption in the Middle Ages, but is a great deal in comparison to 1950, when Germans drank very little.

However, wine consumption in the Federal Republic has stagnated for several years. Still, growth has been predicted for the 1980s. It should be noted that it is in no way only German wine that is drunk between Kiel and Garmisch-Partenkirchen, Trier and Berlin: Foreign wine now has a 40 percent share of the market. But in the long term German wine has shown encouraging growth.

In exports to over one hundred countries this growth has reached sensational levels. Thirty years ago Germany exported 27,000 hectolitres. In 1978 this figure reached 1.4 million; it is still increasing. In Japan, Australia and of course the United States German wine is in great demand.

Poets have praised German wine for centuries. Otto Brües (1897–1967), an enthusiastic wine historian, has the following to say:

> How well I think back on a visit to the poet who gave the Rhine Sagas their beautiful form, and who wrote many an anecdote and wine story. I mean of course Wilhelm Schäfer, who had his summer residence in Friedrichshafen on Lake Constance and who gave me a wine from that area which was mild and clear. . . . That is a completely different wine from the Markgräfler, which grows in Breisgau where the old *Kaiser-Doppeladler* [the Hohenzollern double-eagle] still towers in the vineyards; also different from the Glottertaler, with its volcanic temperament, and the Kaiserstühler, with its heaviness; not to mention the Württemberg wine; which helps to explain the dialect saying "One time I will graze on the Neckar, one time on the Rhine."
>
> How completely different is the wine of Franconia. Not for nothing does it have its own individual bottle shape —the Bocksbeutel—its heavy and strong form in harmony with the stony ground out of which it grows.
>
> Again completely different is that of the Rhine Palatinate, which grows on the Weinstrasse ["wine road"] and deep into the country—what a beginner I was when on my first visit to this area I drank a light Moselle and after a short time found myself in an inn with the room spinning around me.

That is the wine that the knight Franz von Sickingen drank, and he was a real man.

Every river and stream has its own wine: the Nahe, invigorating and sweet according to the position of the vineyard, on steep slate slopes or facing the Rhine—the Saar and Ruwer giving us wine like no other, which the nose should experience before the tongue—the Moselle with its many bends and just as many places forgotten by the world, places that can produce a sweet wine like Rhine wine but also mixed with the refreshing dry wine loved by the connoisseur (in the correct mixture is to be found charm and true pleasure).

Back to Rheinhessen, where the scattered hills (which are covered by short undergrowth) spread out under the rays of the sun, and Oppenheim, Nierstein, Nackenheim and all the places, irrespective of what they are called, over which the bell rings with its clear tone: Every wine—the cheap, the precious, the most expensive—is to be found here in abundance.

Again different is the Rheingau: Every village in which cars, trains or ships stop has a famous name to the connoisseur, the map becomes a wine map.

Here we can find red and white wine, as on the Ahr and as far north as Unkel. The Burgundy grape has also found its place in our country; from Walporzheim to Meersburg and from Ingelheim to Baden many connoisseurs swear by it. To compare, musically speaking, the red to the major key and the white to the weaker minor is an over-simplification, for there are both major and minor in white and in red.

In any case it is still true to say that praise for German wine is inspired only by the characteristics of each individual variety of wine.

It gives us so much because it is more of the earth than other plants and is at the same time like bread, more than just wine. Bread and wine must be mentioned together here, as Hölderlin has done: Bread is the earth's fruit, blessed by light and from the thundering God comes the pleasure of wine.

At the end of his peroration Brües reminds us that wine must be understood spiritually: "When the spirit appears in many forms, that in which spirit and wine meet, should be mentioned—namely, humor."

We know that the human spirit can often unburden itself in the form of humor. Two things which do not necessarily belong together are brought onto one level. Humor provides the strength that enables us, when ideals and reality conflict, to continue to love reality—and love mankind. In German wine, sweet and dry are mixed: Without the acidity that it gets from the north the wine would be just as incomplete as without its southern gift of sweetness.

Here our praise of German wine converges with that for the German way of life: Where it is worth anything it is always to be understood as a good mixture of north and south, east and west, exuberance and serenity, strength and tenderness. Wilhelm Raabe once said that it is the glory of a great person to be spoken of in the same breath as his country. To transfer this to German wine: Its greatest glory is to be brought to mind whenever Germany is thought about.

Sylvaner

Morio Muskat

Riesling

Wanner

Ruländer

S-8

Faber 10375

Müller-Thurgau

Grauburgun

56

(Tokayer)

Gewürztraminer

2845

Sieger

The Character of Wine Comes From the Grape

There are over twenty thousand varieties of grape in the world, of which more than one hundred are cultivated in West Germany. Of these, about thirty white and eight red types are of importance in the market. The great quality of this wine and its high and reliable yield are a direct consequence of successful vine cultivation. Nowadays experiments are being carried out on a large number of new vines with the aim of increasing yield, durability against frost, resistance to pests and, not least, adjustment of the taste to the consumer's wishes.

The most important types of grape and their share of the total German cultivation area are as follows:

White Wine

Müller-Thurgau	26.6%
Riesling	19.8
Sylvaner	12.0

Differences between the types of vine can be seen in the leaves. Some less well known types are also represented here—e.g., Wanner, an old white-wine variety from Lothringen. S88 is the cultivation number for the Scheurebe, and 2845 the number of a variety crossed by Peter Morio which has no official name and is not registered at the official office ("Bundessortenamt"). The similarity between Ruländer and Grauburgunder here is not coincidental, as they are the same type (which by the way has nothing to do with the Hungarian Tokay, although it is sold in France—only in France—under this name).

Ruländer	4.00%
Kerner	4.75
Morio-Muskat	2.5
Scheurebe	3.7

Red Wine

Portugieser	3.7
Blauer Spätburgunder	3.8
Trollinger	2.0
Others	14.0

Riesling

The Riesling grape, which probably comes originally from a wild Rhine vine, produces in a good year the noblest wine. Riesling is a variety which ripens late, giving the wine its acidity. That is not to say, however, that it is a sour wine; this acidity contains the elegant aroma which gives it the flavor of fresh grapes. Without adequate acidity the wine would be dull, the bouquet would be lost. Besides, the acidity is important with regard to the keeping quality of the wine.

Sylvaner

This vine, which supposedly comes from Transylvania, was in 1964 the most cultivated variety in West Germany. It is not as demanding as Riesling with regard to soil and climate, its yield is better and it ripens earlier, giving a pleasant, full-flavored, mild wine with a modest bouquet.

Müller-Thurgau

This, the most dominant German wine at present, was developed in 1882 by the Swiss Hermann Müller from Thurgau at the Geisenheim Teaching and Research Institute. Originally once suspected to be a crossing between Riesling and Sylvaner, in the last few years experts have come to the opinion that it represents a crossing

and recrossing between Rieslings of different viticultural regions.

The yields of this type are very high: 300 hectolitres per hectare are possible, which is more than twice the average. The wine has a pleasant muscat flavor, medium acidity and a strong bouquet.

Morio-Muskat

A crossing between Sylvaner and white Burgundy carried out by Peter Morio. This vine can be grown almost anywhere and produces a relatively high yield. If at harvest the grapes are not ripe enough the muscat bouquet can be a little persistent.

Ruländer

The businessman Johann Ruland from Speyer discovered this variety in 1711 in an overgrown garden and recognized its importance. The Ruländer—also called Grauburgunder—belongs to the family of Burgunder vines. It is found mostly in Baden, and is a well-rounded, full-bodied and robust wine which in good years has a very distinctive bouquet.

Scheurebe

This new vine, a crossing (Sylvaner and Riesling), grown at the research institute in Alzey by Georg Scheu in 1916, has become popular in the last two decades. The wine is mellow and has a bouquet reminiscent of black currant.

Kerner

This is an interesting crossing between the red wine Trollinger and the white Riesling, developed by August Herold and named after the poet Justinus Kerner. This wine

Some of the most important varieties of grape cultivated in Germany.

58

Riesling

Sylvaner

Müller-Thurgau

Ruländer

Morio-Muskat

Scheurebe

Spätburgunder

Trollinger

Portugieser

has many positive attributes, one of which is that it is not demanding as regards either soil or location and has made very spectacular progress in the last few years. The Kerner certainly has a great future.

Traminer

Also known as Gewürztraminer, this is a very old variety, probably known to the Romans, and has been cultivated in Germany for nearly five hundred years. It has a low yield and a pronounced bouquet. In good years it produces a harmonious wine with aroma and body that can be considered of the best.

Gutedel

This type probably comes from Asia Minor and is found in Germany almost exclusively in the Markgräfler area of Baden. It is a light, attractive wine particularly suitable as a dry wine and in Baden is valued as both "drinking wine" and table wine.

Others

Several new vines have achieved positions in the market, especially the Huxelrebe, another crossing by Scheu (Gutedel and Courtillier *musqué*) which produces a lively wine with a decent muscat bouquet.

The Faberrebe can be mentioned as well, yet another Scheu crossing, this time of white Burgundy and Müller-Thurgau, producing a fruity wine with a light muscat taste.

The Ortega is a cross between Müller-Thurgau and Sieger, producing a full wine with a fine bouquet. The Bacchus (Sylvaner and Riesling) produces a fruity wine with a decent muscat bouquet.

Optima (Latin: "the best") is a crossing between Riesling-Sylvaner and Müller-Thurgau which produces a fragrant, lively wine.

Ehrenfelser, another Riesling-Sylvaner cross, is similar to Riesling and is named after the castle on the Rhine. Special types from Baden are the Freisamer (Sylvaner and Ruländer)—full-bodied and harmonious—and the full-bodied Nobling (Sylvaner and Gutedel).

The Kanzler (Müller-Thurgau and Sylvaner) produces a wine full of body whose name should symbolize its position as far as quality is concerned. At present the area under cultivation is small, as with the Albalonga, a specialty native to Franconia that is a crossing in which the lively Rieslaner (Riesling and Sylvaner) is married to the parent Sylvaner vine. This variety produces an elegant, fruity wine with strong acidity.

Spätburgunder

This vine, which produces a pleasing yield, is a Burgundy. Its wine is smooth, full and of a fine almond taste, in good years noble and blessed with a long life. The best Spätburgunders can compete with their great "cousins" from Burgundy.

Trollinger

This specialty from Württemberg produces a fresh, lively wine with pleasant acidity, much in demand as a drinking wine. The name probably comes from "Tirolinger" ("of the Tyrol"). It is a vine very demanding of the soil but very satisfactory in its yield.

Portugieser

This vine comes not from Portugal but from the area around the Danube. It can grow in almost any soil and location and always produces high yields, but is often not quite so good in quality. It is not suitable for laying down and must be drunk "young," often two months after harvest.

Others

The Müller vine (Schwarzriesling) is a mutation of the Spätburgunder, but does not approach its quality. Other German red wines worthy of mention—although of lesser importance than the aforementioned types—are the Blauer Limberger (Lemberger), Deckrot, Rotberger, Helfensteiner and Herold.

The Middle Rhine

Castles and Wine

When building a house one does not begin with the rafters, but perhaps it is allowed when describing the German wine-cultivation areas to begin at the "top," in the most northerly wine village in the Federal Republic—namely, Oberdollendorf just outside Bonn, the capital. The area we are talking about, the Middle Rhine (*Mittelrhein*) is perhaps, together with the Moselle, the most charming wine landscape in the watershed of "Father" Rhine, which here over the course of centuries has carved out its valley. Indeed it is one of the most beautiful river landscapes that we have in all Europe. Heinrich Heine wrote:

> There is a beautiful land of sweetness and sunshine, in the blue river is reflected the river bank, with castle ruins, woodland and ancient towns. There the villagers sit on their doorsteps on summer evenings drinking from large jugs, chatting confidentially as the wine grows.

Naturally, the years have not left this part of the Rhine undisturbed and the river is no longer so blue as in Heine's time, the early nineteenth century, but the magic and romance have to a large extent been

Stahleck Castle on the Middle Rhine has given its name to a "Grosslage."

63

maintained in the twentieth century. The meanderings of the river change unceasingly, as do the images they reveal. Ruins of once-proud castles give evidence of an ever-changing past, as do towns and villages with magnificent churches and cathedrals which show us the advanced architecture of the Middle Ages.

When one walks or drives slowly by car—don't use the bypasses which are sometimes available; they save time but you lose a lot—through the old settlements with their fortified gates and defiant towers, one can easily believe that one is back in the Middle Ages.

Beneath the rocks of the Lorelei—it is ten minutes to the summit, from which, as in legend, one can observe the ships pass—is where the Nibelungs' treasure is supposed to be buried.

At Rhens, the meeting place of the German princes in the fourteenth century, is to be found the famous Königsstuhl ("king's throne"). From here the power of the kings was proclaimed. The Dragon Saga is connected with the Drachenfels ("dragon rock") in the Siebengebirge ("seven mountains"). Perhaps here we should remember Siegfried, the dragon slayer who himself was the victim of a treacherous blow from a spear.

The beauty of this landscape could never be kept secret. Fortunately so, for the romantic Rhine with Binger Loch and the Mäuseturm ("mice tower"), the castle at Kaub, the Lorelei and the Deutsche Eck ("German corner") with its numerous castle ruins is certainly one of the most famous tourist attractions in Germany. Alexander von Humboldt once wrote enthusiastically that it is the Eighth Wonder of the World.

The wine from this area is, however, not so well known as the area itself. Those who do know it know that it in no way has deserved this, and that its quality is such that it should be in every throat. However, wine is not so plentiful here, because perhaps only on the Moselle are there harder working conditions. Steep slopes characterize this region, and therefore the area under cultivation has decreased from about twenty-five hundred hectares (sixty-three hundred acres) in 1850 to two thousand (five thousand acres) in 1927 to nine hundred (twenty-three hundred acres) today. Eighty percent of the area consists of steep slopes and 15 percent is at a very steep angle; only 5 percent is relatively flat.

The classic varieties of Riesling dominate here with a share of 75 percent, followed by Müller-Thurgau with about 11 percent and the new vine Kerner with 4 percent. The conditions that are so unfavorable for the wine-growers are, however, excellent for the wine. Steep slopes, a good angle to the sun, reflection from the Rhine, a balanced humidity level—these are the best conditions for the cultivation of a wine full of character.

Riesling especially shows itself well here. The acidity is quite strong but not unpleasant, indicating to the connoisseur that the wine can expect a long life. The expression *"Stahlig"* ("sinewy," literally "steely") is often used for this wine. Sales are mainly to tourists, who are often invited by road signs on the banks of the Rhine to stop and visit the local wine-growers.

Cooperatives here are only of local importance.

About 25 percent of the harvest goes in barrels directly to the sparkling-wine industry, which makes especially good use

Layers of slate on the Middle Rhine: On such soil the Riesling grows especially well.

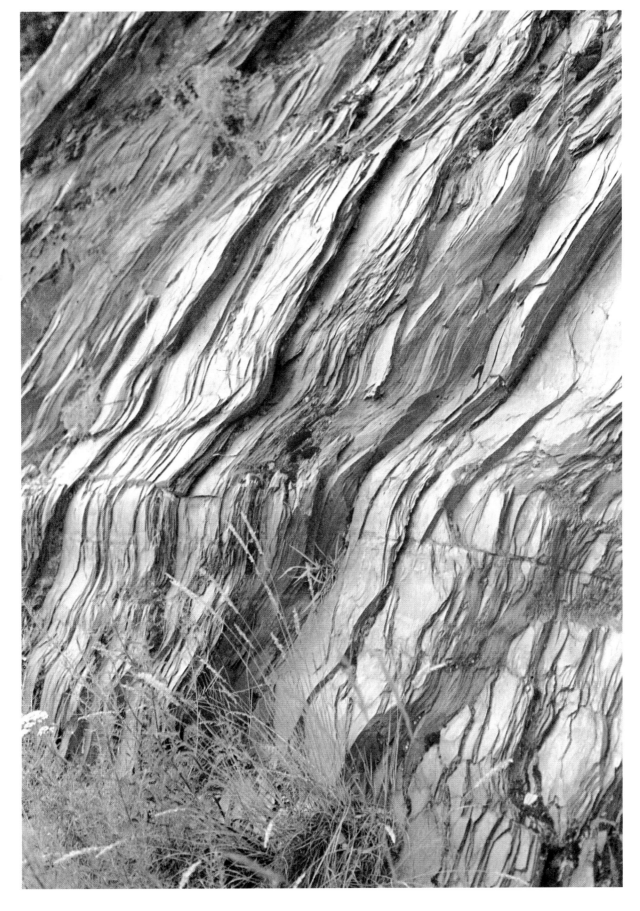

of this wine, high as it is in acidity. Every now and again one finds red wine in this region—for example, the Spätburgunder at Unkel as well as along the Rhine at the Siebengebirge, but these are rare. As regards prices, the local wine-growers have managed to keep them low in spite of the high costs of production caused by the steep slopes of the vineyards.

One of the centers of this area is Bacharach, an old, often-praised wine village which gets its name from a Roman altar to Bacchus which stood on a rock in the Rhine. In the Middle Ages it became the most important wine village in the area. Victor von Scheffel was a great admirer of its wine. However, its good and great reputation is probably owed not to its own wine but to Rheingau wine. If wine from the Rheingau or Rheinhessen or the Palatinate had to be shipped on the river, it first had to be brought in shallow barges to Bacharach and then loaded there onto bigger ships, because it was impossible for ships with a bigger draught to get through Binger Loch. The wine now carried the name of Bacharach; it was sent as such out into the world in much the same way as is normal today with many wines, in particular Spanish wine. When it was claimed that the best wines came from Bacharach one had to accept this, with reservations.

Bacharach has a great many competitors nearby. Numerous wine or tourist villages stretch for about sixty miles along the Rhine Valley like pearls on a string.

Usually a tour of the Middle Rhine begins at Binger Loch, the conjunction of four wine-growing regions—the Middle Rhine, Nahe, Rheingau and Rheinhessen. Here in the middle of the river is the Mäuseturm ("mice tower") to which according to legend Archbishop Hatto II of Mainz fled.

The mice pursued, found and ate him as a punishment for his heartless treatment of poor people.

The customs of those days were indeed harsh. A lot of relics from the past and information about old customs can be found in the Burg Rheinstein ("Rhine-stone castle") near Trechtingshausen, as well as farther north in the museum at the castle Burg Rheinfels ("Rhine-rock castle") above St. Goar.

Going back upstream, a little south of St. Goar is Oberwesel, which attracts the attention of the architecture connoisseur not only because of the town fortifications from the thirteenth and fourteenth centuries, but because of the wine-growing site (*Lage*) Engehöll.

A little farther upstream and across the river is the traditional seat of Rhine pilots at Kaub, where the customs-station Pfalz, built in 1326 on an island in the Rhine, is also to be found. Kaub is also historically famous as the place where Blücher crossed the river on New Year's Eve, 1814, during the War of Liberation against Napoleon.

Going north again, we come upon further stations of the past, of which only fragments remain, the Burg Katz ("cat castle") and Burg Maus ("mouse castle") near St. Goarshausen, separated by a ravine and whose rulers were at one time enemies. In 1250 Count Dietrich of Katzenelnbogen built the strongest fortress here, Burg Rheinfels, of which we have already spoken. The chief town of the district, St. Goar, was founded in 570 by Saint Goar of Aquitaine (patron saint of innkeepers and potters). From here the Rhine narrows more and more into a gorge and one comes

Nearly every settlement has its old castle: St. Goarshausen.

66

to the famous, much-praised Lorelei, which is also the name of a *Grosslage* (an area formed by a number of neighboring vineyards). On the opposite side of the Rhine is Boppard with its countless pretty, half-timbered buildings and the well-known Hamm wine-growing site. Round a hairpin curve we come to Braubach with its Marksburg, a castle still occupied and containing a collection of old weapons and in which one can even "admire" a torture chamber.

The Königsstuhl ("king's throne") at Rhens, Burg Stolzenfels and the Rittersturz are further specimens of magnificent castles. At Lahnstein the Rhine is joined by the Lahn River, on which there are also vineyards, for example at Bad Ems, Fachbach, Dausenau, Nassau, Weinähr and Obernhof. However, wine-growing has suffered a loss of quality here.

Suddenly the romantic scenery is all over when one reaches Coblenz, a town with a lot of tradition and many old buildings (above all, remarkable churches), but also considerable industry in the suburbs. Coblenz is evidence of the ancient Roman settlement of this area: The town (*Confluentes*) was founded as a military camp by Drusus in 9 B.C.

Farther along the Rhine towards Bonn, wine is grown only on the east bank of the river. The next vineyards can be seen from the courtyard of the old fortress Ehrenbreitstein high over Coblenz, from which there is a truly fantastic view of the Rhine and Moselle rivers, the Eifel plateau and the Hunsrück.

In this area the wine-growing has a great tradition. In Leutesdorf, for example, it is over two thousand years old. Farther on are the castle ruins of Hammerstein, which remind us of the Emperor Henry IV (1050–1106) and his feud with Pope Gregory VII, in which at one point he made his famous journey of penance to Canossa to see the Pope, who had excommunicated him.

Passing Rheinbrohl, Bad Hönningen, Leubsdorf, Dattenberg, Linz and Kasbach we come to Unkel, well-known for its half-timbered houses, Bad Honnef, which offers —unofficially—"wine cures," and finally Rhöndorf and Königswinter, a suburb of which, Oberdollendorf, is the most northerly vineyard in the Federal Republic. The climate is of course more severe here than, say, in "sunny" Baden, but nevertheless the wine-growers are able to produce a good wine with refreshing acidity, one which is eagerly sought.

We will leave this, probably the most highly praised wine landscape in the world, with an observation from Matthias Claudius's Rhine-wine song:

So trinkt ihn denn,
Und lasst uns alle Wege
Uns freuen und fröhlich sein!
Und wüssten wir, wo jemand traurig
   läge,
Wir gäben ihm den Wein.

So drink it then,
And let us go on our way,
Happily and full of joy!
And if we knew where someone was
   unhappily lying
We would give him wine.

MIDDLE-RHINE VINEYARD SITES

Divided into three regions:

Siebengebirge
with the *Grosslage* Petersberg;

Rheinburgengau
with the *Grosslagen* Burg Hammerstein, Lahntal, Marksburg, Gedeonseck, Burg Rheinfels, Loreleyfelsen, Schloss Schönburg, Herrenberg; and

Bacharach
with the *Grosslagen* Schloss Stahleck and Schloss Reichenstein.

Another 110 individual sites are registered, with a total cultivated area of 903 hectares (2,230 acres). The average yield between 1975 and 1977 was about 70,000 hecto-litres for the whole area—about 1 percent of the total in Germany.

Steep vineyards near Leutesdorf: The wine-growers' work here is no easy task.

The Ahr

River of German Burgundies

A surprise for the layman: Although this region is known as the classic red-wine area, almost as much white wine is produced here. White wines take up about 43 percent of the area; red, 57 percent. The most popular variety of grape is the Spätburgunder (29 percent), followed by the Portugieser (25 percent), Riesling and Müller-Thurgau (each 22 percent).

In total, then, there is a nice balance in this, the second smallest wine area in Germany. (Its viticulture area is 900 hectares or ca. 2,225 acres.) There is a well-known saying, often heard at wine-tastings, which refers to the "great" size of the area: "Whoever was on the Ahr and knew he was there, wasn't on the Ahr. Whoever didn't know that he was on the Ahr, was on the Ahr."

Yet besides Württemberg this is the greatest single area for red wine in Germany—proof again that everything in life is relative.

Around 900 growers grow wine here—mostly as a second occupation—and more than half of these have an area of less than .25 hectares (ca. ⅗ acre), and only 80 have an area of more than 1 hectare (ca. 2½ acres). Wine-growing as a family business has been known here for generations,

Wine-growing on slate: terraced slopes of the Ahr valley in autumn.

71

the first documentary proof existing from the eighth century. Two other historical dates are of great importance: In 1881 the vine louse made its presence felt for the first time on German soil in the Ahr valley (the cultivated area decreased because of this to 200 hectares or about 500 acres), and in 1868 the first wine cooperative in the world was founded here in Mayschoss. Before that time the quality of Ahr wines was hardly known outside the area. Gottfried Kinkel wrote in 1846 about the Ahr:

> Rocks crowding narrowly together intensify the heat of the sun by reflecting it: Black, mottled slate-stone, intentionally covering the ground in the vineyards, soaks up the heat of the day and lets it act upon the grapes through the cool of the night. And the river, too, gives the wine-growers encouragement: From its lukewarm waters the gentle mists rise up into the night air during the summer, when they can be seen—wonderfully still and brooding—hanging over the valley on a summer's morning; they drench the parched, rocky soil and soften the grapes' skins for the hot ripening rays of the sun.

So observed the professor and writer from Bonn over 130 years ago. Little has changed in the meantime, with the Ahr wines still profiting from the countryside and climate. However, the wine-growers do not have an easy time, for 75 percent of the cultivated area is on steep slopes and 15 percent on extremely steep slopes. Those who enjoy this wine do not often realize how much strenuous effort went into producing it.

This sixteen-mile-long area between Altenahr and Heimersheim with its beautiful volcanic landscape and fiery red wine attracts masses of tourists. They arrive by the busload and, with thirst quenched by cool beer and schnapps, descend into the cool wine cellars, sample the lively red wine or if possible the just as effective red sparkling wine and capitulate to the strength of the wine when they return to the light of day. This is a pity, but the wine industry is forced out of economic necessity to cater to these excesses of the tourists.

Nevertheless, when one samples Ahr wine quietly and attentively one will be well pleased with the full, aromatic Spätburgunder, with its ripe, smooth character, and the lighter Portugieser and Weissherbst (a rosé-type wine). Those who have the staying power to turn to the white wines will notice that their dainty, lively character shows great similarity to the neighboring Moselle wines.

The red wines were first planted about 1680 and for many decades the Burgundy was made into rosé wine and sold under the name "Ahrbleichert."

Connoisseurs value the Samtroten with its mild and powerful flavor. This, a mutation of the Müller grape, is a rarity as is the Frühburgunder, still found in the Ahr region, which originally came from the Spätburgunder.

New vines are also to be found in this area, above all Domina (a crossing of Portugieser and Spätburgunder) and Rotberger (Trollinger and Riesling), which have both gained a lot of ground in the last few years.

What is true in other wine areas is also true here: Wine areas are tourist areas. Bad Neuenahr, the hub of this area, is well known as a spa town. (Many spa guests

Wine determines the face of the countryside and its villages: Dernau in the magical Ahr valley.

72

have confirmed at vacation's end that the daily glass of wine has more beneficial effect than the doctor's medicines and other treatments.) Those who wish to visit this area for a vacation should avoid the peak season and take time to explore it on foot. Eleven wine villages are connected here by a wine footpath indicated by the sign of a red grape. Each of the villages can be recommended for a short stay (accompanied, perhaps, by wine-tasting).

In Ahrweiler, part of Bad Neuenahr, are picturesque side streets with half-timbered houses dating back to the Middle Ages. The local museum is of particular interest, as is the Ahrgau museum. A few miles farther beyond Walporzheim, where the valley narrows, the Bunte Kuh ("spotted cow"), a high cliff, can be seen. It almost appears as if the river has difficulties in winding its way between the cliffs, vineyards and castles. Those who like romantic wine cellars should have a longer stay in Rech—where the oldest stone bridge over the Ahr stands—and in Mayschoss—where, as we have already mentioned, the first wine cooperative was founded.

The last stop on our Ahr tour—which is certainly no hardship—is reached with Altenahr and the castle ruins of Are. Not to worry—all the sightseeing, sampling and wandering will be borne without too much trouble, because on the Ahr the necessary bodily support and fortification are well looked after. The culinary specialties of the area are Neuenahrer Rauchfleisch (smoked meat), Ardennerschinken (ham) from the Eifel and trout from the Ahr itself.

The Ahr-Rotweinstrasse ("red wine road") for motoring tourists is new; this goes from Sinziger Kreisel over routes B266 and B267 as far as Altenahr-Kreuzberg.

AHR VINEYARD SITES

Eleven wine villages are joined together in a single region:

Walporzheim/Ahrtal
with the *Grosslage* Klosterberg.

Forty-three individual sites are also registered. The average regional yield between 1975 and 1977 was about 46,000 hectolitres—about .5 percent of the total in Germany. Of the cultivated area 80 percent is managed as a second occupation. Seven wine cooperatives concern themselves with sales both within and without the area.

Wine harvest on terraced slopes. Less than 10 percent of the Ahr wine-growers have an area of more than 1 hectare (ca. 2½ acres).

Moselle-Saar-Ruwer

*A Splendid Chain of
Vine-Covered Hills*

**Hairpin bend of a wine river: the Moselle near Kröv,
a landscape that seems like a painting.**

There is no better poet to quote concerning the Moselle (*Mosel*) River than Decimus Magnus Ausonius, a Roman from the Bordeaux area. He lived at the emperor's court in Trier, and in the year 386 in his work *Mosella* praised Germany's first wine region in glowing terms. That this poet's original home was Bordeaux led the Moselle locals and their colleagues on the Saar and Ruwer to claim that French wine could not compare with theirs; after all, Ausonius had emigrated from France to remain on the Moselle because he had learned to appreciate the good wine.

Ausonius was perhaps the first to compose poetry about Moselle wine, but certainly not the last. Perhaps the most beautiful words ever to be written about this wine come from Rudolf G. Bindung in his *Moselfahrt aus Liebeskummer* ("Moselle Journey Taken for a Lover's Grief"):

One tastes the slate in the wine, one breathes it in the air, one smells it after a rain shower when the sun dries the porous layers quickly and the velvety, metallic grey glistens once more under the vines as if the grapes had to collect the sun's rays reflected from the ground.

Every wine from each village has its own carefully preserved honor. Similar as they are in their cool, slaty soil which reveals itself on the tongue (as when one licked the slate board as a school boy), in each of them is a liquid . . . presenting according to changing names and locations a matchlessness of a highly individual kind, from candid rusticity to the highest elegance of noble pleasure. The wine is not warming, it is cool and flows without difficulty or reservation. Whilst the heavy Rhine-wine glows and throbs in the veins like

liquid gold transporting the drinker into an ecstasy of happiness and intoxication in which he sits speechless with his glass and forgets the world, the Moselle wine changes, to his advantage, the present to another world. It does not make itself apparent; light, fleeting, fine and clear like lovable music which echoes without burdening body or soul, it hardly takes possession of you. It lets itself be enjoyed: That is its glory, that is its ambition.

To linger on the Moselle and its tributaries —the Sauer, Saar and Ruwer—is a double pleasure: that of the wines and the landscape, so influenced by the rivers.

The fifty thousand people who live here are connected either directly or indirectly with wine. The vineyards cover an area of twelve thousand hectares (ca. thirty thousand acres). Riesling dominates here with 60.5 percent of the cultivated area, but has lost ground in the past few years. Too much so, in the opinion of many; with the creation of a Riesling seal in 1979 the wine promoters hoped to reach a consolidation of Riesling cultivation. This variety, although very demanding on site and soil, produces by far the area's best wine.

Often the wines have a high acidity, which displeases consumers; therefore, one is forced to blend the wine to a certain extent. In the past, before the Wine Laws of 1971 forbade blends using wine from other areas, the wine-growers frequently brought in wine from the Rhine Palatinate for this purpose. As this is no longer possible, the less problematic type Müller-Thurgau is grown more and more instead. This is less acidic, and a small amount blended with

Metternich Castle ruins. Steep slopes on the Moselle make the wine-growers' work more difficult.

the "hard" Riesling produces the desired "rounding off." Müller-Thurgau (21.3 percent of the cultivated area) has also developed its own qualities, but is susceptible to frost damage in winter months. This happened in January 1979 in Franconia and Rheinhessen and on the Nahe, Upper Moselle and Saar when many of the more susceptible vines were destroyed.

A very old type of grape, which in the Middle Ages was planted all over Germany, still has considerable presence on the Moselle: the Elbling. Rich in yield, but not so fine in quality, it is found on the Upper Moselle (*Obermosel*), where it accounts for 8.8 percent of the total Moselle-Saar-Ruwer wine-growing area. This wine is used mostly in the production of sparkling wine. In the experimental stages are also to be found new grape varieties such as Optima. Recently two hectares (ca. five acres) of red wine grapes have again been planted on the Saar.

The wine of Moselle-Saar-Ruwer is produced and sold by fourteen thousand firms. It is a very costly business. According to the Institute of Business Management and Market Research the production cost per hectare (ca. 2½ acres) in 1977 was more than 14,000 Deutsche Marks (ca. $6,720 or £3,500) on the Moselle—by far the highest in Germany—followed by about 6,070 DM (ca. $2,914 or £1,518) in Rheinhessen and 5,269 DM (ca. $2,529 or £1,317) in the Rhine Palatinate.

Reasons for this are the steepness of many vineyard slopes and the splitting up of the growing area. "Here a plot of land, there a plot" seems to be the motto of the small wine-growers here. The economic handicap thus created has been reduced only by the gradual amalgamation of vineyards.

From the border of Luxembourg to Coblenz, the Moselle with all its bends has a length of about 125 miles. As the crow flies, the distance is half this. The river valley has been dug deep into the countryside, in places reaching a depth of 440 yards, its steep sides often crowned with wooded areas. Because of this, climatic zones are formed in which the heat is dammed up, and the constant warmth and humidity provide the best conditions for the vines.

A great difference here to other areas is that because of the steepness of the slopes and the slaty ground the vines are mostly trained to grow up poles and not along trellises. The vines love these slopes with their crumbly slate and colorful sandstone. They produce the best and finest juices and bouquet which give the wine its special characteristic. It is a wonder of nature that the vines put down roots of up to sixteen yards through the cracks in the rock. It is hardly believable that the vine can grow so well in such a normally dry soil, but the slaty ground retains the moisture and as the slate crumbles potash, lime and phosphate serve the vine as nutritive substances. Here in good years can be found some of the best wines in the world.

All these advantages seem to have been recognized by the Romans who brought the art of wine-growing to the Moselle about two thousand years ago. The local people very quickly learned from the legionaries (who didn't want to go far from their homes without a drop of good wine) and increased the cultivation area.

It was the ecclesiastical princes who from the twelfth century supported the wine-growing through their monasteries. The year 1787 was an important date in the history of Moselle wine, when Clemens

The roots of the vine can find their way to a depth of 16 yards.

Wenzeslaus, the last elector of Trier, ordered a changeover to the Riesling.

The wines in the different regions are not the same, and it is therefore not really correct to talk about Moselle wine; one must differentiate between the five different regions—Moseltor, Upper Moselle, Saar-Ruwer, Bernkastel (Middle Moselle) and Zell (Lower Moselle).

Let's begin with the small sub-region Moseltor, consisting only of the wine villages Perl, Sehndorf and Nennig. Then on to the Upper Moselle, stretching from Kreuzweiler to just before Konz. Here the Elbling has its last bastion. The wines are light and dry, sometimes with a pronounced acidity. In good years they can produce good "drinking wines" which find high esteem. Walter Scheel, the ex-President of the German Federal Republic, is reputed to be a lover of the Elbling wine. In the main this variety is much sought after for the making of sparkling wine.

At Konz (on the Moselle) the Saar-Ruwer region begins. Here, many connoisseurs believe, the best Moselle wine is grown. But in this regard there is a lot of room for discussion. Let us content ourselves with recognizing that the Saar district (stretching about nineteen miles from Serrig to the river's confluence with the Moselle at Konz) produces wines of a characteristic individuality. In good years they possess a fine fruitiness, a beautiful mellowness and elegance. A specialty is the Riesling–sparkling wine, the best of which could compete with champagne. Particularly well-known wine localities are Serrig, Saarburg, Ockfen, Ayl, Scharzhofberg, Kanzem, Wiltingen and (not to be forgotten) Oberemmel, Mennig, Filzen and Hamm.

To a certain extent Trier is the hub of the Saar-Ruwer area. This town has ample evidence of its Roman settlement, from the *Porta Nigra* ("black gate") over the emperor's springs to a restaurant which still cooks according to recipes of the Roman Marcus Gavius Apicius. In the Trier Landesmuseum is the famous Neumagen Wine Ship, the gravestone of a Roman wine-trader.

A very aromatic wine grows in places round about Trier, for example Olewig, Kürenz, Eitelsbach and Ruwer. The small wine area to the northeast in and around the valley of the Ruwer, is only about five miles long. Kasel and Eitelsbach produce a good wine full of character, which besides its fine fruity acidity has a pronounced aromatic bouquet and a sometimes light, earthy taste. Grünhaus and Waldrach are also industrious wine villages, hardly to be found on any road map, but of great importance to wine lovers.

The basic principle of one local cellarer can well be taken to heart when considering Ruwer wine: "Every great Ruwer wine should be kept at least four or five years in the bottle so that it has enough time to cultivate its original acidity and develop its sharp, aromatic bouquet."

Proceeding farther down the Moselle we come to the Bernkastel (Middle Moselle) region, whose name is almost certainly the most well known of Germany's wine regions. The normal Bernkastler Riesling, a most pleasant wine, can be found all over Germany, often even in bars selling beer. Concerning the area itself: Flanked by the Hunsrück and Eifel plateaus, the Moselle forces its way through Devon slate, grey slate and, in certain places, red sandstone. Steep slopes increasingly dominate the landscape as we travel eastward from Longuich to Zell. The wines of the Middle Moselle are fuller than those of the river's upper reaches and the Saar and Ruwer—

Bernkastel-Kues on the Moselle, viewed from the famous Doktorberg.

perhaps also a bit softer, according to their age and acidity.

To name some of the towns along the shores of the Moselle going downstream from Longuich (a name derived from the Latin *longus vicus*, "long village"): Schweich, Mehring, Thörnich, Klüsserath, Leiwen and the well-known Trittenheim. Opposite lies

Neumagen, probably the oldest wine village in Germany and site of numerous wine-related artifacts and monuments. Farther ahead lies Piesport, which derives its name from the Celtic goddess of rivers, Bigentia. In 777 this location was known as *Porto Pigontio* ("bridge of Bigentia").

On to Wintrich, Brauneberg, Mühlheim, Veldenz and, on the opposite bank of the river, Lieser and Kues. Depending on the bend of the Moselle, the vineyards are either on the left or right bank, but always on the south slopes. Finally we come to Bernkastel-Kues, truly a historical treasure chest with its small marketplace, a veritable monument to the architecture of the Middle Ages. From here and the neighboring settlement of Wehlen comes the most valuable wine of the whole area; the price of 7,500 DM was recently reached at an auction for a bottle of Trockenbeerenauslese, 1921 vintage, from the vineyard Bernkasteler Doctor. Whoever has the opportunity to sample a vintage wine from 1920, 1921, 1935 or 1937 will be astonished at the freshness; they are still "100 percent." One can sense their ripeness, their age, their having lost nothing of their aroma and piquant character. The Riesling with its fine acidity has preserved them.

It is claimed that the wine from this area has special healing powers. A jug of Bernkasteler is supposed to have cured Bishop Boemund of Trier on his deathbed. The inscription "*Vinum mosselanum omni tempore sanum*" ("Moselle wine is healthy at any time") in one of the wine cellars underlines this recognition of the wine's healing powers. And where should the name "Doctor" for one of the vineyards come from if not the health-giving effects of the drink?

Continuing on our travels, we go past Graach to Wehlen. The vineyard there, Sonnenuhr, is world-famous. Then on to Zeltingen-Rachtig, where the wines are a little fuller and perhaps a little milder; Ürzig; Erden, with its Treppchen; Kröv, whose vineyard has the rather strange name "Nacktarsch" ("bare bottom"), which probably evolved as a coarse jest from the name of an earlier vineyard owner, Nektar, to this ominous but doubtless striking name.

Traben-Trarbach is a wine center in wonderful surroundings, important for tourist traffic. It is followed by Enkirch with its old houses, Reil, Briedel and Pünderich. Then comes the well-known Zell, with its famous Schwarze Katz ("black cat") that belongs already to the last of our four areas, Untermosel (Lower Moselle).

After Alf and Bullay comes Bremm, where we have to really crane our necks if we wish to admire the vineyards—steepest in the world. When one pauses to think how hard the work of the wine-growers is, it is not difficult to understand the current problems with the area's younger generation, who are not to be blamed for thinking that money can be earned elsewhere more easily than on these steep slopes where machinery can be used only to a very small extent.

The Cochem Krampen, a twenty-mile-long loop of the Moselle, which boasts Germany's longest rail tunnel, and the wine villages Eller, Ediger, Senheim, Mesenich, Briedern, Poltersdorf, Beilstein (where many artists got their inspiration from the beautiful landscape), Ellenz, Ebernach, Ernst and Valwig are all places worthy of a visit, either to a wine cellar or directly to the wine-growers.

Beyond the picturesque tourist center of Cochem we turn to Klotten, Pommern, Treis, Karden, Müden and Moselkern, where we admire perhaps the towering Burg Eltz (whose picture appears on 500-

DM notes) and move on to Burgen, Brodenbach, Alken, Lehmen, Gondorf and Kobern. At last we reach the largest concentration of Riesling cultivation in the whole Moselle-Saar-Ruwer area, at Winningen, with its famous wine festival which the Winningen "wine witch" oversees.

The wines are more abundant here, but still maintain their Moselle character, although the proximity of the Rhine can already be detected. At Coblenz is the terminus of our Moselle journey. It can be made not only by car but, since 1964, by passenger ship, with the aid of a dozen locks which have made the Moselle navigable.

MOSELLE-SAAR-RUWER VINEYARD SITES

160 wine communities are divided into five regions:

Zell (Lower Moselle)
with the *Grosslagen* Weinhex, Goldbäumchen, Rosenhang, Grafschaft, Schwarze Katz;

Bernkastel (Middle Moselle)
with the *Grosslagen* Vom Heissen Stein, Schwarzlay, Nacktarsch, Münzlay, Badstube, Beerenlay, Kurfürstlay, Michelsberg, St. Michael, Probstberg;

Saar-Ruwer
with the *Grosslagen* Scharzberg, Römerlay;

Obermosel (Upper Moselle)
with the *Grosslagen* Gipfel and Königsberg; and

Moseltor
with the *Grosslage* Schloss Bübinger.

There are 519 individual sites. The area's total annual yield has in recent years averaged 1.4 million hectolitres, which is about 15 percent of the total in Germany. There is a large proportion of small vineyards, but there are also many producers' cooperatives and large wine cellars which sell the wine at home and abroad. Of total sales, 15 percent are through wine cooperatives.

The Rheingau

Home of World-Famous Wines

The small Rheingau is the heart of all the Rhine wine-growing areas. It is considered so because of the excellent quality and unique character of its wine. Not for nothing do connoisseurs give this area the title "noble" in good years. In general Rheingau wines are full-bodied and elegant; one could easily add a multitude of other descriptive terms. Nature has provided Rheingau wine with a near overabundance of all possible good qualities: bouquet, spice, fruitiness, fineness and ripeness. Good years give a top-quality wine that has made the Rheingau's name world-famous.

From the slopes of the Taunus hills the Rheingau appears as an extended basin. To the east, north and west it is protected by forests and hills, while to the south it is open all day long to the rays of the sun. The Rhine, which for most of its course flows from south to north, makes a turn at Wiesbaden and Mainz towards the west. Only at Rüdesheim and Bingen does it revert to its original course.

The whole Rheingau wine-cultivation area consists of south-facing slopes which are particularly exposed to the intensity of the sun's rays. The surrounding Taunus protects the area against the biting winds from

The wooden presses in the monastery at Eberbach in the Rheingau, in use until only a few decades ago.

the north, east and west. The river here is especially wide—nearly two-thirds of a mile—and the effect of the sun shining on this large expanse of water is that its heat is stored up during the day to be released at night. Evaporation and mist keep the air humid when there has been no rain for a long period. Winter temperatures are seldom extremely low, and late frosts in spring hardly ever occur to dismay the wine-growers.

In fall the combination of adequate warmth and high humidity can have a particularly positive effect. The wine-growers call the thick fall mists which are only dispersed by the sun around midday *Traubendrücker* ("grape trigger"). These mists have a great deal to do with the maturation of the grapes, and above all help start the development of "noble rot" (*Edelfäule*), whose function has already been described in the historical survey in Part I.

With the perfect climate comes fertile soil which is particularly suitable for grape vines. Near the river loamy soils predominate, on the slopes middle to light clays with some gravel and sand deposits, and on the higher levels, weathered layers of Taunus slate interspersed with quartz.

These favorable conditions especially support the Riesling vine which, planted on 75 percent of the cultivated area, is the most important variety here, followed by Müller-Thurgau with about 14 percent and Sylvaner with 5 percent. Additionally, the Spätburgunder is highly valued in the Rheingau, especially in Assmannshausen and here and there in Walluf and Lorch. Approximately two thousand wine-growers earn their livelihood from a scanty three thousand hectares (ca. seventy-five hundred acres).

Charlemagne, who had his palace on the other side of the river in Ingelheim, was one of the first to observe how favorable the opposite slopes would be for wine-growing.

During the course of history it was the monasteries and monks above all who fostered wine-growing and achieved outstanding results. The Rheingau wine-growers have continued to do everything in their power to further the cultivation of wine.

This "paradise," not quite twenty-five miles long, contains only some twenty wine villages, but their names are world-famous. The world's mighty rulers—from the czars of Russia to the presidents of the United States—have loved Rheingau wine and paid for it with gold. Queen Victoria made it the wine of her court. She especially loved the wine from Hochheim, which, although lying on the Main River, belongs viticulturally to the Rheingau area. Its character differs slightly from actual Rheingau wine and to a certain extent displays a connection with the more full-bodied wines of neighboring Franconia. A great deal of wine is still imported by Great Britain from Hochheim as a result of Queen Victoria's interest. In remembrance of a visit by her, a memorial was erected in the middle of the Hochheim vineyards. In fact, one vineyard now bears the name "Königin Viktoriaberg"! (The English term "hock," used very often to describe Rhine wine, comes from the name Hochheim.)

The northern "border" of the Rheingau, with the Middle Rhine, is Lorchhausen. Just south of there, in Lorch and neighboring locales, the wine is noticeably different from the rest of the Rheingau. The reason for this is in the soil. From Kaub in the Middle Rhine onwards, the wines become lighter and tend towards the Moselle wines.

A monument to the most famous lover of Hochheim wine, England's Queen Victoria.

The Spätburgunder has been grown for a very long time in Assmannshausen, mainly at Höllenberg, where as long ago as the twelfth century the Blauburgunder vine was cultivated. Upstream to the east, where the Rhine bends back northward, lies Rüdesheim with its colorful, happy and bustling merrymakers in the Drosselgasse. On the hill behind the town is the Niederwald monument, from which a well-proportioned Germania looks sulkily across the Rhine. She is nicknamed the Prussian Madonna. It is worth it, though, to visit her by cable car; from the foot of the monument one has a uniquely beautiful view of the whole of the Rhine valley towards Rheinhessen, across to the Nahe River and as far as the Odenwald.

A few miles to the east of Rüdesheim is Geisenheim, which houses one of the world's most important wine academies, its only equal being perhaps Montpellier in southern France. Not only are experts from all over the world trained here, but research, including the intensive cultivation of new vines, is carried out.

Between Geisenheim and Winkel, on the slopes of the Taunus, is Schloss Johannisberg, the birthplace of Spätlese wine. Emperor Francis I of Austria presented this palace to Prince Metternich for his services to the Empire. The tithes had to be—and still are—paid by the owners to the Habsburg family.

In the famous Johannisberg wine cellar many great wines of the last century are stored in the *Bibliotheka Subterranea* ("underground wine library"). There one can also find two bottles of the 1748 vintage. Here and in neighboring Schloss Vollrads the Riesling grape finds in the clay, loam and quartzite soils the ideal conditions for a fine, lively growth.

Winkel, Mittelheim and Oestrich have, through administrative change, joined together into one community. In Winkel, the wine has possessed stimulating drawing power for creative spirits: It charmed Clemens Brentano and Achim von Arnim, as well as the brothers Grimm and the poet-prince Goethe.

Near Hattenheim are the extensive vineyards of Schloss Schönborn and Schloss Reichhartshausen, which once belonged to the monastery at Eberbach. Their wines are fruity and elegant, sometimes truly hearty. Inland from here, in the center of a vineyard, is the noted village of Hallgarten, praised not only for its wine but also for the incredibly beautiful Madonna in the local parish church. This work of art from the fifteenth century is a symbol of fertility and motherhood, depicting the Virgin with a grape in her left hand.

Another world-famous name in the vicinity of Hattenheim and Hallgarten is the Cistercian monastery of Eberbach, built from the twelfth to fourteenth centuries. It is not only Hesse's most famous hermitage, but the center of Rheingau wine. It was taken over from the monks by the state in 1803. The Steinberger wine from Eberbach was a particular favorite of Bismarck, who especially liked to drink it as an aperitif. The historical cellar of wine presses in the monastery is now a museum.

Not far east of Eberbach we come to Kiedrich, where Saint Valentine's Church, dedicated to the wine god Dionysus, surprises us with the oldest church organ in Germany. In the center of the picturesque wood-carving dedicated to wine we find a serenely charming Madonna. The grape tendrils on the church pews, carved dur-

A walk in the vineyard: Near Rüdesheim (in the background) one can walk for hours through the vineyards.

90

ing the late Middle Ages, are among the finest works of art inspired by wine.

Returning to the Rhine, our journey takes us to Erbach. Its Marcobrunn is one of the best white-wine vineyards in the world.

In Eltville, the oldest town in the Rheingau, both sparkling and still wines are commercially important. Near Eltville, in the church at Martinsthal we can again admire works of art dedicated to wine. The wines here are full bodied, sometimes earthy and rich. Everywhere in this village are bright green-and-white signs with a large drinking glass—the markings for the "Riesling Route," which diverts drivers away from the heavily-trafficked roads on the riverbank to the charming wine villages.

Onwards to Rauenthal, whose 1861 Baiken Trockenbeerenauslese was once judged the best wine in the world and awarded prizes at the wine exhibitions of Paris, London and Vienna. Today, still, top-quality Rheingau wines are grown in Rauenthal's vineyards of Rothenberg, Nonnenberg and Baiken.

In Wiesbaden, vines grow even in the town itself as well as the suburbs of Schierstein, Biebrich and Frauenstein. Wiesbadener Neroberger is the scarce but much-desired official wine of this country town.

The end of our tour is the previously mentioned town of Hochheim near the confluence of the Main and Rhine. Some of the local wines are characterized by a soft, "smoky" taste similar to many wines from the Saar. One could almost fear a bad cork! In fact, though, a particular slaty taste comes through. The best vineyards at Hochheim are Domdechaney and Königin Viktoriaberg.

RHEINGAU VINEYARD SITES

There is a single region:

Johannisberg
with the *Grosslagen* Steil, Burgweg, Erntebringer, Honigberg, Gottesthal, Deutelsberg, Mehrhölzchen, Heiligenstock, Steinmächer and Daubhaus.

There are 116 smaller, individual sites. The area's total annual yield has averaged around 235,000 hectolitres, which is about 2.5 percent of the total German output. As regards the business organization, most smaller wine-growers deliver their harvest to the sixteen fairly large wine cooperatives.

About five hundred individual growers, a district wine cooperative and a whole series of well-known state firms bottle their own wine and sell it themselves, a great deal of which is exported to, among others, America and Japan.

One of the most famous German vineyards: Schloss Johannisberg in the Rheingau.

The Nahe

Germany's Testing Area

Along the Nahe River the twins of wine and health can be expanded to a harmonious triplet. With the happiness that comes from wine and the effectiveness of the Nahe's healing springs at Bad Kreuznach and Bad Münster can also be associated that most beautiful of raw materials—precious stones, which industry is concentrated around Idar-Oberstein.

Nahe wine as well as gems receives the appellation *"Edelstein"* ("precious stone"), used very often in advertising, as in *"Nahe-wein–Edelstein."*

There is, however, a lot more to be said about this area. One should first know that it was in the fourth century, with the Romans, that viticulture began here. Early tools used at that time in the cultivation of vines have been found—for example, grape knives, wine sieves, wine jars and containers of glass and clay, one bearing the Latin inscription *"Reple me"* ("refill me").

After the passing of the Roman period either viticulture was neglected or there are simply no extant historical records. Only in the eighth century, the early Frankish period, do we again hear anything about wine-growing through inventories concerning Norheim, Waldlaubers-

The Rotenfels, landmark of the Nahe cultivation area.

heim, Langenlonsheim, Hüffelsheim, Weinsheim, Roxheim and Monzingen. The owners at this time were not individual wine-growers, but almost exclusively secular and clerical large landowners. How extensive their ownership was is unclear, as no records remain, but it must have been great because it even survived the chaos of the mass migrations.

One thing is certain: Operations at that time were on a mixed agricultural basis, arable and pasture land being supplemented by vineyards. This is still true today.

The history of Nahe viticulture first becomes dramatic with the Bavarian-Palatinate War of Succession of 1403–1407, when the area was badly damaged and vineyards were destroyed. This devastation was only to be exceeded by that of the Thirty Years' War in the seventeenth century.

As if these catastrophes were not enough, the area had hardly been restored when a new war with France broke out which again destroyed everything. This was the so-called "Palatinate War of Succession" of 1688–1697, in which Louis XIV's soldiers were ordered to devastate the area completely, the troops of General Melac being particularly infamous for their burning of the vineyards. As a result of this, most of the wine-growers gave up; their fear of the future was simply too great.

After the Napoleonic Wars of the nineteenth century, when peace and quiet returned to the area and the Rhineland was ceded to Prussia, a new boom began. Planting was expanded hand-in-hand with progressive wine cultivation. It is evidence of the spirit and versatility of the people of this area that it was here for the first time that a wine-plough was used. Also here the vine louse was successfully resisted, and *Flurbereinigung* (the restructur-

ing and merging of small plots into larger units where mechanization can be effectively employed) was introduced.

With regard to new techniques, it was the Nahe wine-growers who first replaced single-post cultivation with frames. Also, in 1776 in the vineyard of Mönchberg near Bad Kreuznach, one year after its surprising discovery in Johannisberg, the late harvesting of overripe grapes began to be practised. An interest in progress, a will to survive and great knowledge was and still is a characteristic of wine-growers on the Nahe. Their enthusiasm for experimenting can be seen in the fact that nearly all important types of grape are grown here and that time and again new vines are tested. From this comes its nickname, "Germany's testing area."

This wine area, stretching along the Hunsrück as far as Bingen where the Nahe flows into the Rhine had in 1978 a total cultivated area of forty-four hundred hectares (eleven thousand acres) of which only 1 percent was red wine. Müller-Thurgau accounted for 31 percent of the area, the drier and later-ripening Sylvaner 24 percent and the elegant Riesling 23 percent.

Here as everywhere else climate, soil and type of grape form the character of the wine. The landscape has volcanic character and the wine an almost comfortable nature. Free from the hubbub of tourist traffic, one can enjoy it in peace and quiet. One can recuperate in the healing baths at Bad Kreuznach and Bad Münster am Stein, in Sobernheim or in Ebernburg, the home of Franz von Sickingen, and at the same time savor the wine. Perhaps one could even become as euphoric as Goethe, who,

A fruit tree blossoms in a Nahe vineyard. The hill in the background is crowned by the castle ruins of Gutenberg.

speaking of Nahe wine, said, "It's like the name of a great charitable ruler. It will always be mentioned when the talk is of anything excellent."

It is also the wine that impresses on one's memory several curious characters like Schinderhannes (a character resembling Robin Hood whose home was the Hunsrück), or a cavalry commander prominent in the Thirty Years' War, Michael Obentraut (whom the Spanish called "German Michel"), or the "Hunter of Kurpfalz," forestry inspector Friedrich Wilhelm Utsch.

The countryside on the Nahe, whose character is determined by the river and the adjoining forests, is everywhere influenced by the vineyards, as are the people. Contemplative peace reigns, a quiet cheerfulness to be sensed in the small villages with their historic half-timbered buildings. And the wine? Connoisseurs place it somewhere among Moselle, Rheinhessen and Palatinate wines: partly lively, elegant and sometimes of a mild, attractive sort. It is always harmonious and balanced, formed by the many different soils: slate, volcanic porphyry, quartzite, sand, potter's clay, loam and loess which gives the wine an almost metallic taste.

A recent profound judgment of Hugh Johnson, the well-travelled author and holder of the literature prize of the West German Gastronomic Academy, states:

> Its wine seems to capture all the qualities one loves best in German wine. It is very clear and grapy, with all the intensity of the Riesling, like a good Moselle or Saar wine. At the same time it has some of the full flavor which in the Rheingau makes one think of the alchemist's shop, as though rare metals were dissolved in it, possibly gold itself.

On the Nahe one regards such words as a statement of fact. Johnson's judgment has found the agreement of more and more connoisseurs, perhaps because since the last war the most modern cellar technology and business techniques have been developed here with striking success. In Bad Kreuznach is based one of the world's most important firms for cellar technology and filtration.

In the Nahe region the controlled fermentation process was developed, which enables natural fermentation processes to proceed undisturbed. Around Burg Layen *Flurbereinigung* was begun at a very early date and the vine louse was energetically and systematically resisted. In Burg Layen direct selling to wine lovers, the most modern method of distribution, was introduced with great success. Direct delivery of wine was not, however, the only reason for success. There were also the additional advantages of tasting the wine in advance and having expert individual advice before buying. Today the fact that nearly half of all wine sold is sold this way shows how highly wine-drinkers regard these facilities. Progress in cellar and distribution procedure has increased the popularity of Nahe wine considerably. In the recent increase of tourism in its more pleasant forms, the wine festivals which are great attractions and the many unpretentious restaurants and wine cellars have played their parts.

Helping visitors find their way around the area is the Nahe Weinstrasse ("wine road") with its sign of a wine goblet and the letter N displayed on the roadside. Our Nahe tour begins in Bingen where the Nahe (whose source is in the Hunsrück near Birkenfeld and which flows through one

Landmark of the Nahe's "capital" Bad Kreuznach: the Nahe bridge and its bridge-houses, built around 1300.

of the Rhine's most beautiful side-valleys) makes its way between the Scharlachkopf and the Elisenhöhe to join "Father Rhine." Here, just behind Bingerbrück on the west bank of the Nahe is the first of seventy-seven charming wine villages—Münster-Sarmsheim. Above Münster-Sarmsheim, near Laubenheim, one reaches Burg Layen, well known to connoisseurs for its famous vineyards. Those who wish to find out for themselves how wine is made can visit the *Weinlehrpfad*, an informative path through the vineyards. Here a visit to the wine museum is also worthwhile.

Continuing along the Nahe, we come to Langenlonsheim where the valley of the Guldenbach climbs steeply up to Stromberg and further into the Hunsrück. Guldental and Windesheim have extensive areas under cultivation and can boast of very good quality. Guldental is the largest wine community on the Nahe, with clever names like Hölle ("hell") and Teufelsküche ("devil's kitchen") for what is generally understood to be heavenly wine.

Back on the Nahe, only a few miles upstream from the pretty Guldenbach valley is Bad Kreuznach. This spa town, center of the Nahe area, is surrounded by hills covered with extensive vineyards. Without doubt the showpiece among the many hospitable places on the Nahe is the Kauzenburg, a castle on a hill some fifty-five yards above Bad Kreuznach. This was the home of the now-extinct counts of Spanheim (later written Sponheim). In 1689 it was burned and razed by Louis XIV's soldiers, and was "rebuilt" only in the early 1970's through the enterprise of some residents of Bad Kreuznach. Here on what is left of the ruins of the old castle a modern, almost unique wine restaurant has been built, in which several times a month in a huge vault banquets are held as in the Middle Ages.

100

Bad Kreuznach is also the "border town" between the two wine regions on the Nahe, Kreuznach and Schlossböckelheim. In Schlossböckelheim there are also many famous vineyards and enchanting villages. This area gets its name from a historical castle in which Holy Roman Emperor Henry IV was held imprisoned by his son during Christmas 1105 in an attempt to force him to renounce the throne.

Of special interest farther up the Nahe near Niederhausen is the only German "wine hotel," modern but still comfortable and with an exemplary wine list. Not far from here is the village of Hüffelsheim which made history in the Middle Ages. The occasion was a feast held by Count Friedrich Wilhelm in his castle above Bad Münster am Stein. The guests were in good spirits —as was often the case at banquets in the Middle Ages—and as the festivity reached its peak the count ordered a knight's boot to be brought into the room filled with the best Nahe wine, whereupon he said, "Whoever can empty this boot in one draught shall have the village of Hüffelsheim."

As the boot contained several litres of wine the assembled knights and counts were reluctant to try, but finally the knight Boos von Waldeck took heart and emptied the boot in one or two gulps—thereby at one stroke considerably increasing his alcohol level and relieving Count Friedrich Wilhelm of his village.

If we consider the Schlossböckelheim region more closely, there is something that is very striking. Let us look at the names of some of the wine villages: Roxheim, Weinsheim, Rüdesheim, Norheim, Schlossböckelheim, Sponheim, Waldböckelheim, Sobernheim, Staudernheim, Merxheim, Meisenheim. Do you see? They all end with *"heim"* ("home"), thus making it clear that the Nahe can be a real "home away from home" for wine lovers!

NAHE VINEYARD SITES

There are two regions:

Kreuznach
with the *Grosslagen* Pfarrgarten, Sonnenborn, Schlosskapelle and Kronenberg.

Schlossböckelheim
with the *Grosslagen* Rosengarten, Paradiesgarten and Burgweg.

There are 327 individual sites registered, distributed over an area of forty-four hundred hectares (about eleven thousand acres) and worked by some 3,300 winegrowers. The total area's average annual yield has been about 415,000 hectolitres which is about 4.4 percent of the German total. Apart from one or two large firms, medium-size firms dominate here. Approximately 40 percent of the harvest is sold direct and about 20 percent through the wine cooperatives. Much Nahe wine is exported to the English-speaking countries.

Rheinhessen

*Historic Region Between
Worms and Bingen*

The name of this wine-growing area is somewhat misleading. According to the political map, Rheinhessen ("Rhine-Hesse") is not in Hessen at all but in the Rhineland Palatinate (*Rheinland-Pfalz*, of which the Rhine Palatinate—*Rheinpfalz*—is a subsection). Rheinhessen, screened in the west by the Hunsrück and the Pfälzerwald ("Palatinate forest"), in the north by the Taunus and in the east by the Odenwald, has always been involved in a neck-and-neck race with its neighboring wine-growing area to the south, the Rhine Palatinate. The Palatinate has a slight advantage with 21,187 hectares (ca. 53,000 acres) under cultivation to Rheinhessen's 20,789 (ca. 52,000 acres), as with the total yield (in 1978, 2.47 million hectolitres, compared to 2.20 million from Rheinhessen). Be that as it may, this is a healthy state of affairs as it guarantees that barrels will not become empty and glasses will always remain full. That can't be bad, as we know!

Carl Zuckmayer, of Nackenheim, has glorified his area's wine as unqualified *Lachwein* ("laughing wine"), as it makes one happy without intoxicating.

It was in all probability the Romans who brought viticulture to this strip of land in

One of Rheinhessen's most famous wine villages: Oppenheim, with Saint Catherine's Church.

103

the second century, but of this we have no record. The first documentary evidence concerning wine-growing in the Rheinhessen triangle (bounded by Worms, Bingen and Mainz) is dated January 18, 733, on which day the monastery at Fulda bought a vineyard in Bretzenheim near Mainz.

Today some fifteen thousand wine-growers are involved in viticulture here. The Müller-Thurgau is the dominant vine with a share of 34 percent, followed by the Sylvaner with 24 percent and the new variety Scheurebe (7 percent), developed in the Teaching and Experimental Station at Alzey in 1916 by director Georg Scheu. The large share the Müller-Thurgau has in Rheinhessen is also to the credit of this untiring vine cultivator (Sieger, Huxel, Faber and Kanzler are some of his more well-known crossings), as it was Scheu who first realized its potential. Riesling and Morio-Muskat, each with a share of 5 percent, are also of a certain importance in Rheinhessen.

Red wine also plays a part here, mainly with the Portugieser (4 percent), found in the more inland areas. Ingelheim on the Rhine with its Spätburgunder is, next to Assmannshausen, the most famous German "red-wine town." Just north of Ingelheim the ruins of a palace of Charlemagne, where he stayed while travelling through his empire, remind us of this important patron of viticulture, who is said to have been born here.

Rheinhessen is divided into three districts —Bingen, Nierstein and Wonnegau—but one must also differentiate between the hinterland, where milder, agreeable wines predominate, and the Rheinfront, a small strip of land about ten miles long from Guntersblum in southern Rheinhessen to Nackenheim further north. Here the so-called "Rotliegende," reddish sandstone, determines the character of the wine, which comes mainly from the Riesling grape. These wines are rich, full and robust and in good years have a piquant acidity, elegance and maturity. First-class qualities can be achieved in particularly "blessed" years. The red earth found on the Rheinfront colors the roads and even the Rhine after heavy showers. It is especially good for wine-growing because it stores up the sun's warmth during the day and gives it back to the vines at night. The warmth that rises up from the river at night is an added benefit.

The hinterland is characterized by the rolling hills on which typical Rheinhessen wine grows. This tender, flowery wine is seldom made drier, as this would lessen its popularity.

Rheinhessen is the home of Liebfraumilch (also known as Liebfrauenmilch or Liebfraunmilch). More than half of all exported German wines carry this name. In addition it has been copied in other countries. Liebfraumilch has found many friends in America, above all.

The name comes from the monks of the Liebfrauenkirche at Worms, a collegiate church with a chapter (*Stiftskirche*). The German word *"Mönch"* ("monk") was formerly *"Minch"*—*"Milch"* simply being an adaptation of this. Today the name is used for many wines produced in the Nahe, Rheingau, Palatinate and Rheinhessen which are of a mild, agreeable type and good quality.

Those who travel through Rheinhessen should take their time, because there are many original wine cellars and other places of interest to visit. This is particularly true

Dautenheim, a suburb of Alzey, home of one of Germany's most famous wine researchers, Georg Scheu. Scheu is responsible for many hybrids.

of Johann Gutenberg's hometown Mainz (the inventor of printing was also a light-hearted reveller). Here one can visit the cathedral, many churches and museums and perhaps the Haus des Deutschen Weines ("house of German wine"), a restaurant with wines from all eleven German wine-growing areas.

The whole of Rheinhessen is well endowed with cultural monuments, many of which also celebrate wine. The Kaiserdom ("emperor's cathedral") in Worms is perhaps the most striking. One can find in Oppenheim the Katharinenkirche ("church of Saint Catherine"), where Albert Schweitzer often played the world-famous organ. Oppenheim is also the home of an important institution, the Teaching and Experimental Station for Wine and Fruit Cultivation, which has had a great effect on the improvement of quality in this area. The same is true of the Alzey institute.

Nierstein is one of the most famous wine villages. In 1782 Friedrich von Schiller stayed there on his flight from Stuttgart to Mannheim. His companion Andreas Streicher, later a famous piano maker, describes the poet's first acquaintance with Nierstein's wine:

As we reached Nierstein in the morning, neither of us, Friedrich Schiller nor I, could resist the temptation to strengthen ourselves with the wine from the area, wine which we knew only from praise paid to it by the poet and which Schiller in particular seemed to really need. We entered the next inn on the Rhine, and after placing our order received a glass of the oldest wine to be found in the cellar and paid for it with a thaler.

As non-connoisseurs of noble wine, it seemed to us that with this drink, as with other famous things, its reputation was greater than it deserved. However, on returning to the fresh air our footsteps were lighter, our senses wide awake, the future's gloomy clouds dispersed so that we could now face it with more courage than before; we believed that we had found in it comfort for our hearts and gave the wine its full due.

In the hinterland with its many picturesque villages it's well worth while to visit among other places, Wörrstadt, Wöllstein, Selzen, Albig, Gau-Odernheim, Armsheim (with one of the most beautiful village churches in Rheinhessen from the year 1431), Freimersheim and Dalsheim (with its seven-hundred-year-old wall with seven defensive towers).

Gau-Bickelheim, in the center of this rolling landscape, houses the Central Cellars of the Rhenish Wine Cooperative. Some five hundred small holders deliver their wine to this modern cellar, whose barrel capacity is 28 million litres. "Barrel" here does not of course mean wooden barrels; in such highly technical large firms wooden barrels are hardly ever used and are only to be found as ornaments. Using wooden barrels simply takes up too much time. One must set aside romance and accept that using concrete, steel or plastic tanks is the better solution for firms of this size. It is no disadvantage for the wine!

A very special section of vineyards can be found near Bingen, where a ridge, the Rochusberg, extends eastward nearly to Kempten. It is surrounded on all sides by vineyards, even to the north—a situation perhaps unique in all Europe. Its southern

The Liebfrauenkirche in Worms and its surrounding vineyards. Here originated the name of Germany's main exported wine—Liebfraumilch.

slope is the Scharlachberg ("scarlet hill"). The reflection of light from the Nahe and Rhine, which practically encircle it, provide the warmth necessary for growth.

RHEINHESSEN VINEYARD SITES

There are three regions:

Bingen
with the *Grosslagen* Sankt Rochuskapelle, Abtey, Rheingrafenstein, Adelberg, Kurfürstenstück, Kaiserpfalz;

Nierstein
with the *Grosslagen* St. Alban, Domherr, Gutes Domtal, Spiegelberg, Rehbach, Auflangen, Güldenmorgen, Krötenbrunnen, Vogelsgärten, Petersberg, Rheinblick;

Wonnegau
with the *Grosslagen* Sybillenstein, Bergkloster, Pilgerpfad, Gotteshilfe, Burg Rodenstein, Domblick, Liebfrauenmorgen.

Rheinhessen has 435 individual registered vineyard sites on 20,789 hectares (ca. 52,500 acres). With an average annual yield of 2.2 million hectolitres Rheinhessen produces about 23.3 percent of the national total. Mixed farms dominate, but there are also a number of larger, exclusive wine-growers. Through the increase in tourism, which has also reached the smaller villages, the amount of direct selling to the public has increased. Apart from this wine wholesalers and cooperatives provide steady sales.

Bingen on the Rhine. Here the river Nahe meets "Father Rhine." On the opposite bank, in the Rheingau, can be seen the ruins of Ehrenfels Castle.

The Rhine Palatinate

"The Wine Palatinate"

The people from the Rhine Palatinate (*Rheinpfalz*) are proud of their superlatives, and with good cause. Here one finds the most German wine, the earliest spring, the largest wine festival and the biggest wine barrel in the world.

This two-to-six-mile wide area stretching for some fifty miles along the eastern slope of the Haardt mountains is a veritable spring paradise. Valuable because of the abundance of wine, the region had a changeable history until 1214 when it fell to the Bavarian dukes of Wittelsbach. A medieval chronicler honored it by calling it "the wine cellar of the Holy Roman Empire." In the heyday of the empire the emperors lived and died here; eight alone are buried in the cathedral at Speyer. In these early times more than three hundred feudal lords and monasteries shared the blessing of the vine.

On the Rhine Palatinate's 21,000 hectares (ca. 53,000 acres) of vineyards 150 million vines are grown. On the Weinstrasse ("wine road") there are 176 villages. The Weinstrasse's triumphal way through the Palatinate wine country lies between the French border at Schweigen and the Rheinhessen "border" at Bockenheim.

Palatinate countryside in the Südliche Weinstrasse region, between Oberhausen and Hergersweiler.

111

The vine has been a native of these parts for at least two thousand years. The climate, which is similar to that of Italy, has made the Palatinate a Garden of the Gods. At the beginning of May the almond trees start to bloom, closely followed by peach, apple and cherry and finally in June the vines. Even figs and oranges can be found in sheltered places, together with other trees and flowers that appear to bring greetings from Italy.

The vineyards are to be found up to a height of 325 yards on the sides of the Haardt mountains, which protect them against wind and rain and ensure the vineyards a particularly constant and mild climate, with only slight temperature fluctuations, short winters and moderately warm summers. Snow on the ground for longer than a week is a rarity; the Palatinate is renowned as one of the sunniest and driest areas in Germany.

Good soil is a further prerequisite for successful viticulture. In the Vorderpfalz ("front Palatinate") it mainly consists of colored sandstone topped with layers of shell limestone, although limestone, basalt, granite, gneiss and mica slate also occur. In the south, in the Südliche Weinstrasse region ("southern wine road"; formerly Oberhaardt or "upper Haardt"), clay, loess and sand are the main components, while in the Mittelhaardt, where the richest and most noble wines grow, sand and clay predominate. Further north still are areas of clay and loess.

The Palatinate is very versatile as well in the different types of white-wine grapes grown. (White wine takes up 89 percent of the area under cultivation.) The main variety is Müller-Thurgau with 25 percent, followed by Sylvaner with 20 percent, Riesling with 14 percent, Portugieser (the only red wine; Spätburgunder is hardly grown

at all) with 10 percent, Morio-Muskat (8 percent) and Kerner (6 percent).

For every taste the appropriate wine can be found in the Palatinate. Here are light, full-bodied wines, hearty vintages for the men and *Lieblichkeiten* ("lovelinesses") for the women. Walter Kiaulehn, an enthusiastic wine poet, once wrote, "Palatinate wines can be like a loud 'camp follower,' but also like a one true love with whom one stays one's whole life." Another expert on German wine rightly states, "The great value of German wine is its diversity. The Rhine Palatinate adds a great amount of beautiful, precious and rare blooms to the 'vine wreath' made up from all the wine-growing areas."

The fact that one cannot give Palatinate wine a uniform attribute is its great attraction. A wine-tasting of these wines is a journey of discovery with new surprises time and again. On a journey along the Weinstrasse one also gets to know the inhabitants with their friendly and happy but unobtrusive nature, which is really captivating.

That they cook very well in this area needs no longer to be proved. Here homemade specialties rank above the "finer kitchens." *Saumagen* (pig's stomach), *Kartoffelsupp'* (potato soup), *Leberwurst* (liver sausage) and *Weisser Käs'* (white cheese) are diverse tasty tidbits, all of which, cunningly enough, make you thirsty.

The Rhine Palatinate cultivation area is divided into two regions: the Mittelhaardt and, to the south, the Südliche Weinstrasse. Some years ago the latter was scornfully called by critics the "*Süssliche Weinstrasse*" ("sweet wine road") because several wine-growers were placing a little too much

Vineyards such as these at Ilbesheim are not so labor-intensive as those on steep slopes.

112

stress on sweetness. However, with regard to quality the Südliche Weinstrasse has made good progress and is now on a par with all the other areas.

A tour of this area could well begin in Schweigen-Rechtenbach at the Deutsches Weintor ("German wine gate") built in 1936 and rebuilt after World War II. Here a *Weinlehrpfad*, an instructive path through the vineyards, explains the different types of grape and methods of cultivation. On, past Bad Bergzabern and Klingenmünster, the Weinstrasse comes to Leinsweiler, where the great impressionist painter Max Slevogt spent his later life and found his resting place. Here he produced his most beautiful works—dedicated to wine.

The road goes on past Birkweiler to the valley of the Eich-Quellen ("oak springs") near Siebeldingen. Here the road is bounded by many castles, chief of which is Burg Dreifaltigkeit on the Trifels, where once the imperial jewels were kept and in which Richard the Lion-Hearted was imprisoned, if we are to believe the legend.

The way continues past Geilweilerhof, where the Federal Institute for Vine Cultivation is located, past the warmest place in the Palatinate, Gleisweiler, where almond trees, cedars and a whole assortment of other southern plants surprise us, to Rhodt and Edenkoben. Nearby is Villa Ludwigshöhe built by the enthusiastic, art-loving Bavarian king, Ludwig I.

Beyond the large wine villages of Maikammer, Diedesfeld and Hambach we now find ourselves in the Mittelhaardt. Hambacher Schloss (Maxburg) was where in 1077 Henry IV embarked on his journey to Canossa to plead for mercy to the Pope, where five centuries later the local farmers drank three hundred cartloads of wine from the largest, oldest barrel to fortify their spirits during the Peasants' War, and where

in 1832 students demanded the formation of a united German republic.

Our first major stop is Neustadt an der Weinstrasse. In this, the largest wine community in Germany, the Weinlesefest ("wine-harvest festival") has been held since 1929. In the same year the custom of choosing a Wine Queen was introduced. At first this was only relative to the Palatinate and without consistent regard for particular qualifications. However, since 1950 a German Wine Queen has been chosen by an examining committee, and the young aspirants must show knowledge and charm. The competition and selection of the Wine Queen is the climax of the Weinlesefest.

In the Mittelhaardt great wines are grown every year. Full, vigorous vines are associated by connoisseurs with Palatinate wine in general, and at the mention of Mussbach, Königsbach, Ruppertsberg, Deidesheim, Forst, Wachenheim, Ungstein, Kallstadt, Freinsheim and of course Bad Dürkheim wine-lovers eagerly lick their lips.

Bad Dürkheim, a spa town in a wine area, is equally well known for its white and its red wines. The greatest wine festival in the world, the Dürkheimer Wurstmarkt ("Durkheim sausage fair"), held every year just before the wine harvest, attracts up to 400,000 people.

The Palatinate writer August Becker wrote of Bad Dürkheim in 1858 in his sketchbook, entitled *The Rhine Palatinate and Its Inhabitants*:

> Here we are again in the center of the German paradise, the "rapturous district." At the doorway of one of the most beautiful, wild and pleasant places, the most historically rich valley in the Palatinate, in the presence

The Weinstrasse goes for some fifty miles through the Palatinate's sea of vines.

114

of the most magnificent monastery ruins in Germany, in front of the great Rhine plateau, between excellent vine-covered hills, so exactly in the middle of the richest and best wine country, this town has always attracted the attention of all nature lovers and tourists.

Bad Dürkheim, the most beloved town in the whole area, lies in a hilly "wine garden," stretching to a great length along the foothills of the Haardt, which produces the most noble wines. To the north are Ungstein, Kallstadt, Herxheim; to the south, Wachenheim, Forst, Deidesheim, Ruppertsberg and other places known to everyone as plentiful sources of the noble, fiery yet mild Palatinate wine! And who would not place the Dürkheimer as among the best of these?

That Dürkheim has become one of the most visited "brine springs" and most important spa towns should surprise no one, because with its mild southern climate, splendid surroundings, cheerful inhabitants and excellent stock of grapes, all conditions for popularity are fulfilled here.

It gained more advantages for itself when in the last century the princes of Leiningen transferred their palace here. A beautiful palace was built, new roads and pleasure gardens were laid out and—under the artistic Prince Carl Wilhelm, an enthusiastic admirer of the newly blossoming German poetry—a theatre was constructed, at which Iffland von Mannheim, a good friend of the prince, often appeared.

Above the *Brühlwiesen* ("swampy meadows") near Dürkheim the most noble types of grape rise up on the Michelsberg, on which is to be found the Michelskapelle, whose church festival is a part of the Wurstmarkt. It attracts visitors from a

great distance and is always held on the *Brühlwiesen*. Those who wish to get to know the locals in their most merry cheerfulness and joviality, wit and comradeship, verbosity and hearty singing, really amazing appetite for sausages and more amazing drinking capacity, can do no better than visit the Bad Dürkheimer Wurstmarkt. Here is the rejoicing of a normally very lively people: the swirling sound of dance music and barrel organs, the numbing din from the festival booths, the singing of various town and country groups enlivened by wine and the smell of sausages, the bustle around the market stalls, and the extraordinary sincerity which is sometimes expressed a little bluntly. Those looking for jolly times will certainly find them here.

Escaping from all this blissful excitement, we continue further northward past Leistadt, Weisenheim, and the picturesque medieval walled village of Neuleiningen with its castle ruins.

Near the ruins of Altleiningen is the towering Peterskopf, from which one can enjoy a wonderful panorama. Our next stop, Grünstadt, was at one time the residence of the counts of Leiningen. Nearby are Kirchheim, Grosskarlbach and Dirmstein, all well-known wine villages, which in common with all those previously mentioned have wonderfully maintained half-timbered houses. In Bockenheim the Weinstrasse comes to an end, but the tour is well worth carrying on to the area beyond, formerly called "Unterhaardt." North of Bockenheim we find the Zellertal ("Zell valley") with Zell and Niefernheim, where the wines are lighter yet robust. Wachenheim, Gauersheim, Kirchheimbolanden and the most northerly of all, Morschheim, are other wine-growing villages.

One should not forget that while along the

Weinstrasse the Rhine Palatinate wine-growing area is well laid out, occasional "side steps" are to be encouraged. For example, Speyer (about sixteen miles east of Neustadt, on the Rhine) has a truly unique wine museum.

RHINE PALATINATE VINEYARD SITES

The Palatinate can be divided into two regions:

Mittelhaardt/Deutsche Weinstrasse
with the *Grosslagen* Schnepfenpflug vom Zellertal, Grafenstück (Bockenheim), Höllenpfad (Grünstadt), Schwarzerde (Kirchheim), Rosenbühl (Freinsheim), Kobnert (Kallstadt), Feuerberg (Bad Dürkheim), Saumagen (Kallstadt), Honigsäckel (Ungstein), Hochmess (Bad Dürkheim), Schenkenböhl (Wachenheim), Schnepfenpflug an der Weinstrasse (Forst), Mariengarten (Forst), Hofstück (Deidesheim), Meerspinne (Neustadt, Ortsteil Gimmeldingen), Rebstöckel (Neustadt, Ortsteil Diedesfeld), Pfaffengrund (Neustadt, Ortsteil Diedesfeld); and

Südliche Weinstrasse
with the *Grosslagen* Mandelhöhe (Maikammer), Schloss Ludwigshöhe (Edenkoben), Ordensgut (Edesheim), Trappenberg (Hochstadt), Bischofskreuz (Walsheim), Königsgarten (Goldramstein), Herrlich (Eschbach), Kloster Liebfrauenberg (Bad Bergzabern), Guttenberg (Schweigen).

Besides these there are 335 individual sites registered. Two-thirds of all vineyards are part-time businesses. Approximately 27 percent of the grape harvest is taken by the wine cooperatives, a further 25 percent sold directly to the public and the rest sold by the individual wine-growers (among whom there are many old firms, long in tradition) to retailers.

The Hessian Bergstrasse

A Garden of Eden

The wine-growing area in the Hessian Bergstrasse has increased in the last four years by about 100 hectares (ca. 250 acres), giving a total of 370 hectares (ca. 925 acres), of which 99 percent is taken up by white wine. Of this, 52 percent is Riesling, 19 percent Müller-Thurgau, 10 percent the full-bodied and robust Ruländer and a further 10 percent Sylvaner. Wine is grown here by a total of 600 vineyards, with an average size of 0.5 hectares (ca. 1¼ acres). This means that the vast majority of wine-growers have to secure their livelihood mainly by other means; these are the so-called "part-time" wine-growers. Thus there is a strong connection between workers in industry and on the land, a connection confirmed time and time again. The recent increase of the area under cultivation shows how much these people are attached to their vineyards and their wine.

The viticultural area Hessian Bergstrasse —the northern part of the Bergstrasse, a geographical area straddling Hesse and Baden on the west slopes of the Odenwald hills—has existed officially only since the Wine Laws of 1971. Until this date it belonged to the Rheingau (also in Hesse).

These blossoming cherry and walnut trees are an indication of a favorable environment for wine-growing.

119

The southern part—the Baden Bergstrasse—has always belonged to Baden. The main centers of the Hessian Bergstrasse are Umstadt, Bensheim and Heppenheim.

The Bergstrasse ("mountain road") itself is even older than its viticulture, having been built at the time of the Romans, evidence of whom can still be seen. (Its Latin name was *Strada Montana*.) A sandstone relief from Roman times showing grapes has been found during the excavation of a farm in Gross-Umstadt. The first documented evidence of wine-growing dates from 765.

Thanks to the southern slopes and the sheltered sites of this, the smallest German wine area, the grapes ripen well in the fall. However, the area really shows itself a true Garden of Eden in spring.

By March the slopes are covered with white blossoms. This thirty-mile-long area of slopes becomes a spring paradise of almonds and peaches, followed by cherries and other kinds of fruit, ablaze for weeks and months and enrapturing visitors.

There is a superabundance of testimony by famous personalities to this: Emperor Joseph II said on seeing the Bergstrasse that he felt as though he were in Italy. Johanna Schopenhauer, the mother of the philosopher Arthur Schopenhauer wrote:

> Just nearby [is] the friendly little village of Auerbach, a little bit farther the small town of Bensheim not far off from Heppenheim in the center of its vines covering the hillside up to the summit, on which the ruined dark towers of the once-powerful Starkenburg loom up. I don't think that a more beautiful place is to be found in the whole area.

The poet Wilhelm Heinse wrote in 1789:

> Heppenheim is well situated on the Starkenberg. . . . The hill on which the tower stands is the most beautiful part of the whole Bergstrasse: picturesque, covered on many sides with forests of slender beeches, fresh and pleasant everywhere. Next to this, hills full of vines . . .

And Käthe Kollwitz in 1921:

> Fertile and bright. Unbelievably cheerful. Sometimes I was reminded of the hills above Florence when one follows the serpentine paths, now climbing up through vineyards, now going under walnut trees and happily seeing how much can grow in this soil.

From this fertile earth, where fruit and edible chestnuts, almonds and figs ripen besides, the wine simply must be different. One should not assume, however, that in this small area there is only one type of wine. Here again the different types of soil—loess, clay or sandstone—determine the wines, which are nearly always fruity and spicy, sometimes needing to be stored longer for the fine acidity to complete their harmony.

Wine from the Hessian Bergstrasse has one fault, however: There is not enough of it! The demand can hardly be met when wine lovers arrive in the hundreds of thousands in spring, summer and fall, from near and far. Especially they come from nearby Frankfurt, Darmstadt, Heidelberg, Mannheim and Ludwigshafen to enjoy both the countryside and the wine. *Strausswirtschaften* inns kept by wine-growers who sell their own wine or by wine cellars in town (private or owned by the state), cater to visitors.

In practice one can get to know the types

Contemplative weekday in a wine village with many half-timbered houses.

of vineyard and their sites in the course of a walk. For those who wish to look around more carefully the wine cooperative (*Gebietswinzergenossenschaft*) of Heppenheim and the state-controlled cellar in Bensheim organize guided tours, naturally including wine-tasting. These are also offered by the Experimental Vineyard of the Hessischen Landesamt für Landwirt-schaft ("Hesse agricultural department") as well as by the Gross-Umstadt Coopera-tive.

Those wishing to enjoy the wine of the Hessian Bergstrasse must themselves ven-ture there. (It is, incidentally, easy to reach from the Bergstrasse motorway Darmstadt–Weinheim.) One rarely finds these wines in a wine list or shops outside this area.

HESSIAN BERGSTRASSE VINEYARD SITES

The area has two regions:

Umstadt
with only individual sites, no *Grosslagen*; and

Starkenburg
with the *Grosslagen* Rott, Wolfsmagen and Schlossberg.

Twenty-two individual sites are registered. With an average annual yield of 30,000 hectolitres, the Hessian Bergstrasse pro-duces about 0.3 percent of the German total, the vast majority of the grapes being processed and sold by the two cooperatives.

Rows of vines in springtime in the Hessian Berg-strasse between Bensheim, Auerbach and Zwingen-berg.

Württemberg

"Oh blessed land! No hill
without its vines!"

When more evidence has been needed that wine helps the art of poetry, Württemberg has provided it more than once. Experts claim that this is the land of poets and drinkers (wherein normally one and the same person is meant). One thinks of Friedrich von Schiller from Marbach, Eduard Mörike, Justinus Kerner—after whom a new grape was named—and Hermann Hesse from Calw. Great praise for this area also comes from Friedrich Hölderlin of Lauffen on the Neckar and more recently Thaddäus Troll, who has done much to spread the fame of Württemberg wine far beyond the region's borders.

Württembergers, whether with or without talent for poetry, enjoy their wine in large quantities—annual consumption is 40 litres per person—not only because it tastes so good but because they begrudge it to wine-drinkers from elsewhere. Theodor Heuss, ex-president of West Germany and a native of these parts, once answered a guest at a wine-tasting in Bonn as to why one seldom finds Swabian wine outside Württemberg thus: "You know it's quite easy to explain: In the past we drank it because otherwise nobody else would have.

A land nurtured by the sun: Württemberg. Pictured here are rows of vines near Michelbach am Wald.

Today it's so good we don't want to hand it over any more."

Heuss's words show clearly the great change that has taken place in the quality of Württemberg wine. Some decades before Heuss himself had written very critically in his doctoral thesis (1905), "The putting together of good and bad qualities, the harvesting of black and white grapes together . . . was and is a bad habit . . . because the individuality of one variety is destroyed right from the beginning!"

Since 1950 the area under cultivation in Württemberg has increased by over two thousand hectares (ca. five thousand acres), not least because of the decisive work of wine-growers' cooperatives which have resolutely encouraged the improvement of quality and taken care that the mixing of ingredients disappear. Add to this that there have been great advances in modern cellar technology and successful sales planning. Nowadays, in good years Württemberg produces wines of the very best quality and the noblest character.

At present, viticulture here takes up an area of some nine thousand hectares (ca. twenty-three thousand acres). Among the many different sorts of grape one finds two red specialties, to be found only in Württemberg. They are the Trollinger (with a 24 percent share) and the Lemberger (about 3 percent). Other popular wines are the Schwarzriesling (10 percent) and the Portugieser (6 percent). Among white wines Riesling with 23 percent is the most popular, Müller-Thurgau, which predominates almost everywhere else, has only 7 percent, Sylvaner has 10 percent and Kerner, a new grape developed at Weinsberg, has rapidly won a 5 percent share. Although there is already great variety here, the wine-growers are dedicated to new cultivations and love to experiment. In total

there are some eighteen thousand winegrowers, more than half of whom are engaged in mixed farming.

Another particular specialty of Württemberg is the Schillerwein, by which the "must" of both red and white grapes is fermented in a mixture, giving the wine a rosé color. The term for this type of wine is "Rotling," which must not be confused with normal rosé wine or the Weissherbst, which are both produced from red grapes only. Schillerwein is a lively wine—named not after Friedrich von Schiller, as is often supposed, but after its schillernde ("iridescent") color.

As with the wine, the area is also divided into a great variety of smaller regions, due largely to the long connection this area has had with wine-growing. Archeologists have found in excavations between Stuttgart and Heilbronn traces of wine-growing and drinking five thousand years old, showing that viticulture must have been at home here ever since the Stone Age. Although people at that time were usually nomadic, there were some settlements with areas of cultivation.

Württemberg's grapes grow in the many climatically favorable sites alongside rivers and streams; on the slopes of hills, steeper slopes and sometimes more level areas; on different soils, whether shell-limestone, red marl, slate, potter's clay, loam or loess; and at heights of up to nineteen hundred feet. In addition to the deep soil, which makes a good reservoir for water, the climate suits the vines. In Württemberg there are frequent rain showers, and the moisture has a lot to do with the striking aroma of the wine. Lying on south-facing slopes in the various valleys of the Swabian Alps

Difficult terrain bearing enticing fruit: In this vineyard near Esslingen the Spätlese is awaited.

and the Schwarzwald ("black forest"), the vines are protected from the unpleasant influences of the weather.

Visitors to Württemberg should not be weight-watchers. Otherwise they will find it difficult, because the *Spätzle* (Swabian dumplings) and *Brätle* (roast) are so good that no one can resist them. Staying power is also expected from visitors. The theory Theodor Heuss originated—"Whoever tipples wine, sins; whoever drinks wine, prays"—is not agreed with by the locals and should not be by their visitors either; there are many religious people in Württemberg.

The Neckar and the Swabian Weinstrasse serve as orientation for visitors who will in all probability start out from Stuttgart, capital of Baden-Württemberg and the only large city in Germany to lie between hills covered with vineyards incorporated into a whole ring of wine communities, so that after Heilbronn it is the largest wine-growing community in Württemberg. The sites are well protected, and it is forbidden to build on them. If one calculated the value of the soil here in relation to the market price for unprotected land, the wine sites around Stuttgart would be the most expensive in the world.

Red wines dominate the Stuttgart-Esslingen area, with a share of about 70 percent, in particular the Trollinger—to an extent the national wine of Württemberg. The Trollinger is a very demanding vine on site and soil. Where the climate is good it proves itself to be a very generous, fruity, fresh, rich, full and strong wine.

Wine is not only grown on the Neckar, but also along its tributaries, the Rems, Murr, Enz, Bottwar, Zaber, Kocher and Jagst, and the Tauber. In the Remstal ("Rems valley"), which borders in the south on the Schurwald forest and in the north and east

on the Swabian forest, Trollinger is once again of greatest importance, followed by the tenderer Portugieser and—never to be forgotten—the Sylvaner and Riesling.

A little farther north, in the Middle Neckar valley, is Marbach, birthplace of Friedrich von Schiller. Along with one or two sips of Trollinger or Sylvaner one should also take to heart the Schiller Museum and Alexanderkirche. The Bottwar valley above Marbach has fresh Trollinger and fine Riesling wines. Oberstenfeld, a romantic idyll of a village, lies on the Bottwar between hills, castles and slopes of vines.

The Weinsberg valley—formed by the Sulm River—is crowned by Weinsberg with its castle enshrined in legend. Here also is a Teaching and Experimental Institute which has contributed much towards advances in cellar technology. In addition to its Trollinger and Lemberger this area is famous for its Riesling, which demonstrates all its virtues.

Heilbronn, the main city of lower Württemberg, is the starting point for many excursions into the surrounding areas, all of which have a very favorable climate. Reds again predominate: Trollinger, Spätburgunder, Schwarzriesling and Samtrot (a mutation of the Müller grape—which in turn comes from the Spätburgunder—developed at the Weinsberg Institute).

Journeying east of Heilbronn and Weinsberg we come to Ohringen where rich soils bestow on growers and drinkers alike rich wines. Their character is reminiscent of the wine of Franconia, to which this section really belongs. The same goes for the Kocher and Jagst valleys, home of the Knight Goetz von Berlichingen, where the attractive Sylvaner is at home, as are other

Romantic vineyards near Stuttgart: a view of Schnait in the valley.

128

robust white wines, similarly reminding us of Franconian wine.

West of Heilbronn and north of the Zaber River lies the Heuchelberg range (given its name by the mountain dominating the area), where Trollinger and Lemberger reign, red wines full of character and often truly great. Here is Brackenheim, Theodor Heuss's birthplace. The house where he was born has been converted into a co-operative cellar—with his consent. The Trollinger and Lemberger always accompanied Heuss.

To the south, the area of the Stromberg range is also dominated by Trollinger and Lemberger, not so heavy here as in the Heuchelberg, but instead having more scope and lightness. The white wines are valued for their fragrance. A fiery wine with the name "Türkenblut" ("Turk's blood"), produced in the pleasant village of Horrheim, recalls a courageous action by Swabians in the Turkish Wars.

It is said that the hearts of many newly won friends of Württemberg bleed when they have to leave after their first visit. The wine has undoubtedly much to do with this love affair. After all, as the old Swabian motto says, "Never wait until you're thirsty!"

It should be noted that wine legislation and the demarcation of provincial borders have resulted in the fact that far away from the Württemberg wine-growing area are one or two sites legally belonging to Württemberg—for example, Ravensburg far to the south and Kressbronn on Lake Constance—sites which perhaps would be better considered to belong to another area. In this connection we should also mention Nonnenhorn near Lindau, also legally part of Württemberg but displaying on its bottle-label "Bereich Bayerischer Bodensee" ("Region of Bavarian Lake Constance"), a curiosity which we'll say more about in the chapter on Franconian wine.

WÜRTTEMBERG VINEYARD SITES

This area can be divided into four regions:

Kocher-Jagst-Tauber
with the *Grosslagen* Tauberberg and Kocherberg;

Württembergisch Unterland
with the *Grosslagen* Staufenberg, Lindelberg, Salzberg, Schozachtal, Wunnenstein, Kirchenweinberg, Heuchelberg, Stromberg and Schalkstein;

Remstal-Stuttgart
with the *Grosslagen* Weinsteige, Kopf, Wartbühl and Sonnenbühl; and

Tübingen-Reutlingen
with the *Grosslage* Hohenneuffen and many individual sites besides.

In all, 206 individual sites are registered. The whole Württemberg area has in recent years produced an annual average of 900,000 hectolitres of wine, 95 percent of the German total. Of over eighteen thousand vineyards, only forty-two have an area of more than five hectares (ca. thirteen acres) under cultivation.

Baden

*Nearly Two Thousand Hours
of Sunshine*

One thing must be made clear immediately: "Baden wine" does not exist. The Baden wine area, just like Württemberg and Franconia, is not one compact area; rather it is very extensive. It can be found to the north near Mannheim and several hundred miles to the south on the Swiss border. Often it is only small strips of land interspersed with fields and forests, linked by the well-signposted Baden Weinstrasse, which goes from Weil near Basel to Laudenbach north of Weinheim in the Baden Bergstrasse.

Just as the regional wine scenery varies, so does the character of the wine—in taste as well as content. The area under cultivation amounts to 19,000 hectares (47,500 acres); white wines dominate with a share of 80 percent. It should be noted, however, that Baden red wine, including Weissherbst, accounts for some of the best produced in West Germany. As regards individual grapes, Müller-Thurgau has the largest portion with 36 percent followed by Blauer ("blue") Spätburgunder (18 percent); the Ruländer, a derivation of the Burgundy grape here often called "Grauburgunder" (14 percent); the Gutedel, a refreshing light wine which one can't ob-

One of the greatest sites in the Kaiserstuhl region of Baden: the Winklerberg, with its easily worked terraces.

133

tain enough of, ideal to accompany a meal, coming mainly from the Markgräflerland (10 percent); the classic Riesling (7 percent); and Sylvaner (5 percent). The rare Gewürztraminer, which can have extraordinarily good qualities; the Scheurebe, which has won a lot of ground recently; and new cultivations of the State Wine Institute in Freiburg such as the Freisamer (Sylvaner and Ruländer), Nobling (Sylvaner and Gutedel) and Zähringer (Traminer and Riesling) all have local importance. Only rarely will one find the old Weissburgunder and Muskateller, which are very demanding to cultivate but which on the right soil can develop excellently.

Some twenty-five thousand vineyards cultivate grapes in Baden, but only a small percentage produce their own wine, because about half of all the vineyards have an area of less than one "morgen" (less than 0.34 hectare or ⅘ acre). Only seventy-eight vineyards have an area of five hectares or more. Therefore the smaller vineyards are naturally dependent on the cooperatives, which have since World War II initiated a complete reorganization of viticulture in the area. Thus Baden, though one of the oldest wine areas, is at the same time one of the youngest.

It was the Romans who from the year 15 onwards began to spread wine-growing from Lake Constance northward. By the first half of the twentieth century this once-prosperous wine area had shrunk to six thousand hectares (about fifteen thousand acres), mainly because of the disastrous effects of the vine louse, but also for economic reasons. However, in the last three decades no other German wine area has modernized its wine-growing and cellar technology to so revolutionary an extent as here. The uneconomical vineyards which had made the area into a "poorhouse" were

amalgamated. Now Baden has a *flurbereinigten* ("restructured") area that is 75 percent of the total, the most in West Germany. This is only one of the distinctions of Baden.

No other German wine area gets so much sun: in the northern parts, at least 1660 hours of sunshine annually; in the south at Kaiserstuhl, nearly 1900 hours. This climatic advantage has contributed towards Baden's position as the only German wine area incorporated into the European wine-growing "Zone B," which, among other regions, contains Alsace and Champagne. (The classification reflects the high "must weight" for the quality groupings.)

A further specialty of Baden is the Weissherbst wine, made from the Spätburgunder grape—which at one time was found only in Baden (particularly in Glottertal near Freiburg), but which by now has won popularity in other areas, too. It is, as we have already mentioned, fermented like a white wine. An even more recent specialty is the "Badisch Rotgold," really the same as Schillerwein—namely, a mixing of Ruländer and Spätburgunder. (On the label appears the old term "Grauburgunder.")

Since 1949, only to be found in Baden is the Gütezeichen ("quality mark"), which requires the fulfillment of more demanding conditions than the Weinsiegel ("wine seal"). This grading by the Baden Viticulture Association is a prerequisite for placement of a wine as a Gebietsweinprämierung ("area prize winner").

Finally, one last specialty of Baden—its remarkable cooking. There is hardly a Baden wine community which has not been distinguished by this, as can be seen from the judgments of Michelin Guide testers,

While everywhere spring is beginning to show itself, the vineyard is still bare. Pictured here is a site near Schriesheim in the Baden Bergstrasse.

who have spread their stars pretty evenly over the area.

Beginning our journey through this wine area, let us start in the south at Lake Constance with its Seewein ("lake wine"). According to legend it was a "gift of the gods," albeit a rather curious one. As the story goes, Christ and Peter were once walking in the area of Lake Constance. They knocked on many doors looking for accommodation, but were sent away by the locals with a few well-chosen words. Only a poor man opened his doors to them. On the next day he received a small vineyard for his hospitality. The locals then realized what they had done and asked for forgiveness, but at the same time shamelessly begged that grapes should also grow in their gardens. "Return, your wishes have been granted," Christ said. Peter was bewildered and objected, "Not one of them let us in yesterday and for that you give them vines?" Christ, however, smiled and said, "Yes, Peter; but just wait until they taste the wine! . . ."

By now the wine from Lake Constance has a better image, the preferred Müller-Thurgau and Spätburgunder being cultivated as quite dry wines. The Müller-Thurgau is above all an ideal wine to be drunk with the *Felchen* ("white fish") from Lake Constance. The most important wine communities here are Meersburg, with its wine museum, and Hagnau, where in 1881 the first wine cooperative in Baden was founded. Another wine-growing site here is the island of Reichenau.

Following the Rhine northward we come to the Markgräflerland region, which Peter Hebel has described as "a paradise garden" and the Alsatian poet René Schickele as "the most beautiful exile in the world." Schliengen, Laufen and Pfaffenweiler are some of the more well-known wine communities. Here in the Markgräflerland—which extends as far north as Freiburg—the Gutedel grape is of the most importance.

North of Freiburg grow the wines of the Breisgau region, which takes its name from the town Breisach (formerly Breisachgau, and today outside the official wine region that is its namesake). In good years these are very noble wines, similar to those of Franconia. They have a hidden strength; overindulgence can make one weak in the knees.

Visitors to the Breisgau region should not miss visiting Freiburg (in June there is a great wine festival), and of course one must see the Glottertal. In this magical and fertile valley which delves deeply into the hills northwest of Freiburg the vines grow on the ever steepening slopes up to a height of sixteen hundred feet. This is the cradle of the original Weissherbst of Baden.

To the west towards the Rhine the world-famous Kaiserstuhl-Tuniberg region spreads out. On terraces of deep loess and sun-drenched volcanic lava, Baden's strongest wines ripen. Here the Ruländer gets its body, the Gewürztraminer its almost overwhelming bouquet and the Spätburgunder its fire and raciness. Even the normally mild Sylvaner develops temperament here. Achkarren, Oberrotweil, Ihringen and Bickensohl are places in the Kaiserstuhl that wine-lovers have imprinted in their memories.

Most well known of all is Breisach, with its historic minster, from the towers of which one can enjoy a distant view across to Alsace. Here also Europe's largest wine cellar is to be found: Zentralkellerei Bad-

"Flurbereinigte" countryside in the Kaiserstuhl near Oberbergen. Through reorganization the work of the wine-growers has been made considerably easier.

136

ischer Winzergenossenschaften ("central cellerage of Baden wine-growers' cooperatives"), which has a total storage capacity of over 150 million litres. Over three hundred wines of different quality are produced by the ZBW every year, amounting to about half the total in Baden.

Moving northward we come to the Ortenau region lying between Offenburg and Baden-Baden, in which the Riesling grape is much preferred. (Here it is often called "Klingelberger," in the same way that the Traminer is often referred to as "Clevner.")

In Baden-Baden's suburbs Neuweier, Steinbach, Umweg and Varnhalt, Qualitätswein may also be filled into the Bocksbeutel (a distinctively shaped bottle) in accordance with an old law of the Würzburg prince bishop. Although the Franconian winegrowers have protested several times against this privilege, in this case their complaint has had no effect. (Legal action by Franconia has forced other areas to give up all use of this bottle.)

Other well-known wine communities in this area are Durbach (with great Riesling wines), Sasbachwalden, Zell-Weierbach and Kapellrodeck (the latter two well known for their full and rugged Spätburgunder).

In the northern areas of Baden the wine changes its character a little. The Pfinzgau-Enzgau region west of Karlsruhe forms the transition from rolling hills to the steep slopes of the northern Schwarzwald ("black forest"). On differing soils—loess in the valley bottom, shell limestone on the outskirts of the Schwarzwald—Rieslings and powerful red wines grow. The Kraichgau region between Grötzingen and Heidelberg is no longer a small strip of land running alongside the Rhine, but now also contains several offshoots such as Neckarmühlbach and Herbolzheim which bring it close to the Württemberg area. The Kraichgau produces a pleasant and fruity Ruländer and noteworthy Rieslings. On a visit here one must of course make a diversion to the Baden Bergstrasse (which provides above all strong, light wines) and to the Heidelberg Palace with its famous giant barrel in the cellar. Made in 1750, it holds over 220,000 litres.

Wines of a very different nature come from the Badisches-Frankenland region to the east of the Bergstrasse. Although it has belonged to Baden since 1803 it could really belong to Franconia. Wertheim, Tauberbischofsheim, Lauda and Bad Mergentheim are the most important wine communities in this region which produces above all flowery, light, spicy Müller-Thurgau (in the Bocksbeutel), but also soft red wine.

138

BADEN VINEYARD SITES

It consists of seven regions:

Badisches Frankenland
with the *Grosslage* Tauberklinge;

Baden Bergstrasse-Kraichgau
with the *Grosslagen* Hohenberg, Stiftsberg, Mannaberg and Rittersberg;

Ortenau
with the *Grosslagen* Schloss Rodeck and Fürsteneck;

Breisgau
with the *Grosslagen* Schutter-Lindenberg, Burg Lichteneck and Burg Zähringen;

Kaiserstuhl-Tuniberg
with the *Grosslagen* Vulkanfelsen and Attilafelsen;

Markgräflerland
with the *Grosslagen* Lorettoberg, Burg Neuenfels and Vogtei Rötteln; and

Bodensee (Lake Constance)
with the *Grosslage* Sonnenufer.

In total there are 306 individual sites. The entire area produces an annual average of 1.4 million hectolitres, 80 percent of which is produced by the 120 wine cooperatives with some twenty-three thousand members.

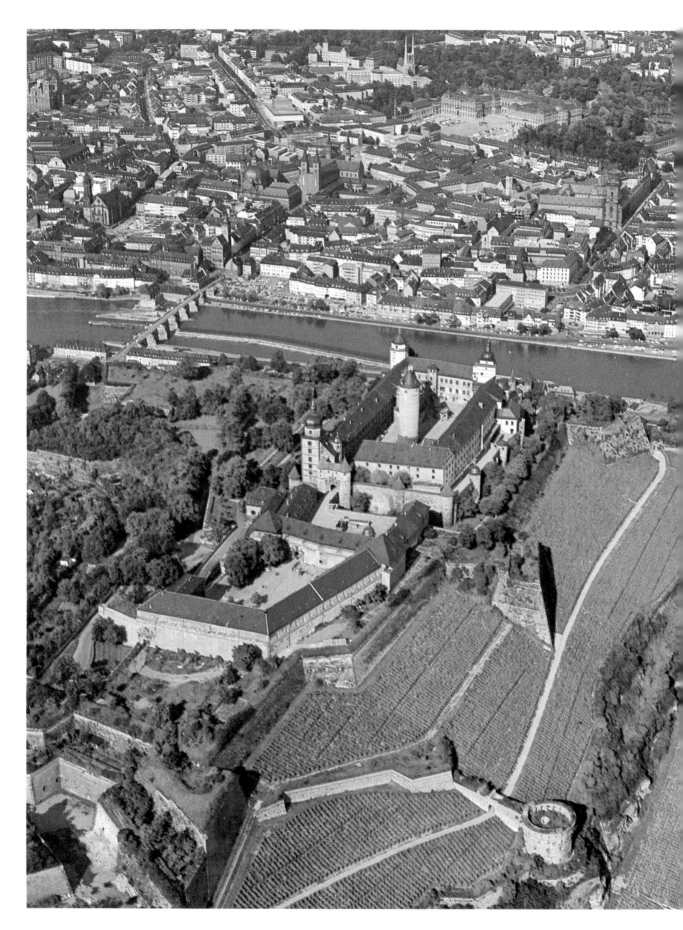

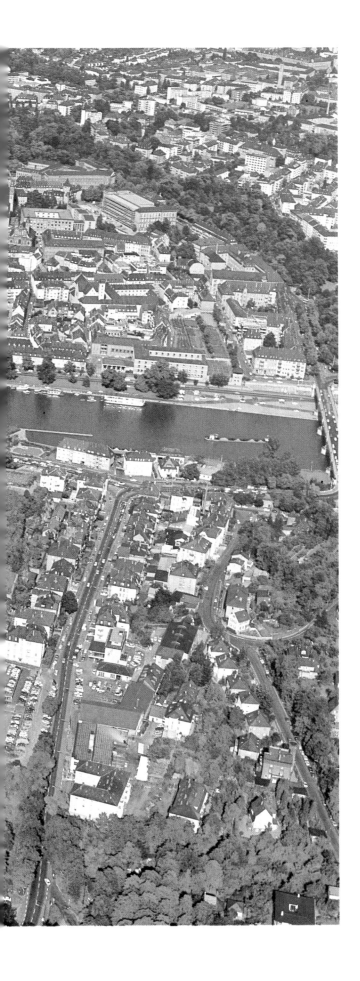

Franconia

The Monks Were Their Teachers

By way of exception it was not the Romans who brought wine to the Main River. When the Irish missionary Saint Cilian, eventually patron saint of Franconian wine-growers, arrived on the Main in 680 he found no wine here and had to have it brought in from other areas in wine skins. The natives of the area, the Franks, were one of the wildest German tribes of that time. Only after years of plundering the settlements along the Rhine had they decided to settle down in this area. Saint Cilian brought Christianity to the region, and soon afterwards Saint Boniface founded the Bishopric of Würzburg. In various documents dated between 775 and 800 vineyards are mentioned: One, for example, dated 779, gave Würzburg permission to celebrate in 1979 the jubilee "1200 Years of Viticulture in Würzburg"!

Monks influenced viticulture in Franconia far more than in other areas. Evidence of this can be seen in the abundance of decorative vines and grapes which appear on wayside shrines, altars and sculptures in royal gardens. In museums and churches one also finds various holy figures, especially madonnas, holding grapes. The Kiliansgruft, Saint Cilian's tomb, in the New

The hub of the Franconian wine area: Würzburg. In the foreground is the fortress of Marienberg, surrounded by vineyards.

141

Minster in Würzburg is a place of pilgrimage for wine-growers and farmers wanting a good harvest. The festival of Saint Cilian is held every year on July 8, and his statue situated below the Marienberg fortress greets Würzburgers and their guests to this day.

In Franconia wine is regarded not simply as a luxury but as a *Heilsbringer* ("bringer of blessings"). This can best be seen by the Würzburger Bürgerspital, a hospital founded in 1319 as a charitable institution and to which vineyard after vineyard was donated "for the refreshment and invigoration of the sick and the weak." Hospital and vineyards still exist in perfect harmony today.

This rather fragmented viticultural region stretching from Zell (near Hassfurt) in the east to beyond Aschaffenburg in the west—administratively part of Bavaria—was in the Middle Ages of considerable size, being approximately 30,000 hectares (75,000 acres). Today it is about one-tenth this, with 3,900 hectares (9,750 acres) under cultivation. Only climatically favorable areas of land are used; they are exploited to the full. The Franconian wine authorities take great care that the area under cultivation not be increased. "Rather a little, but as a result good, wine" seems to be the motto of the Franconian wine-growers, who with this principle wish to fortify themselves against the expected wine-flood after the entry into the EEC of Portugal and Spain.

In particular they are concerned that Portugal has presumed to use the Franconian wine bottle, the Bocksbeutel, for rosé wine. The Franconian wine-growers are conscious of their tradition and hope for European legal protection for this specially shaped bottle—protection for which, as we have already mentioned in the chapter on

Baden, exists in West Germany. In the opinion of Franconians, if the Bocksbeutel could be used in all lands the age-old quality principle would be thrown overboard. Officially this bottle has been used for over 250 years as a way of preventing unscrupulous trading practices.

As to where the Bocksbeutel comes from, there are various versions. Most experts believe that it comes from the scrotum of a he-goat (*Bock*), in which container the wandering monks carried their wine for use at mass or for their own fortification. This is supported by the fact that the he-goat often accompanied the wine god Dionysus in Greek mythology and later, in the Middle Ages, was the Christian symbol for intemperance. Another theory is that the wine-growing Benedictine nuns who were active in the seventh century between Kitzingen and Ochsenfurt were ordered to show restraint in their wine-drinking. According to the story the ladies were very crafty and took bottles that exactly fit their prayer book bags, so equipped, retired to pray. The *Buchbeutel* ("book bag") was called at that time "*Booksbüdel*" from which the word "*Bocksbeutel*" could easily have evolved. However, these are all only theories.

It is certain only that Franconian wine has always had a good reputation among experts. One of these was Goethe, who wrote in 1806, "Send me some Würzburger, because to me no other tastes so good. And I am vexed when my favorite wine is missing." Franconian wine (*Frankenwein*) is often called "*Krankenwein*" ("sick person's wine"). In 1861 Prince Bishop Philipp von Dernbach had a coin minted in gratitude

From this somewhat rounder form was developed the flatter Bocksbeutel. This is a sixteenth-century specimen in the Weinmuseum at Burg Layen.

for his recovery from the plague, with the inscription *"Vincit et sanat"* ("It conquers and heals").

For centuries Franconia was a Sylvaner area; even in the 1960's over 60 percent of the vineyards were taken up by this type. Nowadays the Sylvaner (31 percent) has been overtaken by the Müller-Thurgau (over 46 percent), whose milder nature and flowery bouquet contrasts with the Sylvaner's strong, pithy, aromatic qualities. The Bavarian State Viticultural Institute has been very active in new crossbreeds, and in Franconia many of these varieties are cultivated: Rieslaner (Sylvaner and Riesling), Perle (Gewürztraminer and Müller-Thurgau), Albalonga (Rieslaner and Sylvaner). In good sites and above all in frosty years like 1979, the good old Riesling and the Kerner have shown their worth. A good, rare wine is the Franconian Spätburgunder.

The center of Franconian wine is the Main River Triangle with its shell-limestone, especially the sunny slopes above Würzburg. Near Würzburg—home of the Renaissance sculptor Tilman Riemenschneider—one rejoices in the unique harmony of pleasant countryside, honorable history, rich culture, important scholarly achievement and the cheerful, happy disposition of the people. Without doubt Würzburg is one of the most beautiful German cities. Where one really must visit the Mainfränkisches Museum in the fortress of Marienberg with its many showpieces having to do with wine. Other imposing buildings are the cathedral, the Bürgerspital (hospital), the old university and naturally the former royal residence with its wine cellar, certainly one of the most beautiful in the world.

Franconian wine is often mistakenly called *"Steinwein,"* after a famous site lying directly on the Main River opposite the Marienberg in Würzburg. Running through this site is a *Weinlehrpfad*, a path giving information about wine-growing.

A little farther down the Main is Veitshöchheim with the State Viticultural Institute and the famous wine communities of Thüngersheim, Retzbach and Mühlbach.

In the other direction, upstream from Würzburg, we come to Randersacker, Eibelstadt, Ochsenfurt (with its beautiful Gothic church and magnificent town hall), Frickenhausen and Marktbreit (where one can find excellent examples of Baroque and Renaissance architecture).

The next large wine city on the Main is Kitzingen, with its famous *Grosslage* Hofrat and the oldest German wine cellar. This two-story cellar was built in 745 at the founding of the Benedictine Convent, which at the same time heralded the foundation of the city itself. Beyond Mainstockheim and Dettelbach we come to the *"Weininsel"* ("wine island") which, since 1956, has referred to the area around Nordheim and Sommerach which, because of the building of the Rhine-Main-Danube Canal, now finds itself on a sort of island.

Continuing upstream we come to Volkach —notable because of its historic marketplace and asparagus specialties, served all year round in local restaurants—and its neighboring wine communities Obereisenheim, Untereisenheim, Astheim and Escherndorf with its well-known site Lump.

Far to the north, in a separate section on the Saale River (which eventually joins the Main at Gemünden, well below Würzburg), is the wine town of Hammelburg, where a document dated 777 shows that the Ab-

The cellarer checks the court cellars beneath the Würzburger Residenz, one of the most beautiful German wine cellars.

bey of Fulda was given eight of the vineyards of Charlemagne—the earliest documentary evidence of viticulture in Franconia. The wines from the Schlossberg at Schloss Saaleck near Hammelburg have a good reputation. By the way, here as at Schloss Johannisberg it is claimed that the "noble rot" was discovered, due to the delayed arrival of a messenger bringing permission to begin the harvest.

Southeast of Volkach is the Steigerwald region, whose center is the picturesque town of Iphofen. Almost unchanged since the Middle Ages, it is surrounded by a town wall with four great gates built in 1293. Iphofen wines, especially from the site Julius-Echter-Berg, are exported all over the world. Pope Paul VI was a lover of this wine. Rödelsee, Wiesenbronn, Abtswind, Greuth and Castell are other well-known wine settlements in the vicinity. In Castell an excellent sparkling wine is produced—a rarity in Franconia. An outlying area to the north that belongs to this district is Zell, with the communities Schmachtenberg, Oberschwappach and Ziegelanger and the smaller villages of Zeil, Kammerforst and Donnersdorf where mostly a fresh and lively Müller-Thurgau is to be found.

Finally, it must be pointed out that Franconia has a "colony," in a sense, some hundreds of miles distant: Nonnenhorn, near Lindau on Lake Constance, as already mentioned in the chapter on Württemberg.

Nonnenhorn is an old wine settlement where between 1956 and 1969 no wine was grown—the farmers believing that only a change to fruit-growing would be successful. In the end, however, the locals decided to make a new start at wine-growing. Nonnenhorn is a "colony of Franconia" only in that it is technically in Bavaria and its wine is controlled by Würzburg. This caused problems for the wine authorities in classifying the site, for Bavaria is not a wine-cultivation area. However, as it would be very irregular to offer Lake Constance wine as Franconian wine, the "Nonnenhorner" have been included in the Württemberg area because of their close proximity to Kressbronn. Thus the region officially called "Bayerischer Bodensee" was created. The wine is controlled in Würzburg; Württemberg only provides it with the name. A very complicated state of affairs. Nevertheless, Nonnenhorn is officially recognized as a wine district, which other wine-growers elsewhere have not achieved. For example, vines are grown near Kassel, in the hinterland north of the Rheingau and near Regensburg, but these wine-growers can only sell their mostly harsh-tasting wine as Tafelwein ("table wine"). The step to the Qualitätswein level is a difficult one.

146

FRANCONIAN VINEYARD SITES

There are three regions:

Mainviereck
with the *Grosslagen* Heiligenthal and Reuschberg;

Maindreieck
with the *Grosslagen* Burg (Hammelburg), Rosstal (Karlstadt), Ravensburg (Thüngersheim), Ewig Leben, Ölspiel, Teufelstor, Hofrat (Kitzingen), Honigberg and Kirchberg (Volkach); and

Steigerwald
with the *Grosslagen* Schild (Abtswind), Schlossberg (Rödelsee), Herrenberg (Castell), Burgweg (Iphofen), Schlossstück (Frankenberg) and Kapellenberg.

In all there are 157 individual sites. The whole region produces an annual average of 350,000 hectolitres, 3.7 percent of the German total. (These average figures—as with all other mentioned areas—come from the years 1975–1977.) About 50 percent of Franconian wine production is controlled by wine-growers' cooperatives.

III.
The Long Road from Vine to Glass

From Grape to Wine

A wine journalist once expressed it thus:

> Wine is like a girl with a pretty face. the girl can be tender and coarse, honest and hypocritical, witch and angel. One can't see this at first glance. But when one knows the parentage, family background, education and home, one knows a lot.

Four factors determine the character of wine: Climate, soil, type of vine and the cellarer. German wines have their unique character because these factors nearly always work in complete harmony.

The most southerly extent of viticulture in the world (approximately 40° south latitude) corresponds roughly to a line drawn through Argentina (south of Buenos Aires) to just below the Cape of Good Hope (South Africa) to the southern tip of Australia (near Melbourne). The most northerly limit in America (New York,

San Francisco) and Asia (Peking) is 40° north latitude. Europe, however, is an exception: Here vines grow as far as 51° north on the Middle Rhine and elsewhere in central Germany. This northerly latitude does not present a problem, for climatic conditions are particularly favorable for viticulture as a favorable balance of sun and humidity predominates. More sun or less rain would not be beneficial for the vines; the wine would lose its harmoniousness and longevity.

As for our second factor determining wine character, the soil, slate is probably the best of all. This holds true especially for the Riesling, as slate stores up the sun's heat, holds moisture in the ground and, when it breaks up, provides essential mineral elements for the vine. Other favorable soils which play a decisive role in wine quality are loess, loam and soil containing quartz, red marl, basalt, sandstone, porphyry, potter's clay and granite.

Many connoisseurs even believe they can taste the soil in which the grape was grown.

Early June is usually the blossoming time of the vine. At this time the vines are susceptible to bad weather.

149

Perhaps it would be more true to say that the most the connoisseur can do is make inferences from the taste of the wine.

However, it is not soil alone which determines the character of wine, but also the configuration of the countryside. Here the concept of a microclimate is relevant. It is a matter of significance whether wine grows on a sheltered or sunny slope or flat land open to the wind. Water also plays its part in regulating humidity and temperature, as we have seen in the river valleys of Germany's wine regions and on Lake Constance, whose relatively high altitude (four hundred metres, or thirteen hundred feet, above sea level) favors viticulture although the climatic conditions are not necessarily ideal.

It is said that the vine grows best with an average yearly temperature of at least 9° centigrade (48° Fahrenheit) and with a minimum of thirteen hundred hours of sunshine yearly. Among the German wine areas the average yearly temperature is often more than 10°C., and the yearly hours of sunlight exceed thirteen hundred throughout.

The individual types of vine, which constitute the third factor, have already been described in detail.

The fourth factor is cellar technology, the transformation of grape juice to must and finally to wine. Of first importance is correct timing of the harvest. This is determined from place to place by local wine authorities. The harvest normally begins in September or, in years when growth is not so advanced (as in 1978 and 1980), at the beginning of October. Usually the Rhine Palatinate, with its Mediterranean climate in which almonds and lemons can grow, opens the German wine-harvesting season, which, if the weather is unfavorable, can drag on into late November, particularly in the more northerly areas of the Moselle or Rhine.

Usually, the later the harvest the riper the grape. As long as the sun shines, the grapes continue to take in sugar (between 1° and 2° Oechsle daily), and therefore the truly great wines—the Auslese, Beerenauslese and Trockenbeerenauslese—are all harvested late.

Provided that the vine has bloomed well in July and the wine-grower has successfully combated pests, the harvest becomes his greatest worry. Usually the first visitors to the vineyards in the fall are the starlings which arrive by the hundreds of thousands, even by the millions. They are prevented from doing damage by automatic firecracker devices to scare them, strips of tinfoil or fine-mesh nets of nylon thread to cover the vineyard. However, these methods can keep them in check only for a short time.

Wine harvesting is hard manual labor. Only in a few large flat areas is it possible to use harvesting machines and even then only for the lower and middle qualities of wine, because the machines cannot discriminate and pick only the choicest grapes. The cut grapes are collected and carried, usually by hand, to large tubs. At the foot of the vineyard these tubs are to be found on wagons. Sometimes the collected grapes are crushed then and there into a mash by means of a portable grape mill mounted on a tub. As the grapes are crushed they are also stripped of stalks, skins and pips before pressing.

The mash is then poured into the press and the must pressed out, usually fully automatically. While in the past pressing was hard work with the traditional wooden

Old tools for use in the vineyard, displayed in the Weinmuseum at Burg Layen on the Nahe, near Bingen.

wine presses, it has been made easier by, for example, the use of pneumatic horizontal presses. These operate by having a large, thick-walled rubber hose inflated with compressed air squeeze the grape mash against the stainless-steel wall of a revolving cylinder perforated by a multiplicity of slits.

The must is drawn off from the wine press, not only according to quantity but according to quality (depending on its sugar content), either automatically or by hand. The content is determined by using the Oechsle scale, a thermometer-like hydrometer. The lower the scale sinks into the must the lower is its specific gravity. German wines normally have a "must weight" of between 70° and 80° Oechsle, although for Qualitätswein mit Prädikat the figure is a little higher. From the "must weight" the sugar content and probable alcohol content can be estimated. For example: The specific gravity of the must may be 1080. This means the weight of one litre of must is 1080 grams (one litre of water weighs 1000 grams), representing 80° Oechsle. On conversion, such a must might have a 17 percent sugar content. After fermentation, the wine would then contain about 80 grams of pure alcohol per litre—10.8 percent by volume. In great years record must weights can be obtained. The world record of 326° Oechsle (1326 gm./l.) was achieved in 1971 by a wine-grower in the Rhine Palatinate with wine of the Siegerrebe grape.

Nevertheless, such high levels are not always a blessing. Must weight alone does not always decide the quality of the wine. And with so much sugar in the must it is not always easy to start fermentation. Besides, there is the danger that the high residual sugar content—the amount that cannot be fermented (the yeast-fungi can usually manage up to 100° Oechsle)—

may "kill" many valuable substances in the wine.

Top-quality wines with an Oechsle grade of over 100° need an acidic share of between 8 and 12 parts per thousand for proper balance.

On the other hand, wines with a low must weight can be improved by the addition of sugar. One often hears claims that wine-growers prepare their wine, so to speak, with a sugar sack at their side. But this is often exaggeration; maximum amounts of sugar are officially laid down, and, for example, with Qualitätswein mit Prädikat the adding of sugar is not allowed at all. Besides, the sugar does not remain in the wine, it is changed into alcohol.

This is also true when liquid sugar is added. This "stretches" the wine to a certain extent, and does no harm at all. This traditional practice serves not to increase the wine's alcoholic content but only to reduce acidity in order to make the wine drinkable. For the wine-grower this is often a matter of his very survival. Usually, though, adding liquid sugar is only allowed in the most northerly wine areas and then only for certain types of grape.

To return to the adding of "dry" sugar. It is always astonishing to see how some critics really sink their teeth into this theme. The fact that in the best wine-growing areas and largest sites of France this method is commonplace is denounced by no one.

Let us continue with the wine-making process. The must is cleared of sediment and

ABOVE: **From such partly rotted, carefully selected grapes (Edelfäule —"noble rot"), high-quality wines have been produced for over two hundred years.**

BELOW: **In making Eiswein ("ice-wine") the grapes are often protected by plastic sheets until the necessary temperature below freezing is reached for the harvest.**

deposits before it is allowed to flow into the fermentation tanks. The length of the fermentation period varies according to the must weight of the wine and the amount of yeast which the grapes have naturally received from nature. The alcohol which is the result of fermentation is produced by a metabolic process of the yeast.

The fermentation process itself can be controlled. For example, the warmer the must is during fermentation the quicker it will be. Cooling can delay or even stop fermentation.

Another method of controlling fermentation is through regulating the carbonic acid present. Carbon dioxide is produced during fermentation and allowed to escape through a funnel-shaped spout filled with water. In modern high-pressure tanks the rate at which the gas escapes can be slowed down. This can increase pressure in the tanks up to 8 atmospheres (ca. 118 pounds per square inch). By controlling the pressure the fermentation process can be stopped even before the must is totally fermented, resulting in a high content of unfermented sugar in the finished wine. With controlled residual sugar, a balance can be achieved, so that consumers' taste can always be catered to. This is especially useful in years with a high acidity. Such a total stop is, however, only seldom used, as normally the wine is allowed to ferment and then a sweetening agent (*Süssreserve*) is added.

However, we have still not arrived at our end-product—wine. In the fermentation process, first the must becomes Federweisser ("feather-white"). This is attractive, with a light, bitter taste, and very intoxicating because of its high carbon dioxide content (although it does not contain as much alcohol as wine).

In the fermentation tanks the change from must to wine is completed. The first "racking off" has to be carried out, whereby the wine is run off in order to separate it from the remaining yeast and *Trübstoffen* ("turbid particles"). With more mature and expensive wines a second racking off will also take place. After this the wine remains in a tank, either for a long or short time, according to its proposed use. Before bottling it is filtered several times, clarified and sterilized.

What about the *Süssreserve*? Mostly, this is unfermented grape must, which has been separated and stored under sterile conditions. It is only permitted to add *Süssreserve* from the same source as the wine. Its addition to the wine takes place at bottling in order to give the wine a more balanced form and please thereby all those preferring a flavorful and mild wine.

The legally controlled amount of unfermented sugar for the various quality levels of wine must not be exceeded. The addition of *Süssreserve* must not lead to the wine's basic character being lost.

Wine-growers conscious of tradition let their finished wine mature in barrels. But it can also develop further in the bottle.

Modern machines, with their absolutely sterile bottling conditions, ensure that the wine remain stable and not become cloudy or bad. During this process, wine crystals are occasionally formed (in red wine, tannin deposits), caused by sudden temperature fluctuations—for example, as in a transfer from a warmer cellar into a cooler one or vice versa. Any time wine is transported such fluctuations or vibrations can occur, causing formation of these crystals which are absolutely harmless and influence the taste not at all. The source of these crystals is the alcohol, along with the various substances contained in wine that keep it fresh.

Although the wooden barrel has gone out of fashion, in many firms the practice of storing high-quality wine in wooden barrels is still retained . . .

. . . although steel tanks and other large containers are easier to clean and give the cellarer excellent control over the wine.

Modern bottle-filling plants carry out their work under sterile conditions at tremendous speed, sometimes filling several thousand bottles per hour . . .

. . . and then the wine matures in the bottle at the ideal temperature of 10°C. (50°F.). Qualitätswein mit Prädikat from the Spätlese level upwards must not be made commercially available before March 1 after the year of harvest.

155

Wine is rich in minerals that it gets from the soil. The longer the grapes remain ripening on the vine, the more minerals the vines pass on to them. Potassium contained in the wine tartrate can later appear in the form of minute granules found as a deposit in the bottles. This deposit is formed out of tannin and anthocyase. Often, healthy effects are ascribed to this, as in drinking harsh red wine for gastritis.

These crystals and deposits change neither the taste nor the color of the wine. Wine connoisseurs even value them because they prove that the wine is still "alive" and indicate a fruity acidity in the taste. In old bottles of red wine one finds such deposits, sometimes to a depth of several centimeters. The only change they might effect would be to lighten the red color somewhat.

From Bottle to Glass

The wine has now completed its long "journey" from the vineyard through the cellar of the wine-grower, growers' cooperative or large producer to the home of the wine-drinker.

Here a problem arises. A basic rule for storing wine is that the temperature should vary as little as possible; ideally, it should be between 8° and 12°C. (46°–54°F.). A certain amount of humidity should be present so that the cork does not dry out, the wine evaporate, and, at worst, air (and with it bacteria) find its way into the bottle and spoil the wine. It must also be protected from light, and should always be stored lying horizontally so that the cork is always in contact with the wine to avoid shrinkage, dryness and loss of wine.

All this is very easy to say, but—to be honest with ourselves—where do we have such storage facilities nowadays? It could be, dear reader, that you are one of the lucky ones who has an ideal wine-storage cellar at your disposal. But if so you are in the minority. What should the tenant of a three-room apartment do whose "cellar" is simply a room which cannot even be locked up securely? Should he keep here his remaining stock of '71's or '76's, or the more recent '80's until they are mature?

Of course not! Perhaps it is possible to make a storage corner in a room not normally overheated such as the bedroom or hallway. Another way to achieve a relatively stable temperature is to use earthenware pipes or to cover the wine bottles with polystyrene. This at least is good enough for wine which you intend to keep only a short time—perhaps one or two years—but for a really great wine a cool place in your apartment is not enough.

The best solution is to buy a wine-cooling cupboard. These are not at all expensive and can hold up to four hundred bottles, maintaining the ideal temperature.

The controlled cellar temperature is also the best temperature at which to drink the wine. White wine that is not very old can be kept a little colder than red, down to 8° C. (46° F.). Under no circumstances should it be warmer than 12° C. (54° F.), particularly a "noble wine." Red wine can best be enjoyed at a temperature of 16°–18° C. (61°–64° F.). The fuller and more mature the wine, the warmer it may be. Young red wines can take 2° or 3° C. (4° or 5° F.) less. For example, a sparkling Portugieser from the Palatinate tastes very stale at 18° C., but when a little cooler unfolds its complete freshness. Rosé wine (or Weissherbst) should be drunk like white wine—that is, a normal rosé would be at 8° or 9°C., a Qualitätswein mit Prädikat at 11° or 12°C.

Opening the bottle is a problem for some, but it is really very easy when one uses the right corkscrew. The best type of corkscrew has a hollow, spiral "worm" with the point a continuation of the spiral. The spiral should be long enough to penetrate to the bottom of a two-inch cork; this will help prevent the cork from crumbling. If the cork is very tight it is advantageous to turn either bottle or corkscrew while pulling out the cork. Under no circumstances should it be pulled out abruptly, as violent movement is not good for the wine.

When ordering wine, one has to decide what wine to store. What types of wine? How much and what varieties of each type? There is no general answer to these questions, individual prerequisites and desires are so varied. One individual has only a small cellar or wine-cooling cupboard, another unlimited room. One can spend a lot of money on wine, the other must buy a little at a time. It is, however, always advantageous to have an assortment that one can easily add to. Of the lighter wines the proportion should be especially large. Of Qualitätswein mit Prädikat and Auslese one should perhaps store half as much as of lighter wine. How big the share of "noble wines" should be, which should be kept longer for a special anniversary or other occasion, is best left to the individual's discretion.

The choices among the different wine-growing areas and types of grape is also a matter of taste. The range of German wines is so wide and rich that everyone must choose according to his own wealth and taste. If one entertains frequently one should have many types available, from the simplest to the greatest wines, as nothing is nicer than to round off a pleasant evening with a wine-tasting. Regarding types of grape, one should as far as possible always have Riesling and Müller-Thurgau—in other words, two with very different characteristics which, when desired, can be supplemented with Sylvaner or Ruländer. Each wine-tasting is of course interesting if arranged full of variety with different types of grape including new crossings. Even more exciting is to compare vintages of one type of wine from one site.

In order to enjoy wine at its best, a good wineglass is important. Two types that often adorn cupboards of glassware are the colored *Römer*, a large drinking glass —with whose color one unfortunately cannot see the color of the wine—and the heavy, ostentatious atrocities which are not at all suitable for wine. As far as possible, the glass itself should be thin; whether it is cut-glass or not depends again on the personal wealth of the individual. The wineglass should have the shape of an apple, being slightly narrower at the top, which helps to retain the wine's aromatic qualities. The wineglass should have a stem that allows one to make light, circular movements with it to release the aroma and yet avoid a change in the wine's temperature, which would occur were the glass held in the hand, as well as unsightly fingerprints on the glass. Champagne glasses differ in that they should be much wider; a large area is needed for the bouquet to be released. For red wine, more substantial glasses are better; it is usually fuller, with a decent aroma, and needs, like Champagne, a greater surface area for the aroma to unfold.

Glass was probably invented several thousand years before Christ. Evidence of this has been provided by discoveries in

Even two thousand years ago there was great variety in drinking vessels, as shown in this woodcut from the time of Messalina (first century A.D.).

Egypt. Its possible use was, however, only realized thousands of years later. Until the time of Christ, and persisting until much later, containers for must and wine were made of pottery.

In all probability such containers were used as early as 7000 B.C. as shown by excavations at Megiddo and Jericho in Israel. In a similar type of vessel in Persia have been found the resinated remains of wine from the second century B.C. This container had been shaped on a wheel, and has a round base and a stand. The round-based form was the most widespread style in Near Eastern pottery for hundreds of years. Often these beakers stood on metal or wooden frames. These narrow-based wine containers, to be found from the Sumerian to the Egyptian areas, were popular until about 100 B.C.

Further developments gave wine containers new forms time and again, refinements and improvements running parallel with the migration of viticulture from the Near East around the Mediterranean. Today one can confirm that the more advanced the wine culture and the more esteemed the wine, the more beautifully were the wine containers shaped.

In Greek ceramics the beaker was replaced by the goblet, with which a climax of artistic form was achieved. The vessels were goblets, with either one or two handles, and so large that often both hands were needed to raise them to the mouth. They were impressive not only because of their size, but because of the way they were decorated, with carefully matched colors. Goblets became works of art; so much so, that in Greece vase- and goblet-making became a skilled profession. Artistic wine containers became as important as great masterpieces of architecture and sculpture. The paintings on the goblets changed from black to red figures around 500 B.C. They mostly depicted Dionysian scenes full of vines, grapes and animated drinking. Dionysus triumphs.

In Roman times the form first followed the Greek example, later was simplified and finally disappeared altogether. Only Etruscan ceramics conscientiously followed the Greek example, using the goblet for a very long time, whereas the Romans soon came to prefer the beaker.

Following ceramic pottery, work in glass appeared in Roman times. This material seems to have been first artistically formed around 260 B.C. with the invention of glassblowing, through which glassmaking became an art form that developed further and further.

Many wonderful examples have been maintained from Roman times, examples which clearly show the great ability and sensitivity to style of the glassmakers. The absolute climax of Roman glassmaking was reached with the *diatreta* glasses, of which only seven examples exist in the whole world. They come from the third to the fifth century A.D. Fragments can be seen at the Römisch-Germanischen Museum in Cologne, as well as a complete glass at the Landesmuseum in Trier. An extremely delicate, "woven" glass net, cut in relief, covers the whole glass.

Sixteenth- and seventeenth-century wine containers give us much information about the way of life at that time. Well-rounded shapes with dark colors dominate the scene. The considerable size of these glasses makes it apparent how great a thirst drinkers of the time had. Stoneware mugs were just as popular as glasses at this time. In the sixteenth century, Dutch glassworks

Relic of a bygone wine-drinker: a beautiful glass beaker from Cologne (fourth century A.D.).

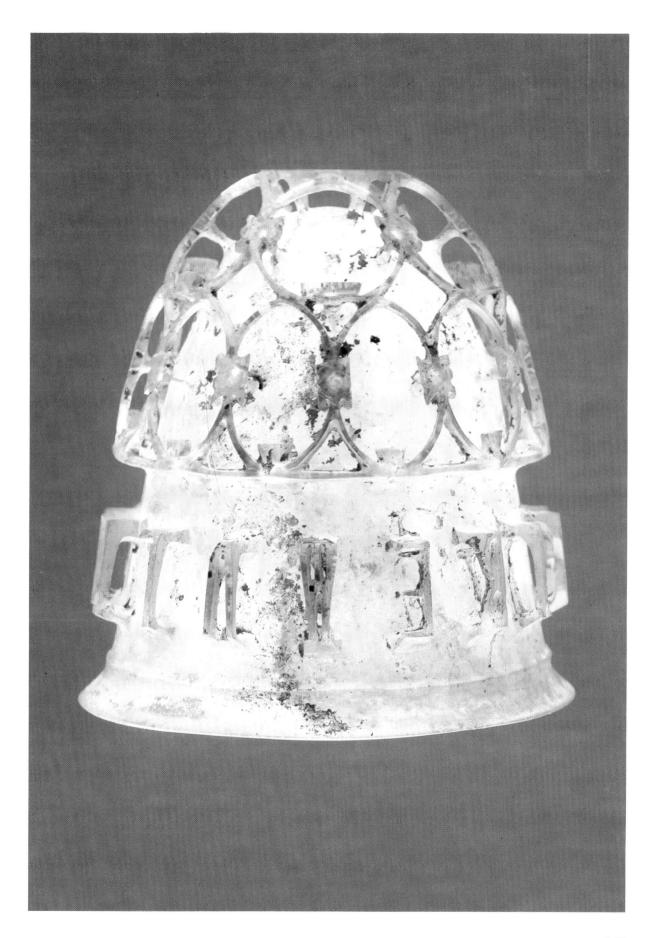

developed the *Römer*, which has remained an ideal glass to the present day. The word comes from the Dutch *roemen* ("praise, boast, glorify"). Thus was the wine drunk, with glasses raised in a toast.

Pompous yet still beautiful are a lidded goblet made in Augsburg at the end of the seventeenth century and a magnificent amber cup from the first quarter of that century.

In the Baroque period wine glasses were absolutely pure and colorless. Enamel colors were still being used until the middle of the eighteenth century, but they had become less and less popular. Cut glass gained in importance. By the end of the seventeenth century reference was already being made to different types of glass cut-

ting. The advantage of this artistic technique was that the glass remained transparent and colorless, and, because of the "cut," the best refraction of light resulted. The wine is thus able to dazzle with its own color. In the eighteenth century ornamental decoration resulted from this cutting, as we still see today in our glassmaking industry.

The shape of the wineglass has been refined again and again, for the glass has been the basis of the whole drinking culture, particularly with wine. Glass bottles also took over from other vessels. The wineglass became nobler and more unpretentious. (However, in the second half of the nineteenth century there was a relapse to trashy, showy work.)

Centuries in contrast. BELOW: Roman drinking utensils in glass and clay, from A.D. 50 to 200. RIGHT: Wine bottles from the eighteenth and early nineteenth centuries on display in the Weinmuseum, Burg Layen.

The Art Nouveau (*Jugendstil*) movement at the turn of the century encouraged more multicolored experiments. The glass became of most importance, the wine secondary. Too often its color could not be seen through the glass.

In the twentieth century simple, pure forms have predominated, with colorless, transparent glass taken for granted. Form is harmonious. The glass serves two purposes, to express artistic feeling and to enhance the pleasurable drinking of good wine.

Wine glasses through the ages. ABOVE, right to left: Beaker (sixth or seventh century A.D.), drinking glass and "Römer" (both fourteenth or fifteenth century A.D.). BELOW, right to left: A Roman beaker from A.D. 200, a Silesian cup from 1700 and a modern crystal glass from the Christinenhütte at Zwiesel.

Varieties of Wine

Of the nearly 90,000 hectares (225,000 acres) of vineyards in the German Federal Republic, approximately 80,000 (200,000 acres) are planted with white-wine grapes and 10,000 (25,000 acres) with red. In these two main categories there are, however, special wines which are precisely described in the Wine Laws.

The Weissherbst, mainly to be found in Baden, is a red-wine grape fermented as a white. It may come from only one type of grape, and must be graded at least as a Qualitätswein according to the official criteria concerning type of vine, and so on. If it comes, on the other hand, from several types of red vine, and is graded Tafelwein then it can only be labeled with the general term "rosé."

Production methods for the three types differ as follows: White wine is fermented right after crushing and pressing. Red wine is crushed into a mash that is left to ferment for several days in an open vat before being pressed. During this process of mash fermentation, the juice of the blue red-wine grapes, which is naturally as colorless as that of the white ones, assumes its color from the tannic acid in the red pigment of the grape skins. In the case of rosé and Weissherbst the blue grapes are instead pressed immediately after gathering; in this way they can, in fermentation, absorb only a limited amount of the tannic acid.

Schillerwein is a native of Württemberg. The name has nothing to do with the poet but is taken from the verb *schillern* ("to be iridescent"). It is made from a mixture of red- and white-wine grapes that are planted on the same plot, ripen at the same time and are picked, pressed and fermented together. Use of this name is allowed only in Württemberg. Wines that are made in this way but do not come from Württemberg can carry only the name "Rotling." Schillerwein must be a Qualitätswein; Rotling, however, need only be a Tafelwein. Although Schillerwein has been known in Württemberg for over three hundred years, since long before there was even a Friedrich von Schiller, the crafty Swabians have made a connection with the great poet by using a Schiller saying in their advertising:

Denn wo das Strenge mit dem Zarten,
Wo Starkes sich und Mildes paarten,
Da gibt es einen guten Klang.

Then where rough with smooth,
Where strong with mild are paired,
There is a good sound.

As with all rosé wine, Schillerwein is drunk

cold at the normal white-wine temperature. This attractive drink goes well with nearly all occasions, especially snacks and meals, because its taste is not too persistent to harmonize well with almost any meal.

Rotgold is a new name for a Baden wine that results from the white-wine Ruländer and the red Blauer Spätburgunder being fermented together.

Another specialty is Federweisser ("feather-white")—also called "Bitzler," "Rauscher," or "Sauser"—young wine that is drunk still muddy with yeast soon after it has reached the height of its fermentation. It is often drunk in large quantities, and, in contrast to finished wine, contains a lot of vitamins. On the other hand, the particular composition of this drink results in large amounts of alcohol finding their way into the blood very quickly. This one notices soon after drinking too much, at the latest the next day. . . .

Perlwein is a wine that at $20°$ C. ($68°$ F.) has a carbonic-acid gas pressure of at least 1.5 and at most 2 atmospheres, and sparkles. The carbonic acid is added to it.

We will concern ourselves with Schaumwein ("sparkling wine") and Sekt in the next chapter. Here we will mention only the legal stipulations regarding their production.

Schaumwein and Sekt are not identical. Sekt belongs to the category Schaumwein but must come from a high quality level—in other words, must be a "Qualitätsschaumwein."

Schaumwein, made from grape must, contains carbonic acid and must have, through alcoholic fermentation, at least 70 grams of alcohol per litre. Its carbon-dioxide pressure in the bottle must be at least 3.5 atmospheres.

The next level is the Qualitätsschaumwein. For this, 80 grams of ˉalcohol are prescribed, no more carbonic acid need be added and the wine must be the result of two fermentation processes and at least nine months of storage.

With Sekt, if a specified wine-growing area, region or site is mentioned on the label, it must be 100 percent from this area and at least 75 percent from the region mentioned. If the year or grape type are mentioned in connection with the geographical position, then at least 75 percent must be from the stated year or grape.

The Sparkling Cousins

Schaumwein, Sekt, Champagne

In the French wine region of Champagne, near Épernay and Reims, by the end of the seventeenth century it had become extremely difficult for the monks—who as in Germany were at that time the most important producers of wine—to sell their products. The wine was very dry and therefore did not correspond to customers' taste. Many attempts to combat this impediment to sales failed. Then, at the turn of the century, the Benedictine cellarer Dom Perignon at the Abbey of Hautvillers produced, after twenty years of vain experimentation, a method of carbonic-acid fermentation. The harsh character of the resultant wine could be tempered, and thereby the product was able to find a market.

The basis for the bottling of carbonic-acid-bearing wine was the use of strong glass bottles and the development of a special stopper made of cork additionally secured with a wire to hold the sparkling wine in the bottle. In the early days Champagne gained the nickname "cork-driver" or "devil's wine."

It was only through the famous Prussian actor Ludwig Devrient, that the word

Two friends of the noble Sekt: E. T. A. Hoffmann, poet and composer (left) with the actor Ludwig Devrient in the Berlin wine bar Lutter und Wegner. (Lithograph from a drawing by Hoffmann.)

169

"Sekt" as a term for a type of Schaumwein entered the German language 150 years ago. After each performance he used to meet with his friends, especially E. T. A. Hoffmann, in the historic wine-tavern Lutter und Wegner on the Gendarmenmarkt in Berlin. He was accustomed to entering the restaurant and addressing the waiter with the quotation from Shakespeare—in German—"*Gebt mir ein Glas Sect, Schurke! —Ist keine Tugend mehr auf Erden?*" ("Bring me a glass of sack, rascal!—Is there no virtue left on earth?").

It was Champagne that would then be served him, probably because it was the most expensive drink on the wine list. Certainly Devrient did not know what kind of drink Shakespeare's "sack" was. The term has its origin in the Spanish name for Sherry, "*vino seco.*" In English usage this finally became "sack," originally an unfermented wine which was turned into a liqueur by adding ingredients like sugar, alcohol and honey.

The ritual between Devrient and the waiter was repeated so often that more and more guests began to say "Sekt" instead of "Champagne." Probably they believed this to be a particularly distinguished mode of expression.

From Berlin the term "Sekt" for Champagne soon spread to the whole of Germany. In Esslingen in 1826 the first German cellarage for Sekt was formed. Some four years later a Schaumwein, Sparkling Rhine Wine (Schäumender Rheinwein), was offered as far afield as Philadelphia.

In 1908 the French established a limited area for the production of Champagne. All importation of wine for processing to become Champagne was prohibited and the word "Champagne" was protected. By the Treaty of Versailles the Germans were forbidden to use the term for their Schaum-wein, a measure that did not cause any damage to its quality. Today it has such a good reputation that it is exported to 124 nations on all continents. The main customer is Great Britain.

The cuvée—that is, the blend of basic wines obligatory for the production of Schaumwein—must, according to law, have a minimum alcoholic content of 8.5 percent. The finished wine must, after the second fermentation, contain at least 9.5 percent alcohol. Qualitätsschaumwein, however, including Sekt, must show a percentage of at least 10 percent alcohol.

Popular brands are expected to taste the same every year. This means that, as the component wines turn out differently every year, the cuvée must be composed anew in such a way that the character of the result does not change. The cellarers responsible must be sensitive—in the truest sense of the word—in order to compose from the different basic wines a product of consistent character.

How is Schaumwein produced? In principle it is very simple. A normally fermented wine is fermented for a second time by the addition of sugar and yeast. From this point on there are three different procedures for the making of Schaumwein, although the final product does not vary greatly.

In the first method—practised in the Champagne area under the name "*méthode champenoise*" and in some of the less modern German cellars—is that of traditional bottle fermentation. The sugar-yeast mixture is added at the first filling of the bottles. As soon as the yeast is fermented, these bottles are shaken once a day and replaced on their shelves at a slightly steeper angle each time. In this way the yeast clot settles slowly in the bottle's neck. After this stage, the yeast deposit is frozen at about $-16°$ C. $(-3°$ F.). The cork used up to now is removed and the carbonic acid drives the yeast out in the form of an ice clot; the space left in the bottle is filled with a flavoring dose of wine— e.g., a "noble-sweet" (*edelsüsser*) wine. This gives to the Schaumwein, whose sugar has been used up by the second fermentation, the desired grade of sweetness.

In contrast to this traditional bottle-fermentation method is the technique of removing the yeast by filtration using counterpressure with nitrogen. The crude Schaumwein is decanted into a container; here the flavoring dose is completely mixed in, and the contents, with carbonic acid preserved, are then bottled again by means of a filter installation. This sort of Schaumwein can also be put on the market as a "bottle fermentation" if it was stored in bottles.

The third method is that of tank fermentation, which accelerates the procedure considerably. After fermentation, the addition of the flavoring dose, removal of yeast under counterpressure by filtration and finally bottling complete the process.

As with all Qualitätswein, in order for Qualitätsschaumwein, including Sekt, to be graded it is subjected to an examination procedure, which ends with the granting of the official inspection number (*Amtliche Prüfungsnummer*). By law, Qualitätsschaumwein must, from the beginning of the second fermentation, be stored at least nine months under an overpressure of 3.5 atmospheres. For the various classifications shown on the label the following percentages of sugar content are specified by the legislation:

Herb (*brut*, "extra dry")	0–15 gm./l.
Sehr Trocken ("very dry")	12–20 gm./l.
Trocken (*sec*, "dry")	17–35 gm./l.
Halbtrocken (*demi-sec*, "half-dry")	35–50 gm./l.
Mild, Süss (*doux*, "sweet")	over 50 gm./l.

The proportion of actual German wine as the basis of German Schaumwein is relatively small, amounting to only a few percent, particularly in good vintages, when the grape must is eagerly and almost exclusively utilized as wine.

This may disconcert many consumers, who read the name "Deutscher Sekt" on the label. But on this point the lawmaker has made a different definition of *Deutsch* ("German"). Deutscher Sekt can be called such when and only when it has been produced in Germany. It is a product considered to belong more to the region where it is processed than to the region whence its components come, and which obtains its characteristics by the producer's adherence to certain norms.

The basic wines for Deutscher Sekt come mainly from Italy. The producers of the lesser qualities make cheap purchases there, and are thus able to compensate for the high tax on sparkling wine—1.50 DM ($.72 or 37d.) per bottle, a relic of the Kaiser's era—in their price to the consumer.

One can argue that consumers are misled by the designation "Deutsch" on the label. Recently there has been a great deal of quarrelling on the subject. The results of sundry inquiries have indeed shown that the overwhelming majority of consumers believe the wine base of their Deutscher Sekt to be from Germany. In reality, Deutscher Sekt made from German wines is only seldom to be found—and then at a substantially higher price than the "industry-product."

Wine Law and Official Quality Levels

The year 1971 was a turning point as far as German wine law is concerned. Even before the long-awaited German Wine Law was completed, new, binding rules of the European Economic Community had come into effect to which the German Federal Republic had to orient itself. This in turn led to the German Wine Law of 1971 being even stronger—German thoroughness!—than the EEC had planned.

The basic principle of the EEC law is the division of wine into two groups: Tafelwein ("table wine") and Qualitätswein Bestimmter Anbaugebiete or QBA ("quality wine of specified cultivation regions"). In the meantime, in France, among other countries, the term "Land Wine" has been introduced as part of the table-wine group. As this book goes to press it is still not clear whether the concept of Land Wine would also be introduced into Germany, as a sort of better Tafelwein.

Let us stay with Tafelwein. There are four areas:

1. Rhine and Moselle, with the sub-areas
   a. Rhine
   b. Moselle
2. Main
3. Neckar
4. Upper Rhine, with the sub-areas
   a. Römerturm
   b. Burgengau

To make this a little clearer and relate it to wine areas already discussed: The sub-area Rhine comprises the Ahr, Middle Rhine, Nahe, Rheingau, Rheinhessen, Hessian Bergstrasse and Rhine Palatinate. The sub-area Moselle is the same as Moselle-Saar-Ruwer. The Tafelwein area Main is Franconia, Neckar is Württemberg and the Upper Rhine is Baden.

In this respect, the German Wine Law differs greatly from that of France or Italy. There the numerous areas are designated from the beginning either as table-wine (Land Wine) areas or quality wine areas (France's Appellation Contrôlée and Italy's Denominazione di Origine Controllata); they do not overlap as is the case in Germany. One could probably do without this division of German wine into four areas, but then of course Tafelwein from different areas could be mixed together, so really it is necessary. As regards quality, however, Tafelwein is of little importance here. In 1979 there were several areas where no Tafelwein was harvested.

The second group, QBA and QBA mit Prädikat (the highest quality) contains eleven areas:

Ahr
Baden
Franconia
Hessian Bergstrasse

Middle Rhine
Moselle-Saar-Ruwer
Nahe
Rheingau
Rheinhessen
Rhine Palatinate
Württemberg

For this Qualitätswein, whether "mit Prädikat" or not, a further division into districts has been carried out:

Ahr: Walporzheim/Ahrtal
Baden: Bodensee, Markgräflerland,
    Kaiserstuhl-Tuniberg, Breisgau,
    Ortenau, Baden Bergstrasse–
    Kraichgau, Badisches Frankenland
Franconia: Steigerwald, Maindreieck,
    Mainviereck
Hessian Bergstrasse: Starkenburg,
    Umstadt
Middle Rhine: Bacharach, Rheinburgengau, Siebengebirge
Moselle-Saar-Ruwer: Zell/Lower Moselle, Bernkastel/Middle Moselle,
    Upper Moselle, Saar-Ruwer, Moseltor
Nahe: Kreuznach, Schlossböckelheim
Rheingau: Johannisberg
Rheinhessen: Bingen, Nierstein,
    Wonnegau
Rhine Palatinate: Südliche Weinstrasse,
    Mittelhaardt/Deutsche Weinstrasse
Württemberg: Remstal-Stuttgart,
    Württembergisch Unterland, Kocher-
    Jagst-Tauber, Tübingen-Reutlingen,
    Bayerischer Bodensee

In these districts growing conditions are, as far as possible, the same, and the wines produced are typical for the district.

The EEC legislation prescribes the following minimum alcoholic contents for table wine: In Zone A, white wine must have 5 percent, corresponding to $44°$ Oechsle; in Zone B, white and red wine 6 percent, cor-

responding to $50°$ Oechsle. This refers to the natural alcoholic content, without consideration for improvement carried out.

If the wines are improved, then their actual alcoholic content must be at least 8.5 percent, corresponding to $67°$ Oechsle. The maximum allowed, after improvement is, in Zone A, 11.5 percent for white wine and 12 percent for red, and, in Zone B, 12 percent for white and 12.5 percent for red.

For Qualitätswein, the minimum allowable alcoholic content in Zone A is 6.5 percent, corresponding to $53°$ Oechsle; in Zone B, 7.5 percent, corresponding to $60°$ Oechsle. It is left to each wine-growing state to decide the particular norms for certain cultivation areas.

For example, Baden, in Zone B, has to achieve higher must weights. This is not a disadvantage; on the contrary, Baden has been in favor of being in this zone, because the great number of sunny days (much referred to in advertising) makes it no problem to reach these high levels.

The must weight is not the most decisive factor with regard to wine quality. But a rugged Ruländer Spätlese from Baden needs a lot of backbone, whereas an elegant Moselle Spätlese best unfolds its typical characteristics with a lower must weight.

The different wine-growing zones help to keep the market well-balanced. The EEC rules do not create uniformity, as they prescribe only minimum amounts and each area is free to fix its minimum higher, as in fact some do.

However, reference to Zone A or B is not allowed on the label. Consumers have enough reading material here as it is.

In discussing the label in detail let us begin with Tafelwein. If it carries the word "Deutsch" ("German") it must originate exclusively from German vineyards; any mixing with wine from other countries is forbidden. This is controlled by the states. If the wine is a blend from different EEC countries, it must be clearly marked *"Wein aus mehreren Mitgliedsstaaten der EG"* ("wines from several member countries of the EEC"). Such wines usually carry colorful, imaginative names.

Qualitätswein must carry the *Amtliche Prüfungsnummer* ("official inspection number"), usually abbreviated to "A. P. Nr." It shows which testing office examined the wine and gives, for the expert's benefit, the code number of the estate and its location.

1. The first individual number or group of digits represents the code number of the testing office, for example:
    a. Coblenz for Lower Moselle, Middle Rhine, Nahe.
    b. Bernkastel for the region Bernkastel.
    c. Trier for Upper Moselle, Saar and Ruwer.
    d. Alzey for Rheinhessen (includes Liebfraumilch).
    e. Neustadt an der Weinstrasse for the Rhine Palatinate.
2. The next two digits make up the code number of the estate.
3. The following three digits represent the code number of the producer.
4. The next three digits form the serial number of the application.
5. The last two digits refer to the year of submission of the application (not the vintage year).

This control number is given only after a double examination. At first, the contents of the wine are examined and pronounced to be in order or not. Then the sensory testing takes place, under official supervision. At this time the final decision is made whether the wine should receive its official number, whether it can be classed

as a Spätlese or at a lower level if it does not come up to expectations. This testing is carried out "blind," meaning that the examiners know the cultivation area, type of grape and year, but not the name of the firm. If a wine is rejected the producer can protest, in which case the wine will again be examined by another group of examiners. Normally, though, wines once rejected have little chance at a second examination.

This type of examination was introduced in 1971 in Germany to the great advantage of consumers. Now every new wine must appear before the examining commission, and no preferential treatment is given wine from famous sites. In the meantime, other European wine countries are taking steps to follow the German example.

To return to the text of the label. In the future any Qualitätswein must show the growing region as well as the quality grade of the wine, in letters of the same size. The growing region and year are shown on German wines not out of habit, but because as a result of climatic changes and different geological structures the wine can be considerably different from year to year and site to site. The detailed information on the label greatly helps wine consumers in their choice.

According to the Wine Law, national and regional bodies can decide to what extent Tafelwein and Qualitätswein are to be improved. "Improving" means adding sugar to the must in order to give balance to the wine and keep it smooth. Again, it must be stressed that this addition takes place before fermentation; adding sugar to finished wine is forbidden. Limits on the degree of improvement differ from grape to grape and year to year. At present the limit is between 20 and 28 grams per litre of must. The maximum for alcohol content in the wine is, depending on place of origin, between 91 and 100 grams per litre. With this very strict legislation it is hoped to prevent the wine becoming too alcoholic and thereby losing its character.

For QBA mit Prädikat the permitted levels are very different. In any case, a quality wine hoping to receive this designation must have a minimum "must weight" of 70 grams. This level can be changed upwards by the state governments according to vintage, vineyard and type of grape.

QBA mit Prädikat may not be "improved." In this they merit the earlier term "*natur-*" ("natural"), as in *Naturwein* or *naturrein*. These terms were abolished in the 1971 legislation, because it is practically impossible to have a naturally pure wine, as sulphur and other substances are necessary in order to make wine clear and stable. The "ecological" wines which have been tried in recent years do not meet the requirements of consumers, one of which is a clear wine.

With QBA and QBA mit Prädikat wines, blending wines from different districts is forbidden. This holds for white and red both. Most of these wines come from one site. Thus the wine connoisseur has the protection of obtaining wine from a narrowly defined and strongly controlled area. Another important rule for buyers of wine is that a Qualitätswein graded Spätlese or better must not be bottled and sold before March 1 after the harvest. This guarantees that the wine is mature enough. In contrast, a Kabinett wine may be sold after January 1.

With Kabinett wine we are at the low end of the scale of *Prädikat* wines. This wine comes from the normal harvest. The minimum must weight varies according to region, from $70°$ to $81°$ Oechsle. The next level up is Spätlese, with a must weight of

between $76°$ and $95°$ Oechsle. Here the grapes are picked after normal harvest time, in a totally ripe condition. The later the harvest, the better the wine can be. There is, however, accompanying risk, for a sudden change for the worse in the weather can damage the grapes and make them rot. On the other hand, a little bit of rot is necessary with the better *Prädikat* wines: This is the Edelfäule ("noble rot") brought about by the *Botrytis cinerea* fungus, which damages the skin of the grapes, whereby water evaporates and the sugar content becomes more concentrated. The typical *Botrytis* aroma is reminiscent of muscat and walnuts.

This concentration can be of particular advantage to the next level, Auslese (minimum must weight: $85°-120°$ Oechsle). For this and the next level, Beerenauslese, the grapes are selected individually; the damaged and excessively rotten grapes are removed and only fully ripened grapes taken. This almost liqueur-like wine is characterized by its *Botrytis* aroma.

With Trockenbeerenauslese wine (minimum $150°$ Oechsle), which in good years with many sunny autumns and adequate Edelfäule is produced in German vineyards we have the best white wine in the world. This is, of course, a rarity and must be correspondingly paid for as well as praised. The work load is enormous: The grapes must be picked individually; only the raisin-like, shrivelled grapes affected with noble rot are selected. They are pressed separately. They contain little water and their extract is particularly highly concentrated.

With the pressing and fermentation of these noble wines a lot of sugar, of course, remains behind. The yeast in the must is not sufficient to fully ferment it. Thereby the pure noble sweetness (*Edelsüsse*) is maintained, a noble sweetness which with these top-quality wines is always coupled with the elegance of their fine acidity. None of these great wines taste too sweet.

Eiswein is not a *Prädikat* wine but an extra category for which all *Prädikat* wines can qualify. This specialty is made with late-harvested grapes that are frozen when picked and pressed, whereby the must in the grapes is especially concentrated. Eiswein production is a great risk for wine-growers because the basic legal require-ment—a temperature in the vineyards of $-7°$ C. $(-19°$ F.)—is seldom reached at the right time of year.

Another indication of quality, apart from the *Prädikat* designation, is the seal on the bottle neck showing success at a regional of national wine competition. Wines that at the annual German National Wine Com-petition receive either gold, silver or bronze awards belong to the best wines produced in German cellars. Only after winning at the regional level are wines ever eligible to compete nationally.

On many wines one can find the red Ger-man Wine Seal, a mark of merit intro-duced in 1950 by the German Agricultural Society. In order to achieve this distinc-tion a wine must be submitted to an addi-tional sensory test at which QBA wines must rate three points higher, and QBA mit Prädikat wines two points higher—out of twenty possible points—than the re-quired number for *Amtliche Prüfungsnum-mer* (A. P. Nr.) approval. Per bottle the seals adds about 2.5 pfennigs (5 cents) to the sales price, an amount that hardly makes it dearer and considerably helps to-wards successful sales. From many opinion polls carried out by the Agricultural So-ciety, it is clear that consumers regard the seal as what it in fact is—namely, a sign of quality.

Some years ago the Agricultural Society took heed of the increasing trend towards drier wine with the introduction of a yel-low wine seal. Originally this was intended only for the so-called "diabetic" wines, which carry an additional label with a more detailed explanation. With this wine detailed description of the contents is very important to the health of drinkers. The label includes the notice, "For use after consultation with a doctor." A litre of wine for diabetics may contain at the most 4 grams of unfermented sugar, 714 calories (2987 joules), 200 milligrams of sulphide and no more than 12 grams of alcohol.

It is understandable that many lovers of dry wine could not get accustomed to the label "diabetic wine," and therefore the German Agricultural Society relaxed the requirements for the yellow seal, introduc-ing it for drier wines that meet the general requirements as laid down in the Wine Law. These wines may not contain more than 9 grams of unfermented, residual sugar (*Restsüsse*) per litre; this gives a rea-sonable relationship to the acidity.

A dry wine can only carry this seal if for every litre it has at most 2 grams more sugar than acid. In other words a wine with acidity of 6 parts per thousand can have at the most 8 gm./l. of residual sugar. If the wine already has acidity of 8 parts per thousand then the residual sugar must not be more than 9 gm./l. The diabetic label is still used, as before, but only for wine with a maximum of 4 gm./l. residual sugar.

The latest innovation in categorization is the green seal, introduced in 1977 for Halb-trocken ("semi-dry") wines, which term is mentioned on the label.

The regulations regarding Halbtrocken wine state that it may contain only up to 18 gm./l. residual sugar. But here also balance in the relationship of acidity to sweetness is important. The formula is, "Total acidity plus ten." If a wine has acidity of only 6 parts per thousand then it can contain a maximum of 16 gm./l. residual sugar. With 17 grams it would no longer be a Halbtrocken wine.

Halbtrocken wine tastes neither flavorful nor mild, neither too sweet nor too harsh. A wine is sour when in relation to sweetness (the unfermented sugar), it has a very large share of acidity; such wine is, however, seldom found on the market today.

It is false, however, to assume that in the past all wines were *durchgegoren* ("fully fermented"), and that therefore there were more dry, acidic wines to be found. The share of dry wines was and is very different in the individual wine areas and also with individual firms. At present it probably amounts to a total of 6–8 percent of total German wine sales. How far the trend towards drier wine will continue is hard to say. A report from the reputable Prognos-Institut in 1979 showed that by 1991 the proportion could rise to 15 percent. At present, however, dry wine is much more spoken about than drunk.

There are wine-lovers who regard those who do not like dry wine as cultural philistines. What nonsense! Taste varies, as does often the physical condition of wine-drinkers. One person's stomach can not take dry, harsh wines; another's, sweeter wines. Those who tend towards milder, more flavorful wines can be as expert as others.

At this stage we should remove two misconceptions: that dry wines mostly contain less alcohol than semi-dry or milder wines; and that Beeren- and Trockenbeerenauslese wines contain more alcohol than others.

Both are incorrect. With dry wine, more sugar is fermented to alcohol. And Beeren- and Trockenbeerenauslese wines often contain less alcohol than their Kabinett, Spätlese and Auslese counterparts, because they have a very large share of unfermented sugar. With these two top-quality wines the ratio of alcohol to sugar remains low. If these wines are still found to be heavier, that has more to do with the fact that they are richer and fuller. One interesting side-light is that they contain ethereal oils that, when one tilts the glass to drink, can show as a "church-window" (*"Kirchenfenster"*), gratifying connoisseurs as a beautiful visual aspect of the enjoyment of wine.

The Wine Label

Birth Certificate and Calling Card

The modern German wine label contains the A. P. Nr., the quality grade—whether Tafelwein, Qualitätswein or Qualitätswein mit Prädikat (Kabinett, Spätlese, Auslese, Beerenauslese or Trockenbeerenauslese). Eiswein is identified as such. The label also identifies the producer or cellar that brought the wine into circulation. The vintage year is given, the wine-growing area, the wine village or town, the vineyard and sometimes the *Grosslage*—e.g., "1979–Rheingau–Hochheimer Stein" in the *Grosslage* Berg. Further, we find on the label the type of grape (Riesling, etc.) and sometimes information concerning taste, such as Trocken ("dry"), Halbtrocken ("semi-dry") or Lieblich ("pleasant").

All the information given on the label is controlled by law. In the past legal labelling regulations were not so firm. At that time sonorous-sounding categories like *naturrein* ("natural-pure") or *Originalabfüllung* ("original bottling") were allowed, as well as *Cabinet* as an extra grade. Basically, in the past the label could contain anything that was not explicitly forbidden. Nowadays the label is a sort of birth certificate for the wine, on which what is written is explicitly required.

Some artistically conceived wine labels of the past.

The evolution of wine labels is part of wine history. On older labels we can find the type of grape, districts and sites, some of which now no longer exist, having been amalgamated into *Grosslagen* or having completely disappeared. Before the enactment of the 1971 German Wine Law there were approximately twenty thousand different sites registered; now there are about twenty-six hundred.

If we follow wine labelling through the last centuries, we see a bit of the history of commercial art. It gives us a survey of the development of various styles and color techniques. It shows very clearly what sort of taste predominated at a given time.

The invention of cylinder-flatbed printing with various colors at the beginning of the nineteenth century facilitated the economical production of labels. In the preceding centuries scratched markings, roller-seals, rubber stamps and similar markings had specified the content of barrels, mugs and other containers. The wine's origin and the year were mentioned as well as the vineyard and even the owner. Also, handwritten gummed labels and attached pieces of paper were quite usual. The Greeks and the Romans had marked their amphoras with pieces of parchment and other, similar materials.

At first, printed labels were in content and

form almost as basic as the handwritten ones. Sometimes they only contained a reference to the region. Later, with the further development of printing techniques, they became more effective as a form of advertising and information. Colored labels with different shapes—narrow or wide, rectangular or square, later round or oval—became widespread. They began to be illustrated with scenes—depictions of grapes, creepers, blossoms, castles, wine-glasses. Later additions were coats-of-arms and medallions won at exhibitions and competitions. For those wine-growers with the luck to supply the court of a prince, king or emperor, the display on the label of the coat-of-arms of the distinguished customer was very effective advertising.

In the course of the last two centuries the form of the labels has become more and more lively. The motifs have ranged from simple and elegant to luxuriant and romantic, even trashy. With the Third Reich the style of the label changed: Healthy-looking people, knights, mercenaries, hard-working wine-growers and their beaming wives appeared more and more. In the years of the Second World War there was hardly any wine for general use, and therefore the labelling became very modest and simple.

Two hundred years of the cultural and artistic vicissitudes of society are mirrored in the labels, as are economic and political changes. The label is a historic document of German wine culture.

Collecting wine labels has become a hobby nowadays in the same way as collecting postage stamps. There are collectors who have labels from several centuries. A living hobby, this, if one can recall the particular wine for which the label once spoke.

Just as the label is full of significance, so are the other markings on the wine bottle. We can find awards and distinctions as well as wine-seals. The Rhine Palatinate has been active above all with its regional categories. The Moselle-Saar-Ruwer in 1979 introduced a Riesling seal. From 1980 on Franconia has also demonstrated its individuality. Older is Baden's *Gutezeichen* behind which, in contrast to the Palatine and Moselle categories, stands a quality assessment, one far more severe than that of the German Wine Seal Commission.

The increase in the amount of information on the bottle has also found its critics, who fear that with the great number of seals the consumer will be more confused than enlightened. Be that as it may, the extra markings show the fierce competition in the domestic market, with each area trying hard to gain its advantage.

The Great Vintages

One of the charms of German wine is that each year presents itself in a different way. Therefore the information on the label identifying vintage has special importance. In contrast, with wine from countries having extremely hot summers their constant climate causes little yearly difference in quality.

A particular year does not always become great when old. The terms "old wine" and "great vintage" are not identical. Under certain circumstances wine from a year of moderate quality but high acidity can become very old. Conversely, a great wine full of noble sweetness but little acidity can keep, despite the alcohol, only for a relatively short time—a few years. A typical example of this was 1959, whose wine deteriorated relatively quickly. On the other hand, even today many "treasures" from the bad years 1963 or '65 are in excellent condition. The vine, climate, soil and cellar care are crucial to the character of wine and its longevity. Sweetness (alcohol) and acidity must be sufficiently in evidence and blended well. If both are present in relatively small amounts the wine will not keep. If acidity alone is sufficiently present then the wine can become old, but will usually be biased and badly balanced.

Some wines only live for a few years despite the best keeping. Others, mainly late-ripening types like Riesling, Sylvaner, Traminer, Ruländer and Spätburgunder become better with maturity when from a good year. Having reached maturity and true greatness they can stay at their "climax" for a while before beginning to age slowly to become an old, mature wine. This has a lot to do with timely bottling and quality and length of cork. The longer the cork the smaller the air space between wine and cork, and the better for the wine. In the great year 1937, large amounts of wine had to be bottled with short corks because of a shortage of cork at the time. A certain number, however, were fitted out with longer corks. Twenty years later, on testing the wine, the bottles with long corks proved wonderfully ripe and healthy, whereas those with shorter corks were too far gone.

Wine is the only luxury article that lives and is subject to the law of old age. It can even become ill—and be cured. However, it is never possible to predict exactly the life of a wine. The alcohol alone does not guarantee long life, above all not when there is too little acidity in the wine. Too much alcohol can indeed "kill" the bouquet and make the wine "burn"—change color, become darker and taste bitter.

Up to what age then are great wines drinkable? We shall focus on great wines because, despite the above-mentioned exceptions, normally those wines that are the most well balanced keep the longest. The oldest wines that are still enjoyed today to any extent come from the years 1920–21. Not for nothing did a bottle of 1921 Trockenbeerenauslese from the Moselle site Bernkastler Doctor reach at auction the price of 7,500 DM ($3,600).

The oldest drinkable German wine, of which some bottles still exist, must be a 1727 Rheingau in the "treasury" of the Bremen town-hall cellar. Also, at the Burg Layen Weinmuseum there is still a half-bottle of the same wine, the value of which can hardly be measured according to normal business standards. Such a wine has a collector's value, as with postage stamps. A blue Mauritius of wine!

Old wines are displayed in the Historical Museum of the Palatinate in Speyer where there is a 1631 Steinwein from Würzburg, and from the same place a Leistenwein from the greatest year in the Middle Ages —reckoned to be a "Year of the Millenium"—1540! At a tasting of wine rarities in London in 1961, a wine of this sort proved still drinkable, whether or not the taste was good. As for the matter of taste, at least we know of the 1727 Rheingau from the Bremen town-hall cellar that those who tasted this wine found its bouquet, its aroma, to enchant with incredible intensity but also with tenderness. Its taste? Let's be content with the bouquet. The reason for this wine's dark color, resembling old sherry, is the fact that it was stored for a long time in oak barrels.

What then of the great vintages of the past in Germany? The 1540 we have already mentioned. In the seventeenth century there were only three or four good vintages, but not one "Wine of the Century." In the

eighteenth century only one wine achieved this title, the 1783.

Then, however, the frequency of excellent wines increased, not least because of constant progress in cellar technique. In the nineteenth century there were seven very good years: 1802, 1807, 1822, 1846, 1857, 1865 and 1868. A more outstanding wine was the 1842; the "Wines of the Century" were 1811—which Goethe called "comet wine"—and 1893. Such wines are still kept in rarity collections in cellars in the Rheingau, the Nahe (at the Burg Layen Weinmuseum), the Moselle and the Palatinate. The last time that such a wine was opened in public was at the famous "Wine Tasting of the Century" on the occasion of the Jubilee of the Ferdinand Pieroth firm at the Kauzenburg in Bad Kreuznach. It was surprisingly fresh, fruity and of course very ripe and well-matured.

The twentieth century began with the triumph of the 1911, magnificent and nobly sweet but with too little acidity to be long-lived and thereby today mostly over-mature and bitter. Then came the 1915—high quality with a great yield— and two "Wines of the Century," the 1920 and 1921. Connoisseurs, particularly on the Moselle, argue as to which is the better. Both are still today blessed with good fortune, the Trockenbeerenauslese of excellent quality, exquisite, nobly sweet, full of finesse and fruit.

In 1933 only half a harvest was achieved, but it brought many outstanding wines. 1934 was a very sunny year, with wine of aromatic sweetness. A lot of this wine was practically given or thrown away to make room for the 1935, which was a plentiful

The world's oldest wine (third century A.D.), in a Roman glass bottle on display at the Historical Museum of the Palatinate in Speyer.

harvest of the best quality—fruity and highly elegant, a noble wine.

The 1937, which one still encounters at wine tastings, is also great because of its very flowery nature, its sweetness and well-ripened acidity; to this day it fills people with enthusiasm. The 1945 is an excellent wine but of a very small harvest. At that time there were hardly enough workers available and very few pesticides. Characteristic of this year is its sweetness and fine nature.

1949 was a year of much sun. There was excellent "noble rot" in the fall which provided the magnificent taste, similar to muscat. 1953 was also an outstanding year, with well-balanced wine of rare elegance and wonderful ripeness. The 1959 has created much soul-searching and dispute among wine connoisseurs. Was it a "Wine of the Century" or not? It had a truly great sweetness; its outstanding wines had record must weights. But acidity was often missing, even with the Riesling. Only in cases where the cellarer was able to stabilize the acidity at the right time have these wines kept. The remainder went off after a few years. Many who speculated financially on this vintage suffered great losses.

The next two decades brought the 1964, the outstanding 1971 and the great 1976. Whether any of these years will be regarded as a "Wine of the Century" remains to be seen. This will depend on what the remainder of this century, with perhaps even greater vintages, bestows upon us.

One regards almost reverentially such old vintages as these from the Burg Layen rarities collection. Left to right: a 1949, 1938, 1910 and the legendary 1921.

6.10.
1976er 12.10.

Mandeler

Dellchen

SPL.

Wine-Tasting

Wine lovers enjoy wine-tasting as one of the most pleasant of spare-time occupations. They not only drink the wine, but concentrate with all their senses on its characteristic qualities.

When then would you taste wine? When you are fortunate enough to be invited to a good wine-tasting, preferably by an expert or at least someone who knows a lot about wine. The wine should be tasted with all your attention and concentration in order to appreciate its quality and freshness and determine whether it is worth buying in large quantity.

In tasting wine the nose and tongue are the most important sensory organs. Over four hundred different aromas have been identified so far in various wines. A pleasant smell is part of a good wine. Therefore, a light circular movement is made with the glass to release the bouquet. The first judgment pertains to what sort of bouquet the wine has and whether it is clear and light or dark (the clearer it is, the younger the wine; the darker, the more mature). Feel through the glass the temperature of the wine. A little too warm is only half as bad as a little too cold. Very cold wines are trying to hide something, so exercise

Tasting—from the barrel—one of this decade's exceptional wines, the 1976.

caution when they are offered. Also, they do not allow the bouquet to be freely released.

Then the taste is tested. At a wine-tasting you may—indeed you must—suck the wine up rather noisily. Only in this way are all taste buds used—the roof of the mouth and the tip and base of the tongue—which can then give a total picture of the wine's taste. Some are of the mistaken opinion that you can taste the sweetness of the wine with the tip of the tongue. Try dipping your tongue into a glass of wine filled to the brim to determine the taste. Apart from the technical difficulties, this will hardly be possible because all you will sense will be the moisture and temperature. Only when the wine has reached all the taste buds in the mouth will you be able to decide whether it is harsh or sweet or something in-between.

If you were to take part in a large wine-tasting, at which thirty, forty or more wines are tasted, then you would not swallow all that is in the glass. It may seem a shame to pour it away—it could be a wonderful Auslese—into one of the containers provided. Take consolation from the thought that at the German National Wine Competition up to a hundred wines are tasted, and the examiners must resist temptation and spit every drop out.

After a wine-tasting take care when driving, even when you think you have drunk only a little wine. Make sure that during the tasting you eat traditional bread or rolls and cheese cubes, preferably Emmentaler (which goes well with all wines). In this way you can both neutralize your tongue and settle your stomach. When Sekt-tasting you must be more careful, as Sekt intoxicates more quickly than wine because of the carbon dioxide. Connoisseurs therefore often drink Sekt before a meal or before a wine-tasting. To close the wine-tasting you should always take again the light, extra-dry wine with which you began, in order to neutralize the taste buds once more.

No wine to be drunk with strongly smelling food, no wine to be stored near strongly smelling food! In the cellar such strong odors could find their way into the wine as it "breathes" through the cork, and at meals they detract from the taste of the wine. From Horace comes the dictum on how wine should be tasted: *"Color, odor, sapor!"* One should test wine according to color, smell and taste.

The aroma can only be checked, of course, when the nose can take it in undisturbed. If cigarettes, cigars or pipes are smoked during the wine-tasting then the sense of smell can be impaired. Every experience would be influenced by the excessive nicotine smell. Therefore at wine-tastings you should not smoke. Because of this, you also are spared the hangover on the next day, and the wine is thus saved from false accusations. Normally one attributes a headache to drinking too much wine. You can be sure, however, that wine is only responsible in a minority of cases.

At every wine-tasting one attempts to grade the wines according to their characteristics. How do we then judge wine?

The philologist Hans Peter Althaus has stated in a survey of connoisseur's jargon that there are about a thousand terms with which to express praise or reproach for wine. Yet language is hardly sufficient to express the numerous sensations possible.

One must differentiate between experts and amateurs. The private wine drinker can grade the wine according to how he likes it; his opinion need not agree with that of the expert. In the end, however, in every judgment of wine, whether by experts or amateurs, one cannot avoid the basic criteria: color, clarity, smell and taste.

The German Agricultural Society has designed a twenty-point scheme for experts which is used at competitions. The color of white wine is graded as pale, deep colored, light or typical; 2 points can and must be given here. Red wine is adjudged bright red, browny red or typical. The wine's clarity is examined; it will be either dull—in which case no points are given—or completely clear—meriting a possible 2 points, which is also the minimum. As far as the aroma is concerned it is judged as either faulty (0 points), expressionless (1 point), clear toned (2 points), fine smelling (3 points) or fragrant and flowery (4 points). Minimum score for aroma is 2 points.

The most points are of course given for taste. Here the wine is graded faulty (0 points), lacking (1–3 points), small but independent (small, thin but clean: 4–6 points), good and balanced (7–9 points) or mature and noble (10–12 points). Minimum number of points necessary for taste is 6.

And now to the characterization: Here fantasy and personal impression have been set no bounds. What one person finds full is perhaps elegant for another. However, for all people faulty wine will always be so

The connoisseur examines the wine's bouquet before tasting (drawing by Allers).

described, and rejected. Above all, a healthy wine must not taste of cork or barrel. (That would, by the way, be reason for complaint in a good restaurant.)

Rudi vom Endt, the unforgettable wine poet of Düsseldorf, wine lover and holder of the German Wine Culture Prize, has made a teasing attempt to grade wine into the following groups:

Feminine virtues: pleasant, agreeable, smooth, mild, soft, full, snug, round, racy, distinguished, elegant

Masculine nature: sinewy, robust, fiery, massive, rugged

Content: light, heavy, full, greasy, or oily

Age: young, raw, mature, fully mature, old, turning, empty, or dead

For the palate and nose: sourish, harsh, sweet, pleasant, juicy, balanced, fruity, flowery, spicy, fresh, lively, piquant, clean, or earthy

But whatever sort of taste a wine shows, it is important that taste and smell complement each other. The wine must be well balanced.

With such specifications on your own wine menu for a private wine-tasting or in your own wine cellar, you can put guests in a good mood even before the first drop has been poured. This is equally true for restaurant owners and wine dealers, whose offers should also be as detailed as possible. What kind of effect this can have has been demonstrated by none other than Carl Zuckmayer. It was 1925 in Berlin, a while before the premiere of his *Fröhlicher Weinberg* (*"The Jolly Vineyard"*), which was the breakthrough for Zuckmayer. The poet was suffering from a shortage of money. One day he had agreed to meet his publisher in a wine bar in Berlin, and had to wait a long time for him. To pass the time he read the wine menu, without, however—his purse was empty—being able to make use of it, and finally wrote in the margin:

Weinkarte, wenn mit Phantasie gelesen,
Ist fast so schön, wie wirklich voll
gewesen.

A wine menu, read with fantasy,
Is almost as nice as being drunk.

To create such wine menus is a worthwhile aim for all wine lovers, wine menus which urge our fantasies on and make anticipated pleasure become real pleasure.

189

Wining and Dining

A Double Pleasure

"Mit Wein schmeckt's besser." ("It tastes better with wine.") This saying has a two-fold significance. A good wine goes with a good meal. In addition, some good dishes can be made even better with wine, because it makes them spicier, more piquant, better balanced and more digestible.

Let us start in the kitchen: Wine for cooking should be found in every good and well-maintained kitchen, just as should vinegar and oil. With it nearly all dishes can be improved. This is true for soup and hors d'oeuvres as well as meat, fish and desserts. Good, simple wine—white and red, sharp and mild—should be a permanent part of the kitchen supplies. Outstanding wines are only necessary as accompaniments to special dishes; they are, in the main, the climax or conclusion of a meal.

For wine soups and wine sauces, for simple, stewed fruits and for the improvement of normal meat or fish dishes a normal white or red Qualitätswein is recommended. Only wine creams and jelly need to be made with high-quality wine, as it brings the necessary elegance and fullness. For puddings and pastry one needs a robust, spicy, strong wine. Only such a

Eating and drinking customs in the Middle Ages sometimes got out of hand. The Dutch painter Jakob Jordaens (1593–1678) has immortalized this in a painting.

191

wine can retain its taste during the long cooking time to which it is subjected in preparation.

Soup, which normally begins a meal, can be made much more appetizing by a drop of wine. Fish, mussel and crab soups are best prepared with white wine. Freshwater fish agree very well with a light, lively wine, whereas saltwater fish are better with a stronger white wine.

For meat soups it is recommended to steam fresh mushrooms and herbs with butter and a light white wine before adding them to the soup. For game soup one needs a spicy red wine, whereas for clear ox-tail soup white wine or dry sherry is better. Turtle soup can be improved with a good Madeira or Sherry, as can the English mock turtle; here also a red wine can be used.

On hot summer days, cold fruit soups are wonderfully refreshing. A cool wine soup can work wonders, and makes even tired spirits wide awake. For fruit soups using dark fruits mild red wine is recommended. For soups using rhubarb, strawberries, raspberries, apricots, peaches, pears and apples a white wine is desirable, as this does not mask the smooth individual taste of fine fruit.

"Fisch will schwimmen" ("Fish will swim") is an old saying which is confirmed again and again, as is *"Aus dem Wasser in den Wein"* ("Out of the water, into the wine"). No modern kitchen can do without wine when preparing a fish dish. Wine brings out the fine flavor of fish and, in particular, underlines the taste of cod, haddock and perch. Even when cleaning, marinating or pickling fish one should not be without it, for it cleans the fish well, neutralizes the smell and in the case of marinating makes the fish itself spicy and firmer.

The better the fish, the better the wine should be. Trout, pike-perch and tench go best with an elegant Riesling wine, whereas the hearty saltwater fish and carp need a stronger companion, even a smooth red wine, above all when baked. The method of preparation is even more important in the choice of wine than the fish itself. A blue trout is considerably more tender and lighter than a *"Müllerin"* ("miller-girl's"). For the former one needs light white or, in certain circumstances, light red wine.

For the preliminary preparation of fish, an extra-dry (*herb*) wine is recommended. For marinating one should use half vinegar and half wine, although one can do it with lemon juice instead of vinegar. In coating fish one should use varying amounts of wine, depending on the type of fish.

For steaming one should turn to a white or red wine of a lighter nature. Carp needs a heavier red wine for a more piquant taste: Here a good Spätburgunder is perhaps best. In preparing herring one can use either red or white wine; after frying for a short while one should finish by steaming them. With sole or plaice one should do the steaming in a mixture half water and half white wine. Haddock or sea-perch are prepared best in a robust white wine, but under no circumstances in a sweet wine.

All meat dishes become delicacies when cooked in a sauce of wine rather than water. Large roasts should be honored with heavy wines. Exacting recipes for the preparation of veal, lamb or pork roasts need a strong Palatinate or Franconian wine. As for darker meats, tender red wines are beneficial.

Tender saddle or fillet of venison should be marinated and otherwise prepared not in red wine but in a few drops of a fine Riesling, if the fine fullness of its taste is to be developed.

Brawn or game pâté prepared with a racy

Wine lovers enjoying their favorite pastime, shown in a picture by Frans Frankken (1581–1642).

white wine is a pleasure not only to eat but to see.

Wild boar, hare or deer, if they are young animals, should be steeped in a white-wine marinade. For older animals, a strong red-wine marinade is better; here the red wine should not be sweet or too heavy.

Poultry dishes, vegetables and even pastry can also be improved through careful use of wine.

Concerning choice of wine to accompany a meal, there is an old rule which modern chefs and gourmets seldom keep: white wine with white meat, red wine with dark meat. A bit of guidance is still contained in this: With veal or pork one should use, according to taste, a dry or semi-dry Riesling, Weissburgunder, Sylvaner, Ruländer or Müller-Thurgau. For the much-loved cured pork the wine can have more body, and even a red wine could be considered. Beef and lamb need a smooth, soft red wine. Fuller red wines go well with nearly all game dishes, although a Riesling can be wonderful with saddle of venison (even a white Spätlese is allowed).

To accompany cold cuts a normal, hearty wine or Weissherbst is best. Together with asparagus—with or without ham—Riesling, Sylvaner, and Müller-Thurgau of medium quality are adequate.

If one has cooked the meal one's-self or knows which wines were used to improve each dish, then the problem of choice is not so great. The wine used in preparing the meal is a good one to accompany it. By the way, no wine is served with soup. Nor does the aperitif always need to be the overworked Sherry. Try instead a good Sekt, perhaps a vintage one, or a full, mature Auslese.

One more basic rule: Under no circumstances should one choose a wine that covers up the smell and taste of the meal. The enjoyment of wine with a meal is that it complements, even improves, but never detracts from the food.

The choice of wine also depends on the time of day. For the morning libation, one should try a dry Sekt, a light, extra-dry white wine, or, if one prefers, a harsh red wine with little residual sweetness. For lunch, as a rule, lighter wines are fitting; this applies to wines drunk after the meal. For the evening tipple a strong wine of the type produced in all our wine-growing areas is recommended. After the evening meal is the time for the truly great wines. Then, to finish off such an evening, to enliven and balance the lasting taste of a great sweet wine one should take when possible a harsh, fruity, dry Riesling.

Cheese is always a good way to round off a good meal. Cheese and wine have always been good partners, complementing each other excellently. The French have developed the coordination of wine and cheese into an art, and a great deal can be learned from them. There is only one cheese that harmonizes well with every wine—Emmentaler. Noble and with a tender, nutty taste, it rounds off light, lively wines, emphasizes the mild character of a soft Sylvaner yet also goes particularly well with rich, outstanding wines. Gouda is similar in this respect. Personal taste alone is the deciding factor here.

Cheese must normally be very carefully harmonized with wine. For extra-dry, racy and light wines, finely spiced cheeses of milder character are suitable. Mature Edam can be as suitable as soft cheese or not-too-ripe Camembert or Brie.

Mild, well-bodied wines find a good companion with many cheeses. All sorts of Camembert and Brie are ideal here. Blue cheeses, mixed slightly with butter and therefore not so strong-tasting, are also excellent. Not to be omitted here is Gervais —heavy-cream cheese whose fresh, light, fine spices develop astonishingly well with wine.

Wines of a lighter, agreeable sort are especially compatible with the splendid Tilsit and even Romadur and Limburger. When these cheeses are cut into small cubes their aroma is quite acceptable. With stronger cheeses one needs stronger wines. Rugged Ruländer wines of full character "prefer" Gouda or Edam. Schillerwein "likes," above all, the more uncomplicated soft cheeses and curds, as does Weissherbst. Red wines come to the fore with Roquefort, Tilsit, Romadur and Limburger.

"Zum Wohle!"

"To Your Health!"

Wine and Health

"Alle Dinge sind giftig. Allein das Mass macht's, dass ein Ding nicht giftig ist." ("All things are poisonous, only the amount makes a thing not poisonous.") This old saying is especially true of wine. Naturally, wine is an alcoholic drink, but German wine has a particularly low alcoholic content, usually between 8 and 10 percent and hardly ever above 12 percent. This is a factor that for many people is decisive in choosing German wine over other drinks or non-German wines, which sometimes have 14 percent alcohol. Apart from alcohol, wine also contains about four hundred other active substances, mainly trace elements. To this number probably as many aromas could be added. These substances endow the wine with its effective palette.

Canadian researchers have found that both grape juice and wine are killers of bacteria and viruses. Professor Schettler of the Heidelberg University Clinic, a heart specialist, explains that drinking a moderate amount of alcohol can be advisable for an individual when healthy. "When my patients ask me if and what they are allowed to drink, then I tell them they should not drink more than a half litre of wine per day." Professor Schettler also explicitly points out that there are different personal levels: One person can take more, the other less. "I know people who have been drinking a bottle of wine daily for more than fifty years, and they are thoroughly healthy."

Does wine lengthen or shorten life? Three authoritative scientists give a very clear answer. Professor Kliewe, head of the Hygiene Institute at the University of Mainz, Professor Hochrein and Dr. Reich together state, "Moderate but regular wine-drinking lends itself to a longer life." Most medical scientists who concern themselves with the effects of wine stress time and again that moderate drinking of light wine in no way overstrains the body through an excess of liquid. Reasonable wine-drinking has an effect not only euphoric but also anti-spastic and anti-neuralgic. All doctors, however, emphasize that you should always drink reasonably. They recommend never to drink on an empty stomach, but to have perhaps well-baked bread and mild cheese. Professor Hochrein demonstrated, in a test comparing wine-drinking with and without cheese, that forty-five minutes and then ninety minutes after eating 250 grams of Emmentaler the alcoholic level in a person's body is lowered by 20 percent and 30 percent respectively. Drivers should take particular note of this.

Dr. Reich refers to an experiment carried out by an American university. In this, three groups were identified:

Total abstainers from alcoholic beverages
Moderate drinkers
Drunkards

Life expectancies were examined for twenty-year-old subjects from each group. Out of a total of a thousand examined in each group the number of men still alive at the age of fifty was as follows:

686 abstainers
717 moderate drinkers
585 drunkards

At the age of seventy:

358 abstainers
367 moderate drinkers
249 drunkards

At the age of ninety:

41 abstainers
61 moderate drinkers
21 drunkards

Corresponding figures for women (again starting at the age of twenty, with a thousand people in each group) were also recorded. At the age of fifty, these numbers were still alive:

669 abstainers
755 moderate drinkers
346 drunkards

At the age of seventy:

310 abstainers
364 moderate drinkers
154 drunkards

At the age of ninety:

16 abstainers
52 moderate drinkers
0 drunkards

On the basis of examinations of thirteen hundred people over the age of eighty, Professor Hochrein concluded that nearly all owed their good physical and mental condition to moderate, regular wine-drinking, and that in general wine-drinking groups of the population have a 10–15 percent higher life expectancy than others. On average, they live from eight to ten years longer. Professor Kliewe's conclusion: "The euphoria that wine releases encourages a positive attitude to life, increases vitality and delays the advance of old age."

What scientists nowadays observe was at least suspected in the past. The Apostle Paul wrote in Timothy:

Drink no longer water, but use a little wine for thy stomach's sake and thine often infirmities.

And St. Augustine of Hippo (354–430) in his text *De Sancta Virginitate* ("On Holy Virginity") said:

In many cases wine is necessary for people. It strengthens weak stomachs, refreshes dulled strength, warms up the body's chills, pours balm onto wounds. Sadness is shunned, tiredness of the soul is driven away, joy is brought and companions are imbued with the desire to converse.

The Greek and Roman god of medicine, Asclepius, is supposed to have prescribed wine. Hippocrates, founder of scientific medicine (460–377 B.C.), introduced wine into medicine and treated wounds and sores with bandages soaked in wine.

196

The Roman legionaries also took wine to heal their wounds. Both Roman and Egyptian warriors used wine as a disinfectant for water in conquered countries. The Greek writer Plutarch (45–125) explained the qualities of wine very simply: "Among drinks wine is the most useful, among medicines the most tasty and among foodstuffs the most agreeable."

Later ages did not forget the healing powers of wine. In a little volume from the year 1709, *On the Excellence, Differences, Uses and Effects of Rhine Wine*, we find the statement, "Wine can be used as in all illnesses for a strong preservative instead of warm baths and mineral water." What Rhine wine can do is described here in the following way:

> As soon as one has tasted such a good wine the whole body is warmed, the pulse goes faster than before, and because the blood is pumped around strongly the veins swell up, one gets a red glow in the face, sweat and urine —whereby all unclean substances are removed from the body—increase, and the whole body—even the spirit —is refreshed.

Justus von Liebig (1803–73), the discoverer of chloroform, developer of artificial fertilizers, inventor of baking powder and meat extract, gives one of the best medical testimonials to wine:

> As a restorative when life's strength is exhausted, firing with enthusiasm and enhancement when melancholy days are to be overcome, correction and equalization when organic disparity appears, and as protection against temporary disturbances caused by inorganic nature, wine is surpassed by no other natural or artificial product.

Nobel prizewinner Emil von Behring (1854–1917), who discovered the serum against diphtheria, and tetanus, states:

> Self-observation as well as comparative observation of people well known to me seems to prove that the level of digestible alcohol in good wine can be considerably extended. On many of my long sea voyages it became obvious to me how much consumers of alcohol surpassed non-drinkers as regards physical performance, spiritual freshness, intellectual fitness, general friendliness and good temper.

Professor Kliewe amplifies this (from a 1961 lecture):

> When speaking about the biological characteristics of wine one must differentiate sharply between psychological and biochemical effects on the human organism. In the same way that music, the color of a room, and so on, affect mood and performance at work, so influences on the senses, which the wine causes through its bouquet, color and taste, can be organically established in a positive way. In connection with the euphoric effect of the low alcoholic content, wine when drunk moderately has a compensatory effect on the psyche. In the present period this is all the more important, as a lot of more-or-less pronounced symptoms of illness can be accredited to the nervous burden on civilized people. Such people suffer from so-called problems of "fitting in" caused by the human organism being unable to adapt to external stimulus. There are indeed numerous medicines with which we have tried to dampen this nervous tension, or cure it, but in wine we have a natural product

which, because of the combination of its many substances, can contribute to a large extent to achieving this aim. A glass of wine drunk in the late afternoon or evening gives the organism harmony again and thereby relaxation and recovery from daily stress.

That older people can often take more wine than younger people is to be attributed, Kliewe maintains, to the reduction in functioning of the thyroid glands in old age.

Both strong and weak hearts are affected by the smallest amount of wine. The pulse can be speeded up by a heavy wine or one rich in bouquet. As with illnesses connnected with the heart or circulation, it is less the wine than the amount of liquid taken in which is decisive; the dosage with such illnesses must be carefully taken into account.

A Professor Hjertland, an American, reports that in a series of checkups on seven thousand people it was proven that small doses of wine had the effect of a preventive against heart attacks. Professor Eppstein from Zurich points out that according to statistics heart attacks are rarer in countries with large alcohol consumption than in northern Europe where less wine is drunk. Recent work by British scientists supports the thesis that it is not the alcohol in wine which has positive effects on the heart, but the mixture of many different aromatic substances, as well as the large amount of various trace elements. These numerous replenishing substances, harmoniously blended in this natural product, raise it above all other medicaments and luxuries. Professor Duesberg's findings confirm,

according to Kliewe, that wine does not have an unfavorable effect on blood pressure. Further, examination of older drinkers shows that the inner wall of their arteries is just as tender and elastic as with young people. Moderate wine drinking has, according to Kliewe, probably no essential significance as regards the formation of arterial sclerosis. On the other hand, people who tend to suffer from apoplexy should be dissuaded from drinking wine.

With pre-existing parenchymatosis and liver and kidney diseases, wine should be completely left alone. Professor Kliewe, answering another important question, says, "It need not be explained in more detail that wines containing sugar—and fortified wines do contain sugar—must not be given to people suffering from diabetes." The same goes for diseases of the nervous system.

Concerning the question of the effect of wine on intellectual performance, Kliewe comes to the conclusion that here no norm can be given. One should go by one's own experiences. For one person, wine stimulates intellectual performance, for another it hinders it.

Kliewe says of wine with regard to infectious diseases:

Outside the human and animal body wine is able to kill germs and bacteria which carry diseases. This has been proven by examination on colitis, typhoid and dysentery bacteria, pyaemia and cholera. That means in normal life that wine drunk at meals helps to prevent the undue increase of bacteria in the mouth.

Wine-drinking has a certain prophylactic effect. Wine is recommended for infectious diseases because it strengthens the resistance often weakened by the infection. However, it should never be drunk in connection with medicine, the effects of which can be thereby dangerously increased.

However, wine is not always the same. Here the opinions of doctors sometimes differ as to what constitutes reasonable drinking. Decisive for this is the physical and mental condition of the wine-drinker and the content of the wine. So the recommendations as to how much wine to drink per day vary from one-eighth or one-quarter to one bottle of light wine. Even in slimming diets wine has a place. One thinks here of the Schroth treatment and the findings of American diet experts. In one experiment a group of subjects was given a quarter of a litre (250 ml.) of wine at meals, and another comparable group, no wine. The result: Without wine weight loss per week was 0.26 percent; with wine, however, the figure was 0.54 percent.

As for wine and driving, one may indeed drive more speedily—but be careful! Above all, never drink before the stomach is well filled with food containing fat and protein. If one empties a glass of wine on an empty stomach the legal alcoholic limit for driving will be reached in forty-five minutes. After a further thirty or forty minutes it will have been reabsorbed. Generally, a one-fifth-litre glass of wine is re-absorbed after approximately an hour. The slower one drinks, the better the liver can keep pace with intake in breaking down the alcohol, and therefore the lower the alcohol level. One can take as a principle that an average person's driving ability will be influenced from an alcohol level of 0.5 parts per thousand upwards. Reaction time becomes longer and longer. At more than 1 part per thousand it becomes dangerous, at over 1.5 the intoxication can no longer be hidden and from 2 upwards one can really speak of drunkenness. With younger people, the alcohol level increases faster than with older, usually heavier, people. Clearly, as a driver it is better to drink one glass fewer than risk an accident and endanger others.

Finally, what about the hangover? A pounding head, dizziness and upset stomach are the symptoms that one has drunk either too much or too much of a mixture. Alcohol is not always the same. Nothing is worse than to mix drinks and then perhaps smoke at the same time. Those, however, who stay with the same wine—a healthy, mature, light wine—can be confident that they will not suffer from a hangover afterwards.

Wine is to be enjoyed and not swilled. Then it gives us joy and health equally.

German-English
Wine-Tasting Glossary

Abgang: aftertaste
Flavor that lingers after tasting wine. In a good wine it will not quickly fade but be lasting and pleasing.

Aroma: aroma
The distinctive odor or perfume of fresh fruit that a wine gives off, typical of its own grape variety.

Ausgebaut: mature
Fully developed, ready to drink.

Art: literally, "type"
Characteristics of a wine's origin.

Bitter: bitter
Tasting of bitter almonds. With red wine this is desirable.

Blank: clear
The wine is clear, as opposed to cloudy.

Blumig: flowery
The fragrance is clearly recognizable.

Brandig: burning
Inharmonious wine having too much alcohol and usually too little acidity.

Bukett: bouquet
Smell or aroma of the wine, determined by grape variety, time of harvest, "noble rot," fermentation and ageing in bottle, among other things.

Charakter: character
Sum of a wine's positive and distinctive smell and taste characteristics.

Delikat: delicate
Delicate, unobtrusive character in a wine.

Dick: lit., "thick, fat"
Full-bodied wine, usually with too much residual sweetness.

Duftig: fragrant
Tender bouquet, more delicate and fine than *blumig* wine.

Dünn: thin
Having too little alcohol and acidity.

Edel: noble
Great compliment for a fine, elegant, top-quality wine.

Elegant: elegant
A seasoned, harmonious, pleasant and not-too-heavy wine.

Erdig: earthy
The wine tastes of the soil.

Fad: flat
Low in acidity, without body or bouquet.

Fein: fine
Above average and with good bouquet.

Feurig: fiery
Strong red wine.

Finesse: finesse
Elegant, fruity, mature, noble; with the breed, class and fine nuances in aroma and taste that distinguish great wine.

Firne: turned
A condition in which old wine is slightly oxidized. This may mean it is past its peak, or it may mean the desirable state of *Edelfirne* has been reached.

Frisch: fresh
Young with good acidity; lively, harmonious wine.

Fruchtig: fruity
With a refreshing flavor and aroma typical of the variety of grape; distinguished by a fine, fruity acidity.

Fülle: fullness
A pleasing fullness in a wine rich and well-balanced in alcohol and extract.

Glatt: smooth
Harmonious, elegant, with mild acidity.

Grasig: lit., "grassy"
The taste of a poor-ripening vintage or any unripe wine in which stalks as well as grapes have been pressed.

Gross: lit., "big, great"
Completely harmonious, exceptionally good wine, above average in quality.

Halbtrocken: semi-dry
Wine with 18 grams or less residual sugar per litre.

Harmonisch: harmonious
Wine that is well balanced as to aroma, flavor, alcohol and acidity.

Hart: hard
Refers to a very acidic wine.
Herb: dry
Wine with a high acidity. This sharpness may prove pleasant providing the tannic acid does not predominate.
Hochfarbig: lit., "highly colored"
Golden yellow and brown, often tainted by air or weak in sulphur.

Jung: young, unripe
Wine which has not yet reached the highest point of maturity.

Korkgeschmack: corky (lit., "cork taste")
Taste imparted to a wine by a defective or mouldy cork. No possible remedy.
Körperreich: robust
Full of body, texture.
Kurz: lit., "short"
Without aftertaste.

Lebendig: lively
Fresh with fruity acidity; mostly young.
Leer: thin (lit., "empty")
Having little body.
Leicht: light
A small wine, little alcohol or extract.
Lieblich: pleasant, agreeable
Light wine of low acidity with a slight sweetness. Also, wine with more than 18 grams residual sugar.

Markant: lit., "striking"
Strong, with distinct characteristics, typical for an area or type of wine.

Nervig: lit., "sinewy"
Having marked acidity, full body.

Rassig: racy
Robust, lively; without excessive acid.
Reif: ripe
Fully mature, at its peak.
Reintönig: clean
Absolutely clean wine without any accompanying non-vinous taste or aroma.
Rund: lit., "round"
A well-balanced wine with good body, without pronounced acidity.

Saftig: rich
Mouth-filling, fruity, with good acidity and sweetness.
Samtig: velvety
Applied to red wine that is harmonious, elegant and full.

Sauber: clean
Perfectly clear wine, without flaws of scent and taste.
Säure: acidity
Together with the aromatic elements produces a lively wine that will last.
Schwanz: aftertaste
Same as *Abgang.*
Schwer: heavy
Full-bodied, powerful wine, with high alcohol and extract. Used mostly in reference to sweet wines.
Spielig: lively (lit., "playful")
Having much character and nuance, with appealingly pungent acidity.
Spritzig: prickly
With a fresh acidity, but not sharp. Carbon dioxide is often present but not necessarily noticeable.
Stahlig: lit., "steely"
Harmonious and full-bodied, with good acidity and a long life. More acidic than a *nervig* or *rassig* wine.
Süffig: lit., "palatable, tasty"
Fresh, lighthearted and pleasant wine rounded off by a hint of sweetness and running lightly over the tongue; usually refers to a small tavern wine.

Tot: flat (lit., "dead")
Old wine with no more life left in it.
Trocken: dry
Wine with no apparent sweetness; has no more than 9 grams of residual sugar.

Vollmundig: lit., "mouth-filling"
Full, rich in alcohol and glycerine; mellow, well balanced.
Vornehm: artistocratic, distinguished
An elegant great wine, well-matured.

Warm: warm
Red wine rich in alcohol.
Weinig: vinous
Fresh, fruity, with the taste and character of grapes.
Wuchtig: rugged
Heavy, full, powerful, rich in alcohol and body.
Würzig: spicy
With much natural fragrance, fine aroma, good bouquet.

Zart: lit., "tender"
Light wine of a fine, delicate, elegant type.
Zukunft: lit., "future"
Wine that has still to reach its peak and will probably have a long life.

Twentieth Century
Vintages

1900   bad spring, small yield, but good quality
1901   beautiful summer, average quality
1902   frosts in May, small yield, average quality
1903   hard frost in April, large harvest, average quality
1904   very hot summer; excellent, abundant harvest
1905   small yield but good quality
1906   much damage by *Peronospora* mildew, small harvest
1907   cold summer, good fall, average quality
1908   average yield, good quality
1909   rainy summer, average quality
1910   rainy summer and fall, small harvest
★1911   excellent weather, excellent quality, a "comet wine" (*see* p. 182)
1912   large harvest, average quality
1913   cold summer, small harvest, poor quality
1914   frosts in May, poor quality
1915   dry hot summer, excellent quality
1916   wet, small harvest, poor quality
1917   frost in spring, abundant harvest, excellent quality
1918   continuous rain in fall, average quality
1919   small harvest, acidic wine
★1920   excellent quantity and quality
★1921   outstanding year, top quality
1922   cold summer, large harvest, poor quality
1923   poor fruit formation, small harvest
1924   large harvest, average quality
1925   small harvest
1926   spring frosts, rainy fall, very small harvest
1927   wet summer, small harvests, average quality
1928   damage by frosts in fall, average quality
1929   widespread damage by frosts in winter, hot summer, average
         yield, good quality
1930   large quantity, average quality
1931   wet summer, abundant crop, average quality
1932   small yield, good quality
1933   excellent year
1934   sunny year, abundant crop, very good quality
1935   abundant, good
1936   abundant harvest, quality not so good
★1937   excellent quality—an exceptional year
1938   good harvest, average quality but some exceptional wines
1939   average
1940   abundant harvest, average quality
1941   average
1942   average
1943   abundant, good

1944	average harvest
★1945	May frosts, very small harvest due to the war, but excellent quality
1946	average quantity, good quality
1947	abundant, very good quality
1948	abundant, average quality
★1949	average quantity, excellent quality
1950	average
1951	abundant, but not so good
1952	a good, average year
1953	excellent year, some outstanding wines
1954	abundant, moderate quality
1955	average
1956	average quality
1957	much frost damage, low yield, good quality
1958	fair quantity, average quality
★1959	at the time considered the outstanding wine of the century, but little acidity
1960	large yield, low quality
1961	small yield, good quality
1962	small yield, average quality
1963	large harvest, moderate quality
1964	abundant, excellent quality
1965	small harvest, poor quality
1966	average harvest; good, sometimes very good, quality
1967	moderate quantity, excellent quality
1968	small yield, indifferent quality
1969	a good, average year
1970	abundant harvest, average-to-good quality
★1971	the outstanding year of the century. (This is the first vintage to which the new wine law is applicable.)
1972	average quality, light and fragrant wines with good acidity
1973	large harvest, average quality
1974	normal harvest, fruity wines of Kabinett quality only
1975	good harvest, above-average quality in all grades of *prädikat* wine
1976	many excellent wines
1977	record harvest, harmonious wine, on the whole good
1978	fresh wine with fine acidity
1979	very harmonious wine with a good future, large amount of *prädikat* wine
1980	modest quantity, medium quality
1981	medium quantity harvested, quality to Auslese level

As far as we can see, up to now the years 1911, 1920, 1921, 1937, 1945, 1949 and 1971 will go down in history as Wines of the Century, as will also the 1959, provided it has enough acidity. Other excellent years are 1929, 1934, 1935, 1953, 1964 and 1976.

Index

acidity, wine's, 32, 55, 58, 60, 64, 66, 68, 78, 156, 176–77, 184; carbonic acid, 154, 167, 169, 171; longevity of wine, 181; wine-making process, 152
additives, wine, 18, 24. *See also* sugaring
adulteration, of wine, 31
Afghanistan: wine's mythic origins, 10–12
Ahr (viticultural area), 52 (map), 55, 70–75, 172–73; cultivation area and yield, 71, 74; cuisine, 74; spas, 72, 74; subregion and *Grosslage* list, 74; tourism, 72; types of grape and wine, 71, 72; vine louse, 30; wine-growing conditions, 72, 74; wine trade, 72, 74
Ahrbleichert (wine), 72
Ahr River, 52 (map), 71–72
Ahrweiler, 52 (map), 74
alcohol content, wine's, 32, 152, 154, 167, 170, 173, 174–75, 177, 181, 195, 199
Althaus, Hans Peter, 188
Alzey, 52 (map); State Research Institute, 58, 104
amphoras, ancient, 10–14, 21, 36
amtliche Prüfungsnummer, 171, 174
An die Freude (Schiller), 50
Anne, Saint, in art, 40
Apicius, Marcus Gavius, and Trier, 82
Are (castle), 74
aroma, wine's, 58, 60, 187, 188
art, wine and, 34–51; in ancient Egypt, 34; Near East, 34–35; Greece, 35, 37, 48–49, 160; Etruria, 36; Rome, 35–38; in Germany, 38–51, 114; Christian, 38–40, 90, 141–42; Renaissance, 39–40, 90; eighteenth- and nineteenth-century, 40–48; twentieth century, 42–44, 50. *See also* ceramics, crafts, literature, mosaics, music, painting, religious uses of wine, sculpture
Asclepius, 196
Asia Minor, early viticulture, 9, 12, 14
Assmanshausen, 88, 90
Athena, 10, 17; mythic origins of wine, 10
Augustine, Saint, on wine and health, 196
Auslese, 30, 32, 150, 175
Ayl, 82

Bacchanalia, 18, 36; bacchanalian revels, 18, 36, 38; in painting, 40, 42, 43
Bacchus, 18; and Dionysus, 18, 19, 35; Erasmus on, 19; invoked by Schiller, 48; and mythic origins of wine, 9; in Renaissance arts and crafts, 40; in Roman art, 35, 36, 37, 38. *See also* Dionysus
Bach, Johann Sebastian, 42
Bacharach, 66
Bacharach (region, Middle Rhine), 69
Bad Dürkheim, 52 (map), 114–16; Dürkheimer Wurstmarkt, 114, 116
Baden (viticultural area), 52 (map), 54, 58, 60, 120, 133–39, 172–73; Baden Viticultural Association, 134; climate, 134; cooperatives, 134, 136–39; cuisine, 134; cultivation area, 133, 134, 139; diversity, 133; *Gütezeichen*, 134, 180; soil, 136; subregion and *Grosslage* list, 139; types of grape and wine, 133–34, 136, 138; viticulture, 134, 138; Weinstrasse, 133; Weissherbst, 166;

Zentralkellerei Badischer Winzergenossenschaften (ZBW), 136–37
Baden-Baden, 52 (map), 138
Baden Bergstrasse, 120, 134, 138
Badische Bergstrasse-Kraichgau (region, Baden), 139, 173. *See also* Kraichgau
Badisches Frankenland, 138, 139, 173
Bad Kreuznach, 52 (map), 95, 96, 100
Bad Münster, 95, 96, 100
Bad Neuenahr, 72, 74
Badstube (*Grosslage*), 85
Baiken (vineyard at Rauenthal), 92, 96
balance, wine's, 32, 55, 58, 154, 174, 181
Baldung, Hans, 40
Bavaria, 24, 29, 111, 142
Bayerischer Bodensee, 130, 146, 173
Beerenauslese, 30, 150, 175, 177
Beethoven, Ludwig van, 43
Behring, Emil von, on wine and health, 197
Benedictines, 22, 142, 144
Bensheim, 52 (map), 120, 122
Bergstrasse, 119, 120
Bernkasteler Doctor, 84, 182
Bernkastel-Kues, 52 (map), 83, 84
Bernkastler Riesling, 82
Bible, the, wine references in: Book of Judges, 10; Exodus, 10; Cana, miracle of, 10, 11; Jesus Christ, 10; Moses, 10; Noah, 9, 10; Satan, 10
Bigentia, 84
Bindung, Rudolf, *Moselfahrt aus Liebeskummer*, 50, 78
Bingen, 52 (map), 98, 108; Rochusberg, 106–8; Rochusfest, 45
Bingen (region), 104, 108, 173
Bismarck, Otto von, 90
blending wine, 24, 31, 32; international, 174; on Moselle, 78–80; and wine laws, 175; in Württemberg, 126. *See also* cuvée
Blessed Virgin. *See* madonna
Blücher, Field Marshal, 66
Böcklin, Arnold, 40–41
Bocksbeutel, 54, 138, 142; origin, 142
Bodensee (region, Baden), 139, 173
Boemund, Bishop, of Trier, 84
Boniface, Saint, 22, 141
Bonn, 63, 68
Boppard, 52 (map), 68
Botrytis cinerea, 29, 175. *See also* Edelfäule, "noble rot"
bottles, wine, 21, 154–58, 163, 170–71, 181, 182
Bottwar River, 128
bouquet, wine's 32, 58, 60, 187, 189
Brackenheim, 130
Braubach: Marksburg (castle), 68
Brauneberg, 84
breeds of grape, 57–67, 149; crossings, 58, 60; new, 32, 57, 60
—Albalonga, 60, 144; Bacchus, 32, 60; Clevner, 138; Courtillier musqué, 60; Deckrot, 61; Domina, 72; Ehrenfelser, 32, 60; Faber, 32, 56, 60; Freisamer, 60, 134; Helfensteiner, 61; Herold, 61; Huxelrebe, 60; Kanzler, 32, 60; Kerner, 32, 58, 60, 64, 112, 126, 144; Lemberger, 61, 126–30; Müller, 61, 72, 128; Muskateller, 134; Nobling, 60, 123; Optima, 32, 60; 80; Ortega, 32, 60; Perle, 144; Rotberger,

61, 72; Samtrot, 72, 128; Scheurebe, 32, 57–59, 104, 134; Schwarzriesling, 61, 126, 128; Sieger, 57, 60, 152; Tokay (Tokayer), 57; Wanner, 57; Zähringer, 134
—*See also* Burgundy; Elbling; Gewürztraminer; Gutedel; Morio-Muskat; Müller-Thurgau; Portugieser; Rieslaner; Riesling; Ruländer; Sylvaner; Traminer; Trollinger; *also* Ahr; Baden; Franconia; Hessian Bergstrasse; Middle Rhine; Moselle-Saar-Ruwer; Nahe; Rheingau; Rheinhessen; Rhine Palatinate; Württemberg
Breisach, 52 (map), 136
Breisachgau, 136
Breisgau (region, Baden), 54, 136, 173
Bremen, 42; old-wine collection, 182
Brentano, Clemens, 90
Bretzenheim, early vineyard at, 104
Bruckner, Anton, 42
Brues, Otto, on German wine, 54
Brühlwiesen, 116
Burg Dreifaltigkeit (castle), 114
Burg Layen, 98, 100, 182, 184
Burgundy *(Burgunder)* grape, 55, 58, 60; Blauburgunder, 90; Blauer Spätburgunder, 58, 133, 167; Frühburgunder, 72; Grauburgunder, 56–58, 133, 134; Weissburgunder, 58, 60, 134. *See also* Ahr; Ruländer; Spätburgunder
Busch, Wilhelm, 42

"Cabinet" wine *(Cabinetwein)*, 30, 32, 179
Caesar, Julius, in Gaul, 20
carbon dioxide, 154, 167
Carl Wilhelm, Prince, 116
cellars, wine: cooperative, 136–37; historic, 90, 144; personal, 158; storage conditions, 157; state-controlled, 106, 122; technology, 150–54
Central Cellars of the Rhenish Wine Cooperative, Gau-Bickelheim, 106
ceramics and wine: ancient, 34, 160; Greek, 35, 37, 160; Roman and Etruscan, 160, 162; Renaissance, 40, 160. *See also* vessels
Champagne, 134, 169, 170
Charlemagne, 23, 88, 104, 146
Charles Theodore, Elector, 29
Christ, Jesus, 36, 38; Eucharist, 38, 39; miracle of Cana, 10; portrayal in art, 38, 39, 40
Christianity: early Christian era, 19, 141–42, 146; patron saints of wine, 22, 141. *See also* art; Christ; Bible; monasteries; religious uses of wine
Christoffel, Karl, *Der Wein in Goethes Leben und Dichtung*, 46
Christus im Kelche (painting), 38
Cilian, Saint: in Franconia, 141
Cistercians, 22, 23
clarity, wine's, 188
Claudius, Matthias, 68
climate, viticulture and, 149–50; drought, 31; frost, 80; "microclimate," 150. *See also* Baden; Moselle-Saar-Ruwer; Nahe; Rheingau; Rhine Palatinate; soil; Württemberg
Coblenz *(Koblenz)*, 23, 52 (map), 68, 85
Cochem, 52 (map), 84

Cochem Krampen, 84
Cologne *(Köln)*, art in, 38, 40
color, wine's, 188
Constance, Lake *(Bodensee)*, 52 (map), 54, 130, 136; wine-growing conditions, 150
cooperatives, wine, 64, 72, 106, 122, 126, 134–39, 147
cork, 157, 158, 169, 171, 181
crafts, wine motifs in: Renaissance, 40
Cranach, Lucas, the elder, *Madonna mit der Traube*, 40
cuisine: Ahr, 74; Baden, 134; Franconia, 144; Palatinate, 112; Württemberg, 128
customhouses in medieval Germany, 26
cuvée, 170

deposits, mineral, in wine, 154, 156
Deutsche Eck, 64
Devrient, Ludwig, 169
diatreta glasses, 160
Dietrich, Count of Katzenelnbogen, 66
Dionysus, 9, 14, 35, 37, 38, 42, 142; in art, with wine, 35, 38; and Bacchus, 18, 19; cult of, in Greece, 18; and mythic origins of wine, 9, 10, 14; and St. Valentine's Church (Kiedrich), 90; and "wine madness," 16
Doctor (vineyard at Bernkastel), 84
Doktorberg (at Bernkastel), 83
Domdechaney (vineyard at Hochheim), 92
Domherr *(Grosslage*, Rheinhessen), 108
Dom Perignon, 169
Don Giovanni (Mozart–Da Ponte), 44
Drachenfels, 64
Dragon Saga, 64
Dreifaltigkeit, Burg (castle), 114
Drusus, as founder of Coblenz, 68
dryness, wine's, 55, 60, 136, 176–77
durchgegoren wine, 177
Dürer, Albrecht, 38, 40

Eberbach (monastery), 23–30, 87, 90
Edelfäule, 30, 152, 175. See also *Botrytis cinerea*; "noble rot"
Edelsüsse, edelsüsser, 171, 175
Egypt, ancient, 12–14; ceramics and wine, 34; early viticulture, 12; mythic origins of wine, 9; religious uses, 12, 14, 34; sculpture, 34; wine making, 12, 14
Ehrenbreitstein (fortress), 68
Ehrenfels Castle, 108
Eich-Quellen, 114
Eifel plateau, 82
Eitelsbach, 82
Elbling grape, 80, 82
Eltville, 92
Eltz, Burg (castle), 84
Enkirch, 82
Engehöll (site at Oberwesel), 66
Enz River, 128
Epictetus, 18
Erbach, 92
Erden, 84
Erntebringer *(Grosslage*, Rheingau), 92
Esslingen, 126, 128, 170
Etruscans, 36; art, 36; ceramics, 160
European Economic Community (EEC), 142, 172, 173; Zone A, 173; Zone B, 134
Exekias, 35

Federweisser, 154, 167
fermentation, 12, 18, 31, 32, 98, 152, 154, 166–67, 170, 171, 177
fertility symbolism of wine, 35, 36, 90
festivals, wine: Dürkheimer Wurstmarkt, 114, 116; at Freiburg, 136; St. Cilian Festival, 142; Weinlesefest at Neustadt, 114; at Winningen, 85; Würzburg's "1200 Years" jubilee, 141
Feuerbach, Anselm, 42
Filzen, 82
filtration, in wine production, 171

Flurbereinigung, 96, 98, 134, 136
Food, wine with, 16, 116, 136, 188, 193–95, 199; as accompaniment to meal, 193–95; in cooking, 191–93
France, 96, 170; EEC wine law, 172
Francis I, Emperor of Austria, 90
Franconia *(Franken*; viticultural area), 52 (map), 54, 60, 128, 138, 141–47, 172–73; cooperatives, 147; cultivation area, 142, 147; subregion and *Grosslage* list, 147; types of grape and wine, 144, 146; viticulture, early, 22, 141–42, 146; Würzburg, 141–42, 146
Frankken, Frans, 193
Franks, 23; in Franconia, 141; on Nahe, 95
Freiburg, 134, 136; wine festival, 136
Friedrich Wilhelm, Count, 100
Fulda, monastery (abbey) of, 104, 144–46

Ganymede, 35
Gau-Bickelheim, 106
Gaul: Celts in, 20; Greek settlement Massilia, 19; Rome and, 20; wine in, 20
Gebietsweinprämierung, 134
Gebietswinzergenossenschaft, 122
Geilweilerhof, 114; Federal Institute, 114
Geisenheim, 32, 40; Teaching and Research Institute, 31, 58, 90
German National Wine Competition, 176, 187
German wine: award-winning, 92; history, 20–33; diversity, 53–55, 112, 166, 181; statistics, 24, 31, 32, 53–54, 80, 166; varieties, 166–67. See also breeds of grape; climate; label; legislation; Qualitätswein; sparkling wine; Tafelwein; vintages; viticulture; wine; wine making
German Wine Seal *(Weinsiegel)*, 134, 176
Germany
—history, wine, 20–33; Romans, 20–22, 38; *Limes Germanicus*, 20; early viticulture, 20–23; monasteries and viticulture, 23–24; Middle Ages, 33–34, 38–39, 64; Renaissance, 24–28, 39, 40; Peasants' War, 26–28; Reformation, 28; Thirty Years' War, 28–29, 96; eighteenth century, 29, 30, 40–48; nineteenth century, 30–31, 40–50; twentieth century, 31–33, 42, 50
—viticulture: areas of, major, 53–147, 179; German way of life and, 55
—*See also* art, wine and; legislation; viticulture; wine; *also* Ahr; Baden; Franconia; Hessian Bergstrasse; Middle Rhine; Moselle-Saar-Ruwer; Nahe; Rheingau; Rheinhessen; Rhine Palatinate; Württemberg
Gewürztraminer grape, 57, 60, 134, 136, 144. *See also* Traminer
Giotto di Bondone, *The Last Supper*, 39
Gleisweiler, 114
Glottertal, 134
Glottertaler wine, 54, 134
Glottertal, the (valley), 136
Goar, Saint, of Aquitaine, 66
Goethe, Johann Wolfgang von, 44–48; drinking habits, 44, 45, 48; *Goetz von Berlichingen*, 44; on Nahe wine, 96–98; Winkler (Rheingau) wine, 90; Würzburg wine, 142. *See also* Christoffel, Karl
Goetz von Berlichingen, 128
Götz, Bruno, 10
Goya, Francisco, *The Wine Harvest*, 40
grapes. *See* breeds of grape; viticulture
Greece, ancient, 14–20; drinking customs, 16; food, wine with, 16; mythic origins of wine, 9, 10, 14; Plato, 16–18; and Rome, 18, 19; Socrates, 16, 18; *Symposium*, 16; symposium as motif, 35; viticulture, 14, 48. *See also* art, wine and; Dionysus; Homer; vessels; wine making
Gregory VII, Pope, 68
Grosslage, 68 (defined), 179

Gross-Umstadt, 120, 122
Grützner, Eduard, 42
Guldenbach Valley, 100
Guldental, 100
Gutedel grape, 60, 133, 134, 136
Gutenberg (castle), 96
Gutenberg, Johann, 106
Gutes Domtal *(Grosslage)*, 108

Haardt Mountains, 111, 112
Halbtrocken wine, 176–77
Hallgarten, 90
Hambacher Schloss (Maxburg), 114
Hamm, 82
Hammelburg, 144, 146
Hammerstein (castle), 68
hangover, 18, 188, 199
Hanseatic League, 26
Harvest, 150; ancient Greek, 48; late, 96, 150, 152, 175, 176; methods, 29, 31–33, 96, 150; tools, 150; *See also* climate; viticulture
Hasenclever, Johann Peter, 42
Hattenheim, 90
Hatto II, Archbishop, of Mainz, 66
Hautvillers, Abbey of, 169
Haydn, Franz Joseph, *Die Jahreszeiten*, 42
Heben, Peter, on Markgräflerland, 136
health, wine and, 33, 68, 74, 156, 194–99; ancient Greece, 18, 196, 197; Hippocrates' views, 18, 196; Caesar's armies, 20, 197; eighteenth and nineteenth centuries, 197; Franconia, 142, 143; Nahe, 95; research, 196, 198
Heidelberg, 52 (map), 120, 138
Heilbronn, 52 (map), 126, 128
Heilsbringer, 142
Henry IV, Emperor, 68, 100, 114
Heppenheim, 120, 122
Hera and mythic origins of wine, 10, 14
Herodotus, 17
Herold, August, 58
Hessian Bergstrasse *(Hessische Bergstrasse*; viticultural area), 52 (map), 119–23, 172–73; cultivation area and yield, 119, 122; Roman relics, 120; subregion and *Grosslage* list, 122; types of grape and wine, 119, 122; viticulture, early, 120; wine-growing conditions, 120
Hessischen Landesamt für Landwirtschaft, 122
Heuchelberg range, the, 130
Heuss, Theodor, 31, 125–28, 130
Hochheim, wine of, 48, 88, 92; "hock," 88
Hoffman, E. T. A., 44, 169, 170
Hofrat *(Grosslage*, Franconia), 144, 147
Holbein, Hans, the younger, 40
Hölle (vineyard at Guldental), 100
Höllenberg (at Assmannshausen), 90
Holy Roman Empire, 111
Homer: description of wine harvest, 48
Humboldt, Alexander von, 64
humor and wine, 55
Hünsruck plateau, 82, 96, 103
hybrids. *See* breeds of grape

Ice Age, 9
Ihringen, 136
Ilbesheim, 112
"improvement" of wine, 174–75
inebriation: in ancient world, 12, 16–18; and driving, 188, 199; in Germany, 24, 46; prevention, 188, 195, 199
Ingelheim, 23, 88, 104
Iphofen, 52 (map), 146
Israel, ancient, wine vessels in, 160
Italy: Denominazione di Origine Controlata, 172; wines, in Sekt, 171

Jagst River, 128
Johannisberg, 23, 48; Cabinetwein, 30; discovery of "noble rot," 29, 90; wine

cellar (*Bibliotheka Subterranea*), 90. *See also* Schloss Johannisberg
Johannisberg (region), 92, 173
Johnson, Hugh, on Nahe wine, 98
Jordaens, Jakob, 191
Joseph II, Emperor, 120
Judaism. *See* Bible
Jugendstil (Art Nouveau) movement, 164
Julius-Echter-Berg (at Iphofen), 146
Jung, Hermann, 35, 36, 37, 42; *Wine in Art*, 35

Kabinett, 32, 175
Kaiserdom (at Worms), 106
Kaiserstuhl-Tuniberg, 133, 136, 139, 173
Katherinenkirche, (at Oppenheim), 103, 106
Katz, Burg, (castle), 66
Kaub, 26, 64, 66, 88
Kauzenberg (castle), 100
Kerner, Justinus, 50, 58, 125
Kiaulehn, Walter, on Palatinate, 112
Kiedrich, 38, 39, 90
Kinkel, Gottfried, on the Ahr, 72
Kitzingen, 144
Kliewe, Professor (Hygiene Institute, University of Mainz), on wine, 195–98
Klingelberger, 138
Kloster Liebfrauenberg (*Grosslage*), 117
Klüsserath, 83
Kocher-Jagst-Tauber (region), 131, 173
Kocher River, 128
Kollwitz, Käthe, on Bergstrasse, 120
Königin Victoriaberg (at Hochheim), 88, 92
Königsstuhl (castle), 64, 68
Königswinter, 52 (map), 68
Konz, 82
Kraichgau, the, 138
Kressbronn, 130, 146
Kreuznach (region, Nahe), 100, 101, 173
Kröv, 77, 84
Kurfürstlay (*Grosslage*), 85
Kusche, Ludwig: on Bach, Haydn, 42; Beethoven, Reger, 43; Mozart, 42–43; "Wine, Music, and Musical Wine," 42

label, wine, 173–74, 178–80; ancient, 10; in ancient Egypt, 14, 179; Greece and Rome, 179; nineteenth and twentieth centuries, 179, 180; and German Wine Law, 179; printed, 180; for Qualitätswein, 174; Schaumwein, 171; Tafelwein, 173. *See also amtliche Prüfungsnummer*
Lahn River, 68
Lahnstein, 68
Land Wine, 172
late harvesting, 96, 150, 152, 175, 176
Leberwurst, 112
legislation, wine, 31, 32; Bocksbeutel, 142; European Economic Community, 172–74; German wines, 166–67; Hammurabi's code, 14; Heilbronn, 19; Rome, ancient, 18–20; vine louse, 30; wine areas, current German, 130, 146; Würzburg, 24, 138. *See also* inebriation; Wine Law, German; women
Leiningen, in Peasants' War, 26
Leiningen, Princes of, 116
Leinsweiler, 114
Leistenwein, 182
Leochares, 35
Leonardo da Vinci, 38; *Last Supper*, 38
Leutesdorf, 68, 69
Liebfrauenkirche (at Worms), 104, 106
Liebfraumilch, 104, 106
Liebig, Justus von, on health, 197
"*Lieblichkeiten*" (wine), 112
literature, wine and, 44–50; Betsch, Roland, 50; *Gilgamesh*, 34; Grimmelshausen, Christoph von, 50; Heine, Heinrich, 63; Hesse, Hermann, 50, 125; Hölderlin, Friedrich, 55, 125; Mann, Thomas, 50; Mörike, Eduard, 125; Troll, Thaddäus, 125; Tucholsky, Kurt, 50; Voltaire, 50; Wilde, Oscar, 50; in Würt-

temberg, 125. *See also* Bindung; Goethe; Greece; Hoffmann; Homer; Kerner; Rome; Schiller; Shakespeare; Zuckmayer
Longuich, 83
Lorch, 88; Christian sculpture in, 39
Lorchhausen, 88
Lorelei (*Loreley*), 52 (map), 64, 68
Lortzing, Albert, "Im Wein liegt Wahrheit nur allein," 44
Louis XIV (France), 29, 96, 100
Louis of Bavaria, 24
Ludwig I of Bavaria, 114
Ludwigsburg, 40
Ludwigshöhe, Villa, 114
Lump (vineyard at Escherndorf), 144
Luther, Martin, 24
Lutter und Wegner, 44, 169, 170

madonna in art with grapes, 39, 40, 90
Madonna mit der Traube ("*Madonna with Grape*," by Lucas Cranach), 40
Maindreick (region, Franconia), 147, 173
Main River, 52 (map), 141, 144
Mainviereck (region, Franconia), 147, 173
Mainz, 38, 52 (map), 106
marc, 14
Marcobrunn (vineyard at Erbach), 92
Marienberg fortress, Würzburg, 141, 142, 144
Markgräfler (Baden), 60
Markgräflerland, 12, 60, 134, 136, 139, 173
Markgräfler wine, 54
Mary, the Virgin. *See* madonna
mash, grape, 150, 152
maturation of grapes, 88. *See also* harvest
maturation of wine, 154–55, 157; in bottles, 157, 181; in vat, 32
Maulbronn, medieval carvings at, 38
Maus, Burg, (castle), 66
Mäuseturm, 64, 66
Maxburg castle (Hambacher Schloss), 114
Mayschoss, 72, 74
Meersburg, 52 (map), 136
Melac, General, 96
Metternich Castle, 78
Metternich, Prince, 30, 90
Michelbach am Wald, 125
Michelsberg (at Bad Dürkheim), 116
Michelsberg (*Grosslage*), 85
Michelskapelle (Bad Dürkheim), 116
Middle Rhine (*Mittelrhein*; viticultural area), 52 (map), 63–69, 172–73; cultivation area, 64, 69; Rhine River, 63, 64; ruins, castles in, 64; subregion and *Grosslage* list, 69; types of grape and wine, 64, 66; viticulture, 64; wine-growing conditions, 64
mildew, 31
Mittelhaardt/Deutsche Weinstrasse (region, Rhine Palatinate), 112, 114, 117, 172
monasteries and wine in early Christian Germany, 22–24, 80, 88, 90
Mönchberg (vineyard, Bad Kreuznach), 96
monks, 141. *See also* Christianity
Morio, Peter, 57, 58
Morio-Muskat grape, 32, 56–59, 104, 112
mosaics, wine in, 38
Moselle, Lower, (*Untermosel*) or Zell (region, Moselle-Saar-Ruwer), 82, 84, 173
Moselle, Middle, or Bernkastel (region, Moselle-Saar-Ruwer), 82, 84, 85, 173
Moselle, Upper, (*Obermosel*; region, Moselle-Saar-Ruwer), 80, 82, 173
Moselle (*Mosel*) River, 21, 52 (map), 77, 78, 80, 82, 84, 85
Moselle-Saar-Ruwer (*Mosel-Saar-Ruwer*; viticultural area), 21, 52 (map), 55, 76–85, 172–73; cultivation area, 78, 85; geology, 82; production costs, 80; Roman influence, 38, 80; subregion and *Grosslage* list, 85; types of grape and wine, 78–80; wine-growing conditions, 78, 80, 84
Moseltor (region), 82, 85, 173

Mozart, Wolfgang Amadeus, 42–44; *Die Zauberflöte* 42, 43; *Don Giovanni*, 44
Müller, Hermann, 32, 58
Müller-Thurgau grape, 32, 56–60, 64, 78, 80, 88, 96, 104, 112, 119, 126, 133, 136, 138, 144, 146
Münzlay (*Grosslage*), 85
Murr River, 128
music, wine and, 42–44; in Bacchanalia, 36; classical, 42–44; in Greek wine harvest, 50; Schubert, Franz, 44; Schumann, Robert, 44; Strauss, Richard, 44; Wolf, Hugo, 44. *See also* Bach; Beethoven; Bruckner; Haydn; Mozart; Offenbach; Reger; Strauss, Johann; Weber, Karl Maria von
must, 134, 150, 152, 154, 173, 175, 195

Nackenheim, 55, 103
Nacktarsch (vineyard at Kröv), 84
Nacktarsch (*Grosslage*), 85
Nahe River, 52 (map), 95, 96, 98, 108
Nahe (viticultural area), 52 (map), 55, 95–101, 172–73; cultivation area, 96, 101; medieval period, 95–96; post-medieval history, 96; Roman period, 95; subregion and *Grosslage* list, 101; types of grape and wine, 96; viticulture, beginnings, 95; viticultural techniques and research, 96; wine-growing conditions, 96; wine making, 98
Napoleonic Wars, 66; in Nahe, 96
Naturrein, 32, 175, 179
Naturwein, 175
Navratil, Joseph, *In the Wine Cellar of Herr Chlumecky*, 50
Neckar River, 52 (map), 54, 128
Neroberg (vineyard at Wiesbaden), 92
Neumagen, 21, 38, 82, 84
Neustadt an der Weinstrasse, 52, 114
New Minster (at Würzburg), 141–42
Nibelungs, 64
Nicetius, Bishop, 23
Niederwald monument (at Rudesheim), 90
Nierstein, 55, 106
Nierstein (region), 104, 108, 173
Nietzsche, Friedrich, 16
"noble rot," 19, 88, 152, 175; discovery of, 29, 90, 146
Nolde, Emil, 38
Nonnenberg (vineyard at Rauenthal), 92
Nonnenhorn, 130, 146

Obentraut, Michael, 98
Oberdollendorf, 63, 68
Oberremel, 82
Ochsenfurt, 144
Ockfen, 82
Odenwald, the, 103, 119
Oechsle, Christian Ferdinand, 30
Oestrich, 90
Offenbach, Jacques, *Tales of Hoffmann*, 44
Offenburg, 52 (map), 138
Öhringen, 128
Oppenheim, 55, 103, 106; Teaching and Experimental Station, 106
Originalabfüllung, 32, 179
Ortenau (region, Baden), 138–39, 173
Osiris: and mythic origins of wine, 9

painting, wine and: in Greek ceramics, 35, 37, 160; Etruscan frescoes, 36; Pompeii, 36–38; in Christian art, 38–40; Renaissance, 38, 40; eighteenth century, 40; nineteenth century, 40, 42; twentieth century, 42; Slevogt, Max, 42, 114
Pasteur, Louis, 31
Paul, the Apostle: on health, 196
Paul VI, Pope, and Franciscan wine, 146
Peace of Westphalia, 28
Peasants' War, 26, 28, 114
Perl, 82
Perle grape, 144
Persephone: mythic origins of wine, 10

206

Persia, ancient: mythic origins of wine, 10; wine-drinking customs, 17, 18; wine vessels, 160
Peterskopf, 116
Pfalz Castle, 26
Pfälzerwald, 103
Pfinzgau-Enzgau, 138
Philipp von Dernbach, Prince Bishop, 142
Picasso, Pablo, *Bacchanal*, 42
Piesport, 84
Plutarch on wine's merits, 197
Pompeii and wine portrayals, 36, 37, 38
Porta nigra (at Trier), 82
Portugieser grape, 58, 59, 60, 72, 104, 112, 126, 128, 157
Potassium in wine, 156
Prädikat wine, 175–76
Praxiteles, 35
press, wine, 150–52; ancient, 10; at Eberbach, 87, 90; introduction in Germany, 23; modern centrifuge, 32, 152
Prussia: ruling Nahe, 96; wine of, 25
Psiax, 35

Qualitätsschaumwein, 167, 170, 171
Qualitätswein (Qualitätswein bestimmter Anbaugebiete or QBA), 32, 146, 171–76
Qualitätswein mit Prädikat (Qualitätswein bestimmter Anbaugebiete or QBA mit Prädikat), 29, 32, 152, 155, 172, 173, 175, 176. *See also* Auslese, Beerenauslese, Kabinett, Spätlese, Trockenbeerenauslese

Raabe, Wilhelm, 55
Rauenthal, 39, 40, 92
Ravensburg, 130
red wine, 55, 57, 58; EEC legislation, 173; for gastritis, 156; production of, 166–67; temperature for, ideal, 157
—in Ahr, 71, 72; Baden, 133, 134, 138; Middle Rhine, 66; Rheingau, 90; Rheinhessen, 104; Rhine Palatinate, 114; Württemberg, 126, 128, 130
Reformation, 28; secularization of vineyards, 28. *See also* Luther, religious uses of wine, Thirty Years' War
Reger, Max, on inebriation, 43
Reichhartshausen, Schloss, 90
religious uses of wine: ancient Egypt, 12, 34; Hittites, 34; ancient Greece, 35; and Bacchus, 36, 38; Etruscan tombs, 36; temple at Baalbek, 36; Roman tombs, 36; early Christian era, 22, 38; Christian art, 38–39, 40; after Reformation, 28; attitudes in eighteenth century Germany, 46–48; *See also* Bacchus; Bible; Christ
Rembrandt van Rijn, 40
Rems River, 128
Remstal, the, 128
Remstal-Stuttgart (region), 131, 173
Retsina, 18
Rheinburgengau (region), 69, 173
Rheinfels, Burg, (castle), 66
Rheinfront, 104
Rheingau (viticultural area), 52 (map), 55, 78–93, 119, 172–73; art in, 38, 39, 40, 90; cultivation area, 88, 92; geography, 87, 88; Peasants' War, 26, 28; subregion and *Grosslage* list, 92; types of grape and wine, 88, 90. *See also* Johannisberg, Eberbach
Rheinhessen (viticultural area), 52 (map), 55, 103–9, 172–73; cooperatives, 106, 108; cultivation area and yield, 103, 104, 108; Roman influence, 103; monasteries and wine, 104; subregion and *Grosslage* list, 108; types of grape and wine, 104; viticultural research, 104, 106; wine-growing conditions, 104
Rheinstein, Burg, (castle), 66
Rhens, 64, 68
Rhine Palatinate (*Rheinpfalz*; viticultural area), 52 (map), 54, 111–17, 172–73;

Bavarian-Palatinate War of Succession, 96; cultivation area and yield, 103, 111, 117; Dürkheimer Wurstmarkt, 116; geology, 111, 112; invaded by Louis XIV, 29; medieval period, 111; Palatinate War of Succession, 96; in Peasants' War, 26; subregion and *Grosslage* list, 117; types of grape and vine, 112; wine-growing conditions, 112, 150. *See* Bad Dürkheim; Weinstrasse
Rhine Palatinate and its Inhabitants, The (August Becker), 114
Rhine (*Rhein*) River, 52 (map), 54, 63–68, 88, 108; Heine on, 63
Rhine Wine, On the Excellence, Differences, Uses and Effects of, 197
Richard the Lion-Hearted, 114
Rieslaner grape, 32, 60, 144
Riesling grape, 32, 56–60, 64, 71, 78–85, 88, 90, 96, 104, 112, 119, 134, 138, 144, 149, 181
"Riesling route" (in Rheingau), 92
Riesling seal, 78
Ritterstursz (castle), 68
roller seals, 10
Rome, ancient, 18–20; Ausonius, Decimus Magnus, *Mosella*, 21, 78; Cato, 19; Columella, 19; Domitian, 20; drinking habits, 18, 20, 36; drinking vessels, 158, 162, 182; drunkenness and crime, 18; and Gaul, wines of, 20; in Germany, 20–22, 38, 66, 68, 78–82, 95, 103, 120, 134; and Greece, 18; Horace, 20; *Limes Germanicus*, 20; and mythic origins of wine, 9; Pliny, 20; Probus, 20; Romulus, 19; Tacitus, *Germania*, 20; Virgil, 20; viticulture, 19; wine making, 19. *See also* art; Bacchanalia; Bacchus; legislation
Römer glass, 158, 162, 164–65
Rosé wine, 126, 157, 166. *See also* Schillerwein; Weissherbst
Rotenfels, 95
Rotgold, Badisch, (wine), 134, 167
Rothenberg (vineyard at Rauenthal), 92
Rotliegende, 104
Rotling. *See* Schillerwein
Rubens, 40; *Drunken Silenus*, 45
Rüdesheim, 46, 48, 52 (map), 90
Ruland, Johann, 58
Ruländer (Grauburgunder) grape, 56, 57, 58, 59, 60, 119, 133, 134, 136, 138, 167, 181. *See also* Burgundy
Ruwer River, 52 (map), 78; wine, 82

Saale River, 144
Saarburg, 52 (map), 82
Saar River, 52 (map), 78; wine, 82
Saar-Ruwer (region), 82, 85, 173
St. Catherine's Church, 103, 106
St. Goar, 66
St. Goarshausen, 66
St. Michael (*Grosslage*), 85
Saint Urban's Day, 22
St. Valentine's Church (Kiedrich), 38, 90
Sankt Rochuskappele (*Grosslage*), 108
Sauer River, 78
Schäfer, Wilhelm, 54
Scharlachberg, 108
Scharlachkopf, 100
Scharzberg (*Grosslage*), 85
Scharzhofberg, 82
Schaumwein, 167, 170–71
Scheel, Walter, 82
Scheun, Georg, 31, 58, 60, 104
Schickele, René, on Markgräflerland, 136
Schikaneder, Emanuel, and Mozart, 42–43
Schiller, Friedrich von, 48–50, 106, 125, 128, 166; *An die Freude* ("To Joy"), 50; and Goethe, 48
Schillerwein, 126, 134, 166–67
Schinderhannes, 98
Schlossberg (near Hammelburg), 146
Schlossböckelheim (region), 100, 101, 173
Schloss Bübinger (*Grosslage*), 85

Schloss Johannisberg (vineyard at Johannisberg), 30, 90, 92. *See also* Johannisberg Schloss Reichhartshausen (Hattenheim), 90
Schloss Saaleck (castle), 146
Schloss Schönborn (at Hattenheim), 90
Schloss Stahleck (*Grosslage*), 67, 69
Schloss Vollrads, 40, 90
Schopenhauer, Johanna, 120
Schurwald, the, 128
Schwarze Katz (*Grosslage*), 85
Schwarze Katz (vineyard at Zell), 84
Schwarzlay (*Grosslage*), 85
Schwarzwald, 128, 138
Schweigen, 52 (map), 112
Scout, the (religious-art motif), 38
sculpture, wine and, 34–40; Egyptian, 34; Hittite, 34; at Nineveh, 35; Greek, 35; Roman 36; in medieval Germany, 38; in Christian art, 38–40, 90, 141–42
Seewein, 136
Sekt, 167, 169–70, 171, 188
Shakespeare, 50, 170
Shiva, and mythic origins of wine, 9
Sickingen, Franz von, 55, 96
Siebengebirge, 64, 66
Siebengebirge (region), 69, 173
Siegfried, 64
Silenus, 35, 38, 45
soil, 149; fertilization, 32; slate, 71–72, 78–82, 88
—Ahr, 71, 72; Baden, 138; Franconia, 144; Hessian Bergstrasse, 120; Moselle-Saar-Ruwer, 78, 80, 82; Nahe, 96, 98; Rheingau, 88, 90; Rheinhessen, 104; Rhine Palatinate, 112; Württemberg, 126, 128
Sonnenuhr (vineyard at Wehlen), 84
Spanheim (now Sponheim), counts of, 100
sparkling wine, 167, 169–71; Perlwein, 167; production techniques, 170–71; Riesling, 82
—Ahr (red wine), 72; Franconia, 146; Middle Rhine, 64; Moselle-Saar-Ruwer (Elbling), 80, 82; Rheingau, 92
—*See also* Schaumwein, Sekt, Champagne spas, 72; at Bad Dürkheim, 116
Spätburgunder grape, 59, 60, 61, 181; Ahr, 72; Baden, 134, 136, 138; Franconia, 144; Middle Rhine, 64; Rheingau, 88, 90; Rheinhessen, 104; Württemberg, 128. *See also* Burgundy
Spätlese, 21, 30, 32, 126, 174, 175
Speyer, 38, 52 (map), 111, 117, 182
spoilage of bottled wine, 157
Stahleck Castle, 63
"*Stahlig*," 64
Starkenburg (at Heppenheim), 120
Starkenburg (region), 122, 173
Steigerwald (region), 146, 147, 173
Steinberg (vineyard at Hattenheim), 90
Steinmächer (*Grosslage*, Rheingau), 92
Steinwein, 144, 182
Stiftskirche, 104
Stolzenfels, Burg, (castle), 68
storage, wine, 155, 157, 158; in Egypt, 12
Strauss, Johann, 48
Strausswirtschaften, 23, 120
Streicher, Andreas, on Nierstein, 106
Stromberg range, 130
Stuttgart, 52 (map), 126, 128
Südliche Weinstrasse (region), 111, 112, 114, 117, 173
sugar content, wine's, 55, 152, 181; and longevity, 181; residual, 152, 154, 176–77; *Restsüsse*, 176; in sparkling wine, 170–71; *Süssreserve*, 32, 154
sugaring of wine, 31, 152, 154, 174–75
Sulm River, 128
Sumer, 10; *Gilgamesh*, 34; Utnapishtim, 34
Swabia: Alps, 126; forest, 128; Weinstrasse, 128; wine patron saint, 22
Sybillenstein (*Grosslage*), 108
Sylvaner (*Silvaner*) grape, 56–60, 88, 96, 104, 112, 119, 126–28, 134–36, 144, 181

table wine, 60, 172. *See also* Tafelwein
Tafelwein, 32, 146, 172, 173
tannin, 154, 156
tartrate, wine, 156
taste, wine's, 187–88. *See also* wine tasting
Taunus hills, 87, 90, 103
temperature for wine, 157, 187
Teufelsküche (at Guldental), 100
Thirty Years' War, 28–29; in Nahe, 96
Titian: *Bacchanale*, 40, 43; *Bacchus and Ariadne*, 40
tourism: in Ahr, 72; Hessian Bergstrasse, 120, 122; Middle Rhine, 64; Nahe, 98, 100; Rheinhessen, 108
Traben-Trarbach, 84
Traminer grape, 60, 134, 138, 181. *See also* Gewürztraminer
Traubendrücker, 88
Treppchen (vineyard at Erden), 84
Trier, 22, 38, 40, 52 (map), 82
Trifels, 114
Trockenbeerenauslese, 30, 84, 150, 175–77, 182. *See also* harvest, "noble rot"
Troll, Thaddäus, 125
Trollinger grape, 58, 59, 60, 126–28, 130
Trübstoffen, 154
Truttas, 23
Tübingen-Reutlingen (region), 131, 173
Tucholsky, Kurt, 50
Türkenblut (wine), 130
Turmaier, Hans, on Bavarian drinking, 24

Uhde, Fritz von, 38
Umstadt, 120
Umstadt (region), 122, 173
Unkel, 55, 66, 68
Urban, Saint (Pope), 22, 40
Ürzig, 84
Utsch, Friedrich Wilhelm, 98

Veitshochheim, 40, 144
Velasquez, Diego Rodriguez de Silva y, 40
Venus and Bacchus, 36
vessels, wine, 157–64; ancient, 10, 12, 160; Egyptian, 16; Greek, 18, 21, 160; Roman, 21; Roman, in Germany, 95, 160, 164–65; German, 21, 28, 32, 106, 138, 154–55; Renaissance and Baroque, 160–62; eighteenth- and nineteenth-century, 162–64; modern, 32, 106. *See also* bottles, ceramics, wineglasses
Victoria, Queen, and Hochheimer wine, 88
vine, grape: paleontology of, 9; varieties, 57–61; wild, 9, 58. *See also* breeds of grape, viticulture
vineyards: eminent, 48; most northerly, 68. *See also* German wine; wine
vintages: old, 90, 181, 182; outstanding, 84, 92, 181, 182, 202–3
vinum francium, 24
vinum hunicum, 24
Virgin Mary. *See* madonna
Viticultural Institute, Bavarian State (Veitschöchheim, Franconia), 144
viticulture, 149–50; consolidation of vineyards, 31, 96, 98; *Oidium*, 31; *Peronospora*, 31; pest control, 29–31, 96, 98, 150; scientific approaches, 29, 96;

terracing, 23; training vines, 23, 96; vine louse (*Phylloxera vastatrix*), 30, 72, 96, 98, 134
—history: beginnings, 9–14, 19; German beginnings, 20–23, 95, 126; under Charlemagne, 23, 88; Middle Ages, 23–24, 95–96; Renaissance, 24–28, 96; Napoleonic secularization, 30; nineteenth century, 30–31, 96; twentieth century, 31–33
—*See also* breeds of grape; climate; German wine; Germany; harvest; "noble rot"; vine; *also* Ahr; Baden; Hessian Bergstrasse; Middle Rhine; Moselle-Saar-Ruwer; Nahe; Rheinhessen; Rhine Palatinate; Württemberg
Vorderpfalz, 112
Vulkanfelsen (*Grosslage*, Baden), 139

Wachenheim, 114, 116
Waldeck, Boos von, (knight), 100
Waldrach, 82
Walporzheim, 74
Walporzheim-Ahrtal (region), 74, 173
Wandsbeker Boten, 53
Weber, Karl Maria von, 44
Wehlen, 84
"Weininsel," 144
Weinsberg, 126, 128; Teaching and Experimental Institute, 128
Weinsberg Valley, 128
Weinstrasse ("wine road"): Ahr Rotweinstrasse, 74; in Baden, 133; Nahe, 98; Rhine Palatinate, 54, 110, 114
Weissherbst, 72, 126, 133, 134, 136, 157, 166. *See also* rosé
Weistum, 26
Wenzeslaus, Elector Clemens, (Trier), 80
white wine, 55, 57, 58; EEC legislation and, 173; production of, 166–67; temperature for, ideal, 157
—Ahr, 71, 72; Baden, 133, 134; Hessian Bergstrasse, 119; Rhine Palatinate, 112, 114; Württemberg, 126
Wiesbaden, 52 (map), 92
Wiltingen, 82
wine: "diabetic," 176; "ecological," 175; Eiswein, 152, 176; old, 21; origins, mythic, 9, 10, 11, 12, 136; outstanding, 48, 152, 175, 182; virgin, 10. *See also* bottles; cellars; cooperatives; festivals; food; German wine; German wine seal; health; label; legislation; press; Qualitätswein; red wine; religious uses; storage; Tafelwein; table wine; vessels; viticulture; white wine
wine drinking: ideal temperatures, 157; with food, 193–95
wine-drinking customs: medieval Germany, 24, 100, 191; sixteenth- and seventeenth-century, 160; eighteenth- and nineteenth-century, 40, 44, 46; current, 54. *See also* Egypt, Greece, Persia, Rome; *also* Ahr; Moselle-Saar-Ruwer; Nahe; Rhine Palatinate; Württemberg
wineglasses, 40, 158–65; Roman, 95, 160, 164–65; Renaissance and Baroque, 160, 162, 164–65; eighteenth- and nineteenth-

century, 162–65; twentieth-century, 164–65; ideal, 158; cut glass, 162
wine growing. *See* viticulture; wine making
Wine Institute, State, (at Freiburg), 134
Wine Law, German: *1892, 1901, 1930,* 31; *1971,* 32, 78, 119, 172, 174–75, 179
wine making, 32, 98, 150–55, 166–67, 170–71; artificial wine, 31; mechanization, 32, 150, 154, 155; mineral deposits, 156; Oechsle scale, 30, 152; Pasteurization, 31. *See also* acidity; alcohol content; balance; blending; bottles; cellar technology; Egypt; fermentation; Greece; "improvement"; maturation; Middle East; must; press; Qualitätswein mit Prädikat; Rome; sparkling wine; sugaring; vessels; viticulture
"Wine of the Millenium," 44–45, 182
Wines of the Century, 182, 184, 203
wine tasting, 122, 187–89; jargon of, 188, 200–1. *See also* acidity; alcohol; aroma; bouquet; clarity; color; taste
Wines of the Century, 182, 184, 203
"Wine Tasting of the Century," 182
wine trade, 32–33; artificial wine, 31; Leibfraumilch, 104; in Renaissance Germany, 26, 28. *See also* Ahr; Hessian Bergstrasse; Middle Rhine; Nahe; Rheinhessen; Rhine Palatinate; *also* cooperatives; viticulture
Winkel, 90
Winklerberg (vineyard at Ihringen), 133
Winzerbuch (Georg Scheu), 31
Wittelsbach, dukes of, 111
Wolfskeel, Otto von, Prince Bishop of Würzburg, 24
women, role of, and wine: Hammurabi's code, 14; in Greece, 16; Rome, 19; Heilbronn, 19
Wonnegau (region), 104, 108, 173
World Wars: I, 31; II, 31
Worms, 52 (map), 104, 106
Württemberg (viticultural area), 52 (map), 60, 125–31, 146, 172–73; cultivation area, 126, 131; drinking habits, 125, 128; quality of wine, 126; subregion and *Grosslage* list, 131; types of grape and wine, 126, 128, 130, 136; wine-growing conditions, 126; writers, 125
Württembergisch Unterland, 131, 173
Würzburg, 52 (map), 141, 144; and Bayerischer Bodensee region, 146; and Bocksbeutel, 138; Burgerspital, 142, 144; early Christian art in, 141–42; Saint Cilian and, 141–42; founding of diocese, 22, 141; Marienberg fortress, 141; New Minster, 141–42; Renaissance art in, 40; Residenz, 144

Yeast, in fermentation, 12, 170, 171

Zaber River, 128, 130
Zell (Moselle-Saar-Ruwer), 84
Zeller Schwartze Katz, 84
Zellertal, 116
Zeltinger-Rachtig, 84
Zeus and mythical origins of wine, 10, 14
Zuckmayer, Carl, 50, 103, 189; *Fröhlicher Weinberg*, 50, 189